The Roman Empire and the Wider World

About the Author

I was educated at the universities of Hull and Southampton, where I took degrees in classics, and at Sorbonne University, Paris. After that I worked in medical publishing, much of the time as an international sales director for one market or another while latterly creating medical educational programmes for the pharmaceutical industry.

I am a contributor to a number of history and archaeology magazines, and the author of over 180 books, a number of which are on classical history. I have had features published in the *Daily Express* and *The Observer*.

I am a regular reviewer for 'Classics for All', an editorial advisor for Yale University Press and have contributed the chapter on *Death* to the classics section of 'Bibliographies Online' published by Oxford University Press.

I appear frequently on BBC local radio and have broadcast on the World Service, BBC PM show and contributed to programmes broadcast on BBC iPlayer.

My books have been translated into Chinese and Japanese. I have a website, am on Facebook, Instagram, X, and WhatsApp. I do signings, webinars, I blog and give talks to societies and schools.

paul.chrystal@btinternet.com
www.paulchrystal.com

By the same author

Roman Military Disasters: Dark Days and Lost Legions (2015)

In Bed with the Romans (2015)

In Bed with the Ancient Greeks (2018)

Emperors of Rome – The Monsters: From Tiberius to Theodora, AD 14–548 (2018)

Women at War in the Classical World (2020)

War in Greek Mythology (2020)

A Historical Guide to Roman York (2021)

The History of the World in 100 Pandemics, Plagues and Epidemics (2021)

'Two Case Studies on Receptions of Sex & Power: Lucretia and Verginia' in *The Routledge Companion to the Reception of Ancient Greek and Roman Gender and Sexuality* (2022)

Bioterrorism and Biological Warfare: Disease as a Weapon of War (2023)

World-Changing Women: 150 Women who Rewrote the Histories of Ancient Egypt, Israel, Greece and Rome (2024)

The Book in the Ancient World: How the Wisdom of the Ages was Preserved (2025)

Miracula: Weird and Wonderful Stories of Ancient Greece and Rome (2025)

The Roman Empire and the Wider World

The Two-way Trade of Goods, Culture, Knowledge and Religion

Paul Chrystal

First published in Great Britain in 2025 by
Pen & Sword History
An imprint of Pen & Sword Books Limited
Yorkshire – Philadelphia

Copyright © Paul Chrystal 2025

ISBN 978 1 39903 571 2

The right of Paul Chrystal to be identified as
Author of this Work has been asserted by him in accordance
with the Copyright, Designs and Patents Act 1988.

A CIP catalogue record for this book is
available from the British Library.

All rights reserved. No part of this book may be reproduced, transmitted, downloaded, decompiled or reverse engineered in any form or by any means, electronic or mechanical including photocopying, recording or by any information storage and retrieval system, without permission from the Publisher in writing. NO AI TRAINING: Without in any way limiting the Author's and Publisher's exclusive rights under copyright, any use of this publication to "train" generative artificial intelligence (AI) technologies to generate text is expressly prohibited. The Author and Publisher reserve all rights to license uses of this work for generative AI training and development of machine learning language models.

Typeset by Mac Style
Printed in the UK by CPI Group (UK) Ltd, Croydon, CR0 4YY.

The Publisher's authorised representative in the EU for product safety is Authorised Rep Compliance Ltd., Ground Floor, 71 Lower Baggot Street, Dublin D02 P593, Ireland.
www.arccompliance.com

For a complete list of Pen & Sword titles please contact

PEN & SWORD BOOKS LIMITED
47 Church Street, Barnsley, South Yorkshire, S70 2AS, England
E-mail: enquiries@pen-and-sword.co.uk
Website: www.pen-and-sword.co.uk
or
PEN AND SWORD BOOKS
1950 Lawrence Road, Havertown, PA 19083, USA
E-mail: uspen-and-sword@casematepublishers.com
Website: www.penandswordbooks.com

Contents

Acknowledgements		vii
List of Illustrations		viii
Maps		x
Preface		xvi
Introduction		xvii
Chapter 1	Where in the World Am I? The Roman and his Geography	1
Chapter 2	Roman Trade	10
Chapter 3	The Borders of Empire (*Limes*)	43
Chapter 4	Communications – Getting Goods to and from Market	45
Chapter 5	The Romans' Attitude to Foreigners: Roman-ness and *Romanitas*, Xenophobia and Barbarians	49
Chapter 6	The Celts and the Germani	54
Chapter 7	Rome and the Nordic Countries	68
Chapter 8	Eastern Europe; the Amber Road	79
Chapter 9	Britannia	91
Chapter 10	Africa – Sub-Sahara and West Africa, Egypt, Nubia, Lake Chad	112
Chapter 11	Arabia	146
Chapter 12	Parthia and the Sasanian Empire	156
Chapter 13	India	164
Chapter 14	Sri Lanka and Myanmar (Burma)	174
Chapter 15	China and the Silk Road	176

Chapter 16	The Assimilation and Adoption of Foreign Ideas and Culture through Trade	182
Chapter 17	Eastern Religions in the Roman Empire	187

Epilogue	197
Appendix: The Second-Hand Book Trade in Brundisium	199
Notes	201
Further Reading by Chapter	214
Index	229

Acknowledgements

No book is the work of one man or woman; this one certainly is not. So my thanks go out to Dr Caitlin Green FSA, Institute of Continuing Education, University of Cambridge, for permission to quote from her 'Were There Camels in Roman Britain?' published in *Forbes Magazine*.

List of Illustrations

1. Replica of the famous statue of Mercury by Flemish sculptor Giovanni da Bologna on the island of Källskär, Finland. (*ReinerausH via Wikimedia Commons/CC BY-SA 3.0*)
2. Amphorae recovered from shipwrecks of the Bronze Age, on display in the Museum of Underwater Archaeology at Bodrum Castle, Turkey. (*Ad Meskens via Wikimedia Commons/CC BY-SA 3.0*)
3. The title page of the *Description of Greece* by Pausanias housed in the Laurentian Library collection in Florence. (*Public domain*)
4. A mosaic of an actor's mask of an old slave; Altes Museum, Berlin.
5. Fragment of a limestone mosaic depicting a Roman *venatio* fighting a tiger, c.300–400 CE. (*Daderot/Wikipedia*).
6. Bust of Teuta, pirate queen from Illyria, housed in the Skanderbeg Museum in Kruja, Albania. (*Hyjnesha via Wikimedia Commons/CC BY-SA 4.0*)
7. Roman stone carving depicting mail coach on the *cursus publicus*.
8. Fresco depicting the Isis Geminiana, a small river vessel being loaded from the columbarium 31 of the necropolis at Via Laurentina, Ostia, 200–250 CE. (*Vatican Museums, inv. 79638/Joel Bellviure*)
9. Floor mosaic in the Aula dei Mensores (hall of the grain weighers) in Ostia showing grain measurers (*mensores frumentarii*) at work.
10. Roman mosaic from Veii (Isola Farnese, Italy), depicting an African elephant being loaded onto a ship, third-fourth century CE, Badisches Landesmuseum Karlsruhe, Germany. (*Carole Raddato via Wikimedia Commons/CC BY-SA 2.0*)
11. Sarcophagus found at Porta Latina in Rome showing a busy port scene. Now in the Vatican Museum (inv. 927).
12. Fresco depicting the distribution of bread by a candidate for office to the plebs. (*Public domain*)
13. Trajan's Market in Rome. (*Adobe Stock*)
14. Ostia today: former harbour town of Rome. (*Adobe Stock*)
15. Mosaic showing the bow of a large cargo ship in the quay at Portus, in the Portus Collection Musei Capitolini, Rome (third century CE).
16. NASA Earth Observatory image by Jesse Allen showing the ancient Roman Portus.

List of Illustrations   ix

17. Portrait of Caspar, one of the Three Wise Men, mentioned in the Gospel of Matthew. Painted by Jan Hermansz van Bijlert, c.1640.
18. Bas-relief from Cabrières-d'Aigues showing the transport of barrels and amphorae, pulled by three *halciarii* (boatmen), of which only two have survived. (*Fabrice Philibert-Caillat via Wikmedia Commons/CC BY-SA 3.0*)
19. Floor mosaic with two different approaching ships in the harbour of Portus, most probably a Cladivata and a Corbita.
20. Mosaic from Basrah showing a caravan merchant leading a camel train through the desert. (*Jadd Haidar via Wikimedia Commons/CC BY-SA 4.0*).
21. The Three Wise Men journeying to Bethlehem carrying their gold, frankincense and myrrh as gifts for the infant Jesus. (*Painting by James Tissot/Brooklyn Museum*).
22. Byzantine mosaic c.565, depicting the Three Magi. (*Nina Aldin Thune via Wikimedia Commons/CC BY-SA 2.5*)
23. Trekking along the Amber Road.
24. Roman glassware found in the grave of a rich man in Himlingøje in present-day Denmark. Dated to second-third century CE.
25. A reconstruction of the interior of the Bronze Age *Uluburun* shipwreck, 1330–1300 BCE. (*Bodrum Museum of Underwater Archaeology, Turkey*)
26. A mural showing women dressed in traditional Hanfu silk robes, from the Dahuting Tomb of the Late-Eastern Han Dynasty (25–220 CE), located in Zhengzhou, Henan province, China. (*Public domain*)
27. Roman mosaic depicting two female slaves (*ancillae*) attending their mistress and assisting with their make-up. (*Fabien Dany via Wikimedia Commons/CC BY-SA 2.5*)
28. Roman mosaic from a house in Pompeii depicting fruits, meat and poultry, second century BCE. (*Naples National Archaeological Museum*)
29. Roman bronze incense burner.
30. An ivory statuette of Lakshmi (first century CE), discovered in the ruins of Pompeii, 1930–1938. (*Sailko via Wikimedia Commons/CC BY-SA 3.0*)
31. Zhang Qian taking leave of Emperor Han Wudi for his expedition to Central Asia from 138 to 126 BCE, Mogao Caves mural, 618–712. (*Public domain*)
32. Mosaics discovered in Lod, near Tel Aviv, dating from 300 CE. (*Public domain*)
33. A Roman fresco from the Casa del Naviglio in Pompeii, first century CE, showing a Maenad (female follower of Bacchus) in a silk dress. (*Naples National Museum*)
34. Sarcophagus showing the wedding of Dionysos and Ariadne. (*Getty Museum, Pacific Pallisades CA*)
35. Bona Dea marble statue. *CIL.* XIV 2251. Antoninian, *Ager Albanus*, Italy.

Maps

1. What the map of the world by Hecataeus of Miletus might have looked like (sixth century BCE). (*Public domain*) — xi
2. A reconstructed map of the known world according to Eratosthenes (276–195 BCE), the Greek Alexandrian scholar from Cyrene. (*Public domain*) — xii
3. World map of Herodotus – possibly what Herodotus believed the world looked like (fifth century BCE) based on his *Histories*. (*Public domain*) — xiii
4. The Roman Empire (dark grey) and its clients (light grey) in 117 CE during the reign of Emperor Trajan. (*Tataryn via Wikimedia Commons/CC BY-SA 3.0*) — xiii
5. The Amber Road (east route). (*Richard Resch via Wikimedia Commons*) — xiv
6. Canal of the Pharaohs, precursor of the modern Suez Canal, started in Pharaoh Sesostris' I reign, c.1960 BCE but not completed until at least Darius I. (*Annie Brocolie via Wikimedia Commons/CC BY-SA 2.5*) — xv

Map 1. What the map of the world by Hecataeus of Miletus might have looked like (sixth century BCE). (*Public domain*)

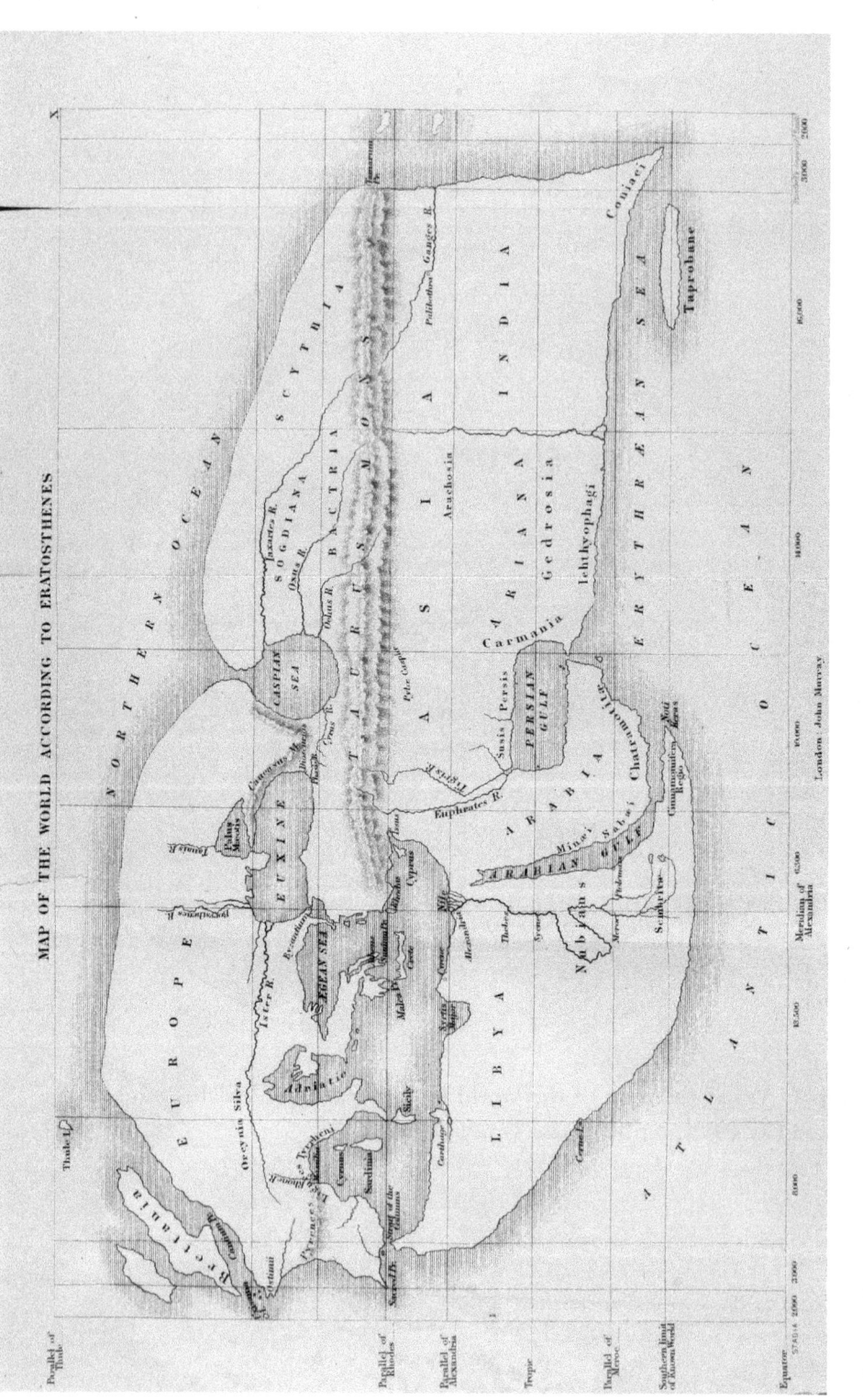

Map 2. A reconstructed map of the known world according to Eratosthenes (276–195 BCE), the Greek Alexandrian scholar from Cyrene. (*Public domain*)

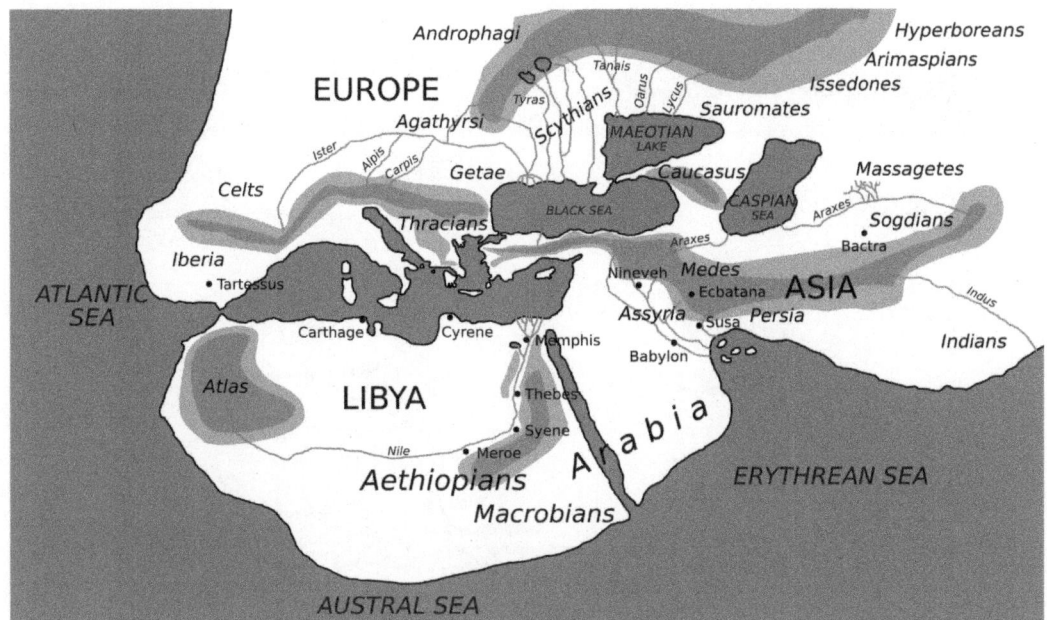

Map 3. World map of Herodotus – possibly what Herodotus believed the world looked like (fifth century BCE) based on his *Histories*. (*Public domain*)

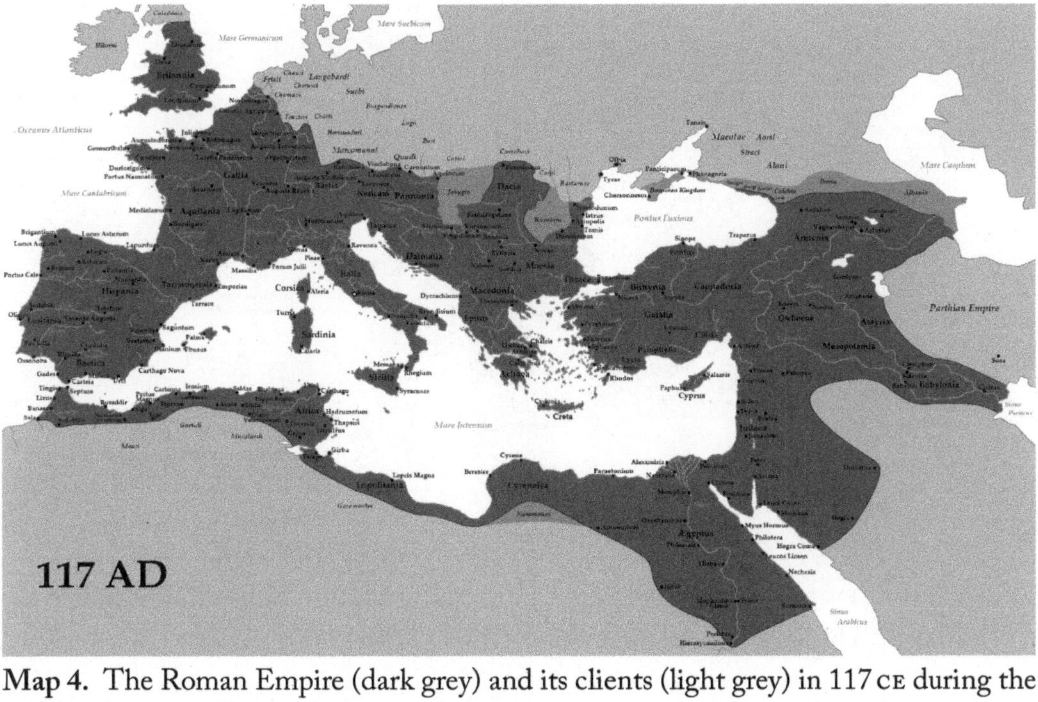

Map 4. The Roman Empire (dark grey) and its clients (light grey) in 117 CE during the reign of Emperor Trajan. (*Tataryn via Wikimedia Commons/CC BY-SA 3.0*)

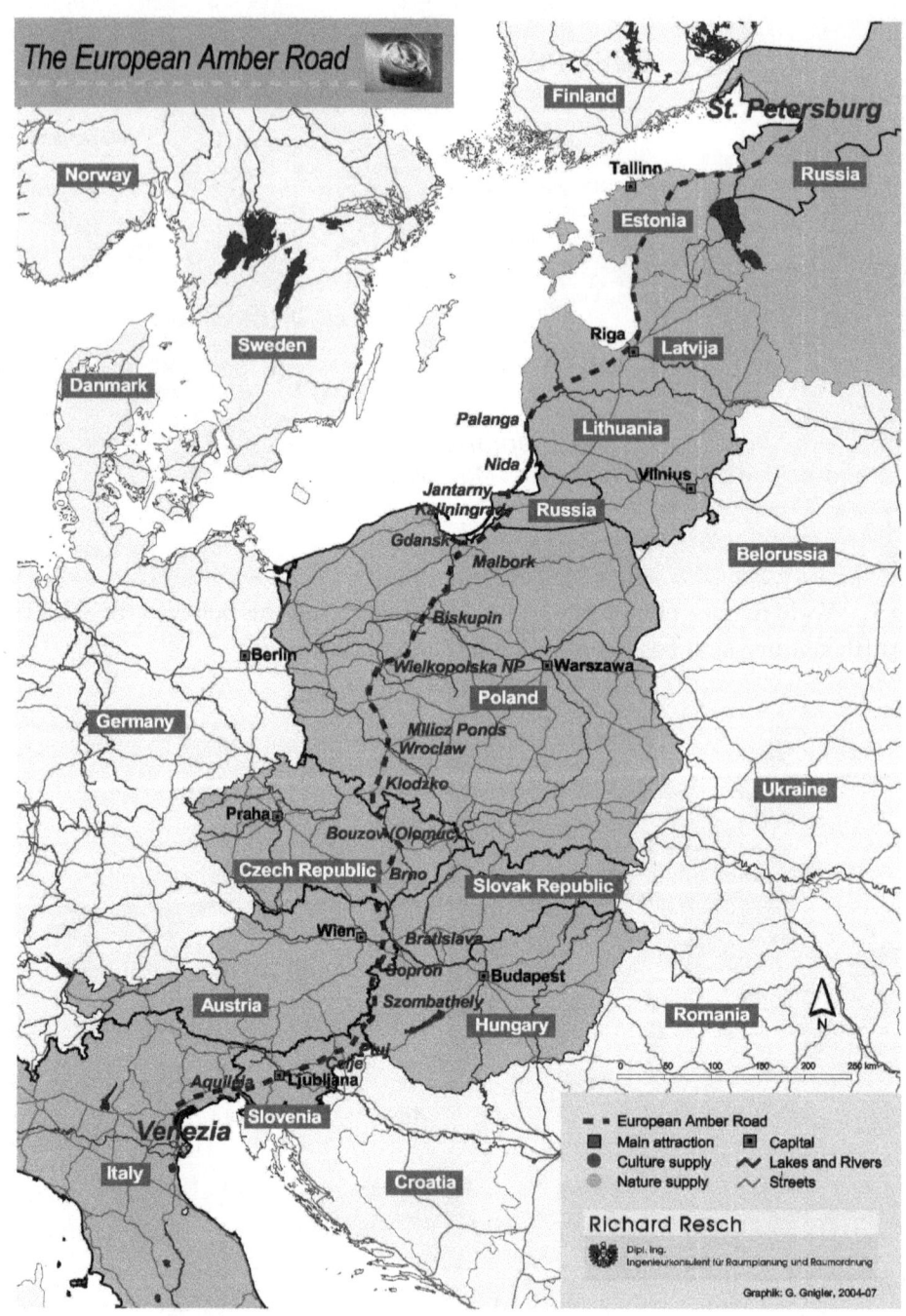

Map 5. The Amber Road (east route). (*Richard Resch via Wikimedia Commons*)

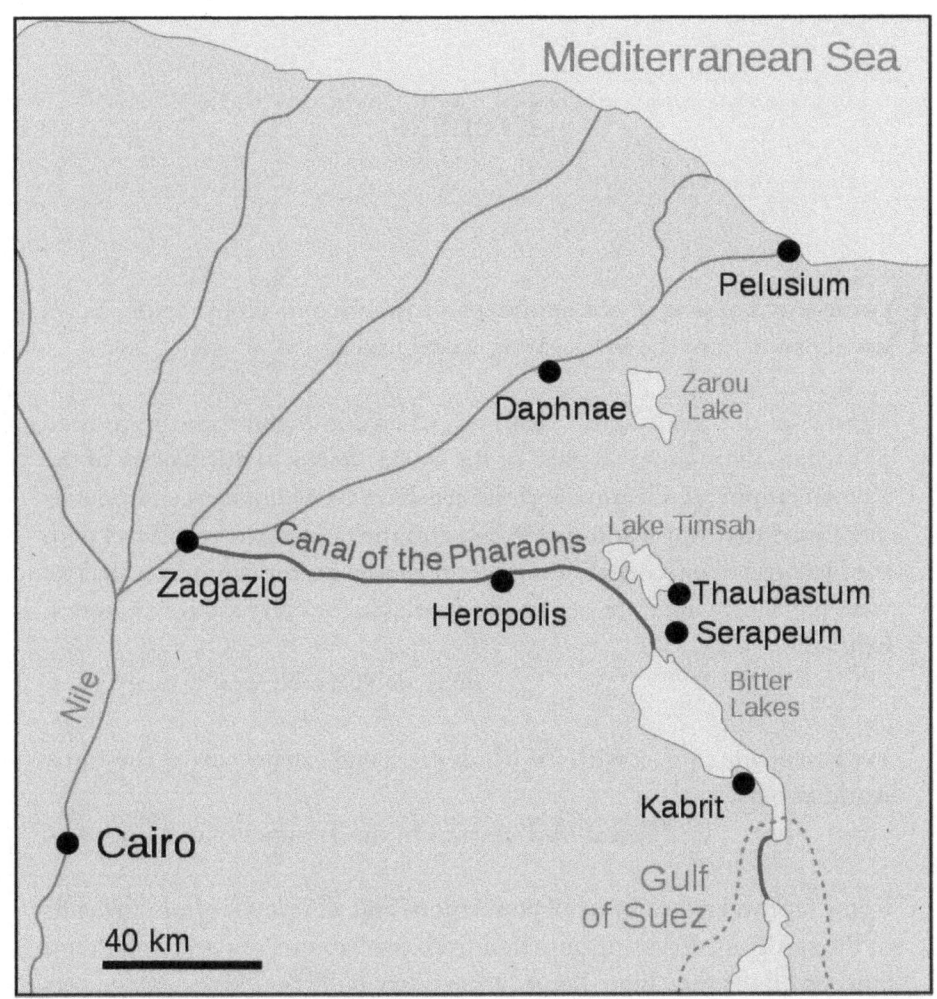

Map 6. Canal of the Pharaohs, precursor of the modern Suez Canal, started in Pharaoh Sesostris' I reign, c.1960 BCE but not completed until at least Darius I. (*Annie Brocolie via Wikimedia Commons/CC BY-SA 2.5*)

Preface

Rome was nothing if not confident of its place in global trade, as these statements from the first century CE remind us:

'Who does not freely admit that now, when communications have been opened up throughout all parts of the world, thanks to the majesty of the Roman empire, civilization and the arts have come on leaps and bounds due to the two-way trading of goods and the enjoyment we all feel with the blessings of peace that brings? At the same time, many goods that we were previously unaware of are now available for everyday consumption by us all?'

Pliny the Elder, Natural History *14, 1.*

'We have made contact with the whole earth and can now claim the entire world as ours.'

Seneca the Younger, On the Tranquility of Mind, *4, 4.*

'Rome received riches from all populations and all revenues from the ends of the earth ... everything garnered from the harvests of Africa, all that is crushed on the threshing-floors of the sultry Nile; the gleanings of divers in Eastern seas; the citron-wood of Massylia; the glory of the Indian tusk.'

Statius, Silvae *3, 3, 89–98.*

Introduction

The more curious and worldly man or woman of the Roman Empire may have wondered as he or she jostled their way through the clamorous and hectic markets and shops of their cosmopolitan cities and towns: where on earth does all this stuff come from?

The exotic fruits and vegetables, the equally exotic animals, bizarre reptiles and colourful birds, the aromatic spices, the luxurious silks, the heady perfumes, ivory, the staple grain supplies and precious metals, all of them may have had their origin in other parts of the existing Empire, through trade within the diverse markets in occupied countries, but a good deal of it was from lands beyond Rome's established borders, in strange lands populated with and run by so-called 'barbarians', as far-flung as the Baltic region, sub-Saharan Africa, Arabia, India, Burma and China, home to the *seres* or 'silk people'.

The goods from these nations did not just turn up at the nearest port: no, they were the result of decades, centuries even, of trade missions, commercial import-export negotiations and deals conducted with other civilizations, and of a general compulsion to explore the outside and largely unknown worlds the Romans came to know generically and metaphorically as *Ultima Thule*.[1]

Nigel Sitwell, in his 1986 *Outside the Empire: The World the Romans Knew*, bemoans the fact that many histories of the Roman Empire all too often 'treat it as if it existed in complete isolation'; just like the market produce referred to above (it just showed up), with contemporary maps showing the Empire to be surrounded by blank space – liminalising, erasing even, the rest of the known world as if the traveller who dared to explore this nothingness would surely fall off the end of a world familiar to the Romans.

This book aims to restore and reinstate the rest of the world, and at the same time to bring the huge influence it had on Rome into sharp focus. In doing so we get a more rounded and complete history of Rome and her empire.

The lands and their cultures annexed and absorbed by the Romans in their relentless expansionism and warmongering over the centuries are very familiar to us. In 100 CE, for example, we could travel from Britannia to Babylonia, from Aegyptus to Armenia, without ever leaving the Roman Empire: and we would, to some extent, expect to encounter Latin being spoken and written, Roman politics prevailing at a local and international level; we would be subject to Roman law; there would be Roman soldiers in the streets and in camps; and we would encounter variations of Roman religion, Roman trade, Roman architecture and Roman literature and drama in Roman theatres.

The empire, at its broadest extent under the emperor Trajan (r.98–117 CE), encompassed some 3.125 million square miles; the traditional population estimate of 55–60 million inhabitants accounted for between 16.6 per cent and 25 per cent of the known world's total population at the time, making it the largest population of any one political entity in the West until the mid-nineteenth century. However, recent demographic studies go so far as a population peak ranging from 70 million to more than 100 million.[2] At the beginning of the seventeenth century CE the three largest cities in the Empire – Rome, Alexandria, and Antioch – were still nearly twice the size of any European city. From Eboracum (York) to Carthage, and from Toledo to Jerusalem, up to one in every four people on earth lived and died under Roman law, worshipped Roman gods, and read Catullus, Livy, Lucan, Lucian and Libanius.

Rome's seemingly inexhaustible quest for new trade opportunities, war booty and buffer states to protect their borders, meant that they were regularly pushing their frontiers eastwards, westwards, northwards and southwards, testing the waters here with new alliances, annexing and conquering there. Often this brought conflict, but just as often it resulted in trade deals, amicable diplomatic relations, and two-way military support through extensive local recruitment, replenishing the legions and bolstering the auxiliary forces.

This book traces Roman activity in the wider world, from modern-day Finland to Nubia, in central and southern Asia and along the trade routes through Arabia, India, the Eurasian steppes and deserts, and China, all with one thing in common: they were beyond the fringes of the Roman Empire. The geographical parameters are given by the extent of the empire in the reign of the emperor Trajan and details what the various nations and cultures outside the empire did for the Romans in terms of commercial and cultural exchange.

It is often assumed that the borders of the Roman empire were inviolable, clean cut and never to be crossed. But these borders were porous on both sides. This 'fluidity' and cross-border communication had the effect of permitting, in the words of Mortimer Wheeler, 'a constant awareness of more distant horizons, of greater riches, more marvels, fresh menaces'.[3] In Rome, Horace tells how there was anxiety amongst the ruling classes relating to what was going on beyond the borders: Maecenas, for example, was worrying about what the Seres (Chinese and central Asians) were up to, and the same with Bactria, once the domain of the Persian King Cyrus, and the troublesome tribes on the banks of Tanais:[4]

> 'tu civitatem quis deceat status
> curas et Vrbi sollicitus times
> quid Seres et regnata Cyro
> Bactra parent Tanaisque discors'
>
> [You obsess over the state of the
> nation and you're anxious about the
> city of Rome; you fear the Seres and
> the Bactrians, once ruled by Cyrus,
> and what fractious Tanai is up to.]
>
> Horace, *Odes* 3, 29.

An ever-vigilant Cicero had his eye on the economic impact of over-the-border activity: 'The credit of the Roman bourse is inextricably bound up with the prosperity of Asia. There cannot be a crisis there without shaking our credit to its foundations'.[5]

This book describes the many 'foreign' territories the Romans visited, the various cultures and social and economic arrangements which the Romans encountered in each, and the particular reasons why, politically, economically and militarily they merited more than just a casual interest. It reveals the impact that their often-speculative forays had back within the borders of the Roman empire and on the Romans. It describes what the Roman brought to these foreign lands and what they took from them. Following in the footsteps of the Roman explorers and merchants, our long and circuitous journey takes us from the misty and dark forests of Britannia and Germania, the bleak steppes of Russia, the unforgiving Sahara Desert and the life-giving Nile, the arid and rocky spice routes to Lake Chad and back, to the hugely influential and powerful civilizations of India and China.

There are, of course, a number of books currently available on the footprint left by the Romans beyond their borders (*limes*).[6] This book looks at the subject with a fresh pair of eyes and takes in the latest research. When the Romans ventured beyond their borders the prime motivation was economic: they had to satisfy a constant demand at home for grain, exotic spices, silks and incense in exchange for home-grown Roman commodities, so it follows that our observations on what the Romans did beyond their frontiers has much to do with Roman trade and economics generally. However, eastern culture and religions were an important by-product of these commercial forays, so we also look at the impact of foreign culture and religions on traditional Roman Olympian polytheism and on society as a whole.

The book will be of interest and value to historians of ancient Rome; the Roman empire and her neighbours; classicists with a specific interest in Roman trade and commerce; economic and social historians; geographers; lecturers; researchers; and students working in Chinese studies, Indian sub-continental studies; South-East-Asian studies; Middle East and North African studies; ancient religion studies; and ethnologists. Anyone with an interest in the global impact of the Silk Road and other trade routes will also find it valuable.

Chapter 1

Where in the World Am I? The Roman and his Geography

This chapter attempts to locate the Romans in the known world. It shows how the trader, as he prepared for an expedition to the ends of Empire, might be helped by various reference books and maps possibly available in local libraries or from fellow merchants.

Romans from very early days, like other civilizations before them, had no choice but to trade with other nations and other civilizations. There were at least three cardinal reasons for this. The first is existential: to make good any deficiencies in local resources, such as metals for weaponry and grain for bread; to offset payments for imports by negotiating and bartering with Roman goods for export; to achieve a trade surplus, the revenues from which and the associated taxes would (or should) go into the national exchequer; and to satisfy demands at home for exotic spices and food, jewellery, textiles, incense, slaves and strange animals. Trade revenues were, like militarism and expansionism, an existential issue for Rome: trade surpluses helped pay for the armies which pushed further from Rome's ever evolving borders to enable more global trade which helped finance more legions and the cost of occupying new territories. And so it was that on the accession of Augustus and the dawning of the Roman Empire, the Pax Romana and the relative stability it brought fostered more trade further afield, the revenues from which helped finance the administration of provinces and protectorates, at least up to the reign of Trajan (98 to 117 CE).

What then, and where, was on the agenda? The Romans were aware of the existence of India but only 'discovered' the Far east and China in the first century BCE, when glorious silks started turning up in the Empire to the delight, no doubt, of fashionable, peacocking, elite Roman women. The trouble was the seemingly endless miles of desert and steppes between Rome and these markets, blocked off, as we shall see, by a decidedly uncooperative Parthian Empire jealously guarding the Silk Road and the Incense Route where they traversed what is now Iran.

So, the impulse to trade as widely as possible to satisfy the needs of an extensive empire was a given with the Romans, as it was with their neighbours in the Mediterranean basin and with their contacts further afield. These neighbours and other traders, often middle-men in the prevailing economic situation, would have demonstrated to eager-to-learn Romans the obvious benefits of reciprocal trade by showing off the goods they brought back with them to Rome, and their associated profits. It would not have taken very long for a Roman merchant to realize that he could eliminate his middle man entirely by hiring a boat, purchasing some Roman commodities in demand abroad to barter with, buying an abacus and setting sail for one of the ports or foreign markets on one trade route or another which were springing up all over the place, north, south, east and west.

Less crucially, it was, and still is, generally believed that travel and adventure – a pre-requisite of trade – are a very good thing for all sorts of reasons:

> *Adventure is worthwhile* – Aesop
> *Travel and change of place impart new vigour to the mind* – Seneca the Younger
> *I did not tell half of what I saw, for I knew I would not be believed* – Marco Polo
> *Man cannot discover new oceans unless he has the courage to lose sight of the shore* – André Gide
> *Not all who wander are lost* – J. R. R. Tolkien
> *Borders? I have never seen one. But I have heard they exist in the minds of some people* – Thor Heyerdahl

Distance and direction did not, it seems, present so great a problem for the more adventurous and committed merchant, nor did deception and fraud, piracy, mutiny, being murdered by the locals, shipwreck, getting hopelessly lost or dying from thirst or starvation. The potential monetary benefits were well worth all of this. After all, the more literate of traders may have been aware that the Etruscans, Egyptians, Phoenicians, Carthaginians, Greeks, Celts, the Northmen, Africans, Arabs and Indians, and the Chinese, had been trading for centuries – like them, the Romans were obliged to if they wanted to survive.

Shipwrecks can tell us much about Roman sea trade, as we shall see frequently below; perhaps one of the most helpful of wrecks is the *Uluburun Shipwreck*; the *Uluburun* was a Bronze Age vessel discovered sunk off the coast of Kas, Turkey. The vessel was probably originally from Phoenicia, and dates around 1300 BCE. Despite its pre-dating the Roman period by some 600 years we can glean much from it which will have still been relevant when the Romans were sea-trading. Most excitingly, the ship was laden with a full cargo of goods, and may have left a port in Lycia on its way to a port on the Greek mainland. Since 1984 archaeologists have reclaimed over 17 tons of artefacts – 'a treasure trove of goods and information on the trade and cultural interaction across the ancient Bronze Age Mediterranean' in the words of Mark Cartwright. Cartwright adds more useful detail: 'It is estimated the *Uluburun* wreck was once around 15 metres in length, 5 metres wide and capable of carrying up to 20 tons of cargo. The hull and keel were made from Lebanese cedar with fixtures and fastenings in oak'.

At a depth of 60 or so metres and with a cargo of over some 250 square metres, the first marine archaeology project on the wreck by the Institute of Nautical Archaeology of Texas A&M University required 22,400 dives to locate and bring up those 17 tons of fascinating artefacts.

Cartwright gives a fascinating description of the cargo manifest:

> 'The main cargo of the ship was raw materials. The largest item was copper ingots, 348 of them, totalling 10 tons in weight. These took the form of 'oxhide' and circular buns, which refers to the shape they had, forms common in the Bronze Age Mediterranean. Lead isotope analysis revealed the ingots were pure copper and from Cyprus. The ingots were placed in four rows along the length of the ship's hold in a herringbone arrangement to minimise their movement while at sea.
>
> 'The next biggest load was 120 pure tin ingots (also in 'oxhide' or bun shape) weighing over a ton in total. Analysis showed that these ingots were originally from mines in the Taurus mountains in Turkey and a source in Afghanistan or nearby; although the fact many of them were cut into four pieces suggests they were not taken directly from the mines but had already been traded elsewhere. There were around 150 Canaanite jars [*pithoi*] of terebinth resin, the largest such find ever. Analysis of pollen within the resin indicates it came from [modern-day] Israel.'

Moving on to the contents of the *pithoi*: nine Cypriot *pithoi* contained olive oil or pomegranates; there was 175 glass disk ingots, weighing 350 kilos in four colours: dark blue, turquoise, purple, and yellow. No doubt these were destined to be cut into beads or used as inlay in jewellery. There were also some 70,000 beads on board in glass and faience. Finally, there was about one ton of cobble ballast in the ship.

Miscellaneous goods on the ship included:

- 24 ebony logs.
- a single ivory elephant tusk and fourteen hippopotamus teeth in addition to various goods made from ivory.
- jewellery, figurines, vessels, and weapons made from gold, silver, bronze, tin, and faience.
- On the exotic side there was Baltic amber, an Italian sword, three ostrich eggshell vases, and cylinder seals from Mesopotamia.

- Perishable goods including spices (cumin, sumac), herbs (coriander, sage), condiments (safflower), olives, almonds, grapes, figs, grain, murex shells, and orpiment, a yellow mineral used as a dye.

Cartwright concludes that:

'It is no surprise that many excavated artefacts relate to the actual running of the ship such as galley wares, lamps, fishing tools, and scrap gold and silver jewellery to be used as payments. The discovery of four balances and their accompanying weights would suggest there were four Phoenician/Canaanite merchants on board. That one was senior, perhaps even the captain, is hinted at by the presence of one superior set of weights being in the form of animals and a single Phoenician sword with an ivory and ebony inlay handle. Mycenaean goods, notably seals and double axes, as wells as pairs of personal effects from mainland Greece, suggest that at least two other people on board were Mycenaean.

'The *Uluburun* wreck is one of those rarest of occurrences in archaeology of an undisturbed time capsule of the past, providing, in this case, a unique window into Bronze age maritime trade and those who pursued it.'

Its antiquity in relation to Roman trading activity is not significant given that most features of the *Uluburun* wreck would have been much the same: type of ship and cargo we know were very much the same for centuries afterwards.

What other resources were available to the Roman merchant if he wanted to make the most of his business trips? Valuable information relating to destinations and the type of marketable goods to be found at one's destination would have been handed down between merchants in the Roman ports, including Ostia and Portus, and by other anecdotal means. The more ardent trader might have had recourse to works of reference, including atlases, to be found in libraries and archives, some of which we can assume are no longer extant. Traders in Alexandria, for example, may have been able to refer to useful books in the great library there. Although there is no real evidence for the existence of the equivalent of ships' chandlers in the ancient world, it is hard to believe that there were not establishments specialising in ship supply in the larger ports around the Mediterranean.

The book trade, such as it was, may have been able to help in some rare instances although the market was, of course, limited by it being largely the preserve of the very rich, general low levels of literacy and the painfully slow process of book production which involved finding the original and then having it laboriously copied. What bookshops there were catered for an on-demand service and generally focussed on literature rather than non-fiction, although technical and military catalogues and encyclopaedic works were increasingly popular – the concept of stockholding to any degree simply did not exist.

So, while there was no indication of any significant organised and flourishing book trade with authors, publishers, booksellers, library and school suppliers interacting, there were signs of a nascent commercial trade in books. Kenyon asserts that 'at the end of the fifth century BCE and in the early part of the fourth, books existed in Athens in considerable quantity, and were cheap and easily accessible'. In *Frogs*, Aristophanes (optimistically perhaps) tells us that everyone in the audience had a copy of the play to hand, while Xenophon includes 'many books' in the cargoes of wrecked ships. Later we find researchers at Alexandria requesting copies of individual titles be made for them, while one prospective customer tells that 'according to Harpocraton, Demetrius the bookseller has them'.

In his *Anabasis*, describing events between 401 and 399 BCE, Xenophon reported that books (in the form of papyrus rolls) made up part of the cargo of ships wrecked off Salmydessus on the north coast of Thrace. This is evidence that books were probably exported from Athens to the Euxine coast by this date and, according to Reynolds and Wilson, indicative of an international book trade:

'Here [Salmydessus] many vessels sailing to the Pontus run aground and are wrecked; for there are shoals that extend far and wide. And the Thracians who live on this coast have boundary stones set up and each of them plunder the ships that are wrecked within their own limits; but in earlier days, before they fixed the boundaries, it was said that in the course of their plundering many of them used to be killed by one another. Here there were found great numbers of beds and boxes, quantities of written books, and lots of all the other commodities that shipowners carry in wooden chests.'

Xenophon, Anabasis, 7,5, 12–14; *trans. adapted from Carleton L. Brownson*

As well as referring to books going down with the stricken ship, Xenophon gives us an interesting description of one way in which vessels on the point of setting sail might provision their vessels in the absence of a handy ships' chandler:

'After him Xenophon rose and spoke as follows: "Cheirisophus, then, is setting off to acquire some ships, and we are to stay here; … In the first place, we must obtain provisions from hostile territory, for we neither have an adequate market, nor have we, with some few exceptions, the means of buying goods; but the territory is hostile, and so there is danger that many of you will die if you set out to get provisions carelessly and without caution. Rather, it seems to me that you ought to get your provisions in foraging parties and not roam about at random, in order that you may be kept safe, and that we generals ought to have charge of this matter." This proposal was adopted.'

Xenophon, Anabasis 7, 5, 1; trans. adapted from Carleton L. Brownson

We can now look at what sources of information were available to the Roman explorer and merchant should he be able and diligent enough to look them out.

Geographies

Strabo opens his *Geography* with the assertion that Homer is the founder of geography; indeed the *Iliad* and the *Odyssey* are mines of geographical information: Homer gives us a circular world ringed by a single huge ocean, indicating that by the eighth century BCE the Greeks had a good hold on the geography of the eastern Mediterranean. This circularity is predicated on the establishment of the borders of the known, and inhabited world – οἰκουμένη, (*oikumene*) as in (Herodotus 3.114): χώρη ἐσχάτη τῶν οἰκεομένων χωρῶν, 'the furthest country of the inhabited countries'. As such it is not dissimilar from the Latin terms, *orbis terrarum* and *Ultima Thule*.

Anaximander of Miletus is the first we know to have attempted a scale map of the known world, while Hecataeus of Miletus summarised earlier knowledge by assessing previous works on the subject and by speaking to the sailors passing through the busy port of Miletus. Herodotus' *Histories* is replete with geographic descriptions of much of the known world; Egypt, Scythia, Persia, and Asia Minor are all described, as well as a passing mention of India.

Pythagoras may have been the first to suggest a spherical world, a notion taken up by Plato, while Aristotle supplied the empirical evidence to support this.

Oikoumene (the whole inhabited world) defined, ancient mapmakers set about wrangling with incorporating essential topography, such as rivers, lakes, mountains and cities. Aristagoras' map is an early example of this, cited at Herodotus 5, 49. Comprehensiveness and detail were a problem because the maps had to be sufficiently big to accommodate all that detail, and so had had to be large scale wall-maps (*pinax* or *tabula*) displayed on a large wall or floor. Alternatively, the maps might be manipulated by increasing the size of densely populated areas and reducing the size of deserts, as in Ptolemy, *Geography*, 8, 1, *Location of Belgica Gallia*.

Explorers added to the growing information: we shall meet Hanno the Navigator, Pharaoh Necho II and Pytheas below. Military men too had something to say, not least Alexander the Great who was on a mission to discover more about the east and included geographers in his train; Julius Caesar expatiated on Gaul and Germany, and Augustus described Arabia Felix and what has become known as Ethiopia (*Res Gestae* 26). Tacitus too supplied invaluable information on Britannia and Germania, particularly in his *Agricola* and *Germania* respectively.

The ancient Greeks had carved up the world into three continents: Europe, Asia, and Libya (Africa). The Hellespont formed the border between Europe and Asia. The border between Asia and Libya was the Nile. The southern part of Africa was *terra incognita*, as was northern Europe and Asia; hence it was believed that they were encircled by a sea and uninhabitable. Eratosthenes calculated the Earth's circumference quite accurately, and the distance from the Atlantic to India was more or less known, raising the vital question of what was out there in the lands east of Asia and to the west of Europe. Crates of Mallus (fl. second century BCE) responded that there were actually four inhabitable land masses, two in each hemisphere. He is remembered for making the earliest known globe of the Earth, in Rome.

Much of this knowledge is now lost, but before it disappeared it would have been available and discussed in the Roman period, and may well have provided invaluable information (or some confusion?) about regions close to and far from Rome. Helpfully, a significant amount is referenced by Strabo (64 BCE–ca. 24 CE) in his seventeen-volume tour de force, the *Geography*.

None of Strabo's maps are extant, but his detailed descriptions give a unique snapshot of geographical knowledge at the time. Pliny the Elder's (23–79 CE) *Natural History* also has useful sections on geography, while, 100 years after Strabo, Ptolemy (90–168 CE) mapped the now-extensive Roman empire in his *Geographia*, including Britannia. Ptolemy's work is a list of about 8,000 place names in the Roman Empire of the second century CE; every place is located with latitude and longitude, with the objective being to produce the complete map of Ptolemy's world.

https://www.ancientportsantiques.com/ancientmaps/#1 tells us that: 'His latitudes are related to the equator, like we do today, and the value of one minute of latitude is 1852m (or one nautical mile, by definition)'.

Marinus of Tyre had paved the way for Ptolemy, who used Marinus' work as a source for his *Geography* and acknowledges his great debt to him. Ptolemy (33) said: 'Marinus says of the merchant class generally that they are only intent on their business, and have little interest in exploration, and that often through their love of boasting they magnify distances.' Marinus' geographical treatise is lost and known to us only from Ptolemy's remarks, from which we glean that he 'introduced improvements to the construction of maps and developed a system of nautical charts'. Pausanias (c. 110 – c. 180 CE) provided the discerning

8 The Roman Empire and the Wider World

merchant with much valuable information on Greece, gleaned from personal visits and published in his *Description of Greece* ('Ελλάδος Περιήγησις). Michael C. Howard describes it as the world's first travel guide.

Around 400 CE, the *Peutinger Table*, perhaps the first road atlas, was published delineating the entire Roman road network, the *cursus publicus*, from Britain to the Middle East and Africa, as well as including India, Sri Lanka and China. Another useful tool for Roman traders travelling by road.

Other gazetteers of places, place names and Roman roads can be found in the *Ravenna Cosmography*, a list of place-names covering the world from India to Ireland, compiled by an anonymous and fastidious cleric in Ravenna around 700 CE. We know from textual evidence that the author often used maps as his source.

And there is the *Antonine Itinerary*: an *itinerarium* was a register of the stations and their distances from each other along various roads. Presumably the data for this came from official documents, possibly from a survey carried out under Augustus. We can assume that they all three played a part in overland trade within the empire to one degree or another.

Maps

The following maps may have been available for merchants to consult at one time or another:

- A reconstructed map of the known world according to Eratosthenes (276–195 BCE), the Greek Alexandrian scholar from Cyrene. (Bunbury, E.H., 1811–1895, *A History of Ancient Geography among the Greeks and Romans from the Earliest Ages till the Fall of the Roman Empire*. London: John Murray, 1883 CE)
- Detail of the *Tabula Peutingeriana*: This shows a section of the *Tabula Peutingeriana*, a thirteenth-century map of the world believed to be based on a Roman original. This detail includes Rome, the heart of the Roman Empire. The scroll measures a huge 1ft 1in x 22ft 1in, and is divided into eleven segments.
- Ptolemy's world map, reconstituted from Ptolemy's *Geography* (circa 150 CE) in the fifteenth century, depicting 'Sinae' (China) at the extreme right, beyond the island of 'Taprobane' (Ceylon or Sri Lanka, oversized) and the 'Aurea Chersonesus' (Southeast Asian peninsula).
- A mid-fifteenth century Florentine map of the world based on Jacobus Angelus' 1406 Latin translation of Maximus Planudes' late-thirteenth

century rediscovered Greek manuscripts of Ptolemy's second-century *Geography*. Ptolemy's first (modified conic) projection.
- The Eleventh Map of Asia (*Descriptio Undecimae Tabulae Asiae*) from Ptolemy's *Geography*, depicting India beyond the Ganges (*India extra Gangem*) and the land of the Sinae in south-east Asia.
- British Library Harley MS 7182, fifteenth century. Detail of East and Southeast Asia in Ptolemy's world map. Gulf of the Ganges (Bay of Bengal) to the left, Southeast Asian peninsula in the centre, South China Sea to the right, with 'Sinae' (China).

The *World Map of Herodotus*, published on 26 April 2012, is an attempt to show what Herodotus believed the world looked like in the fifth century BCE based on his writings.

The *Periplus of the Erythraean Sea* and others

This *peripli* were references tailor-made for the trader and explorer, depicting as they do ports and harbours in various regions. Details of the *Periplus of the Erythraean Sea* and eight others are detailed below.

Chapter 2

Roman Trade

Pliny the Elder sums it up nicely: abridged from *Natural History*, 37, 78:

'The most valuable of all from among the products of the sea, are pearls: of objects that lie on the surface of the earth, it is crystals that are most highly esteemed: and of those under the ground, smaragdus, precious stones, and murrhine, are the things upon which the highest value is placed. The most costly things that are gathered from trees, nard and that are derived from the trunks of trees, logs of citrus-wood; that are produced by shrubs, cinnamon and cassia, that are yielded by the sap of trees or of shrubs, amber, balsamum, myrrh, and frankincense; the most valuable products furnished by living animals, on land, are the teeth of elephants; by animals in the sea, tortoise-shell; by the coats of animals, the skins which the Chinese dye, and the substance gathered from the hair of the she-goats of Arabia, by amphibious creatures the purple of the murex. We must mention that gold, for which there is such a mania with all mankind, hardly holds the tenth rank as an object of value, and silver, with which we purchase gold, hardly the twentieth!'

Roman trade, like war, was an ever-present facet of Roman life in the monarchy, republic and empire. Like war it was existential: trade and commerce prevented the Romans from starving while surpluses helped finance the army and navy to enable them in turn to fight the wars, inculcate 'Romanization' and deploy the diplomacy which enabled Rome to expand and secure her borders or eliminate threats from enemies. To understand the trade-related impact of extra-empire commerce we need to explain the ways in which the Romans were conducting trade within their own borders, borders which started small and limiting, safeguarding a small but expansionist monarchy, but which grew inexorably and exponentially over the following 750 years or so.

Rome traded within her own borders from her early days as an aggressive expansionist people in the Italian peninsula to the vast extent of empire under Emperor Trajan in the second century CE. As the borders extended relentlessly into the unknown world so then did trade expand. Imported goods for domestic consumption and exports would, over time, have included: olives, fish, meat, cereals, salt, fish sauce (*garum*), olive oil, wine and beer, leather, furs and hides, dogs for hunting, objects made from wood, glass, or metals, textiles, pottery, and materials for manufacturing and construction such as glass, marble, wood, wool, bricks, gold, silver, copper, and tin. Finally, there was, of course, a thriving trade in slaves – men, women and children.

Roman trade beyond its borders would, in most respects, be an extension of the commercial activity already going on within Rome's borders, its domestic trade, if you like. Ships, ports, merchants, warehousing, taxation inside the empire and their functions would have been much the same when Roman traders ventured beyond.

In the beginning, the Roman monarchy engaged in regular commerce by way of the river Tiber. We get a sense of local Italian trade with the Samnites according to Rafael Scopacasa in his *An Allied View of Integration: Samnite Elites, Consumption and Ceramics in the 2nd Century BC*, recording that evidence has been found at Montano Vatrano of 'specialised craft production, including textile production' demonstrating 'organised manufacturing activity' and evidence for the consumption of Greek wine from Rhodes and Cnidus showing that 'the local aristocracies were carefully cultivating new styles of consumption'.

Trade with Carthage

Carthage was born of trade – founded as it was in 814 BCE by Phoenician merchant colonists from Tyre: by the sixth century BCE, the ships and merchants of Carthage were a familiar sight throughout the western Mediterranean. Two hundred years later, after a series of military conquests, Carthage controlled most territories west of the gulf of Sirte, (in present-day Libya), and much of the coasts of Numidia and Iberia.

The Punic Wars between Rome and Carthage changed everything to do with commerce in the Mediterranean; before the destruction of Carthage the Republic had enjoyed important commercial exchanges with Carthage, regulated by a number of commercial and political agreements. As powerful, competing movers in the Mediterranean region both empires saw the sense in formalising and regulating their respective interests and influence, especially with regard to trade. In the early days of the Republic it was clear that Rome and Carthage differed widely in their perceptions of sea-borne trade: their economic interests and methods of expansion were very different. Rome was much more focussed on defending itself against her neighbours on the Italian peninsula: Samnites, Etruscans, Gauls, and Greeks, and then on conquering them. Carthage, on the other hand, was torn between the aristocratic party, which was inclined to extend the power of the city into surrounding lands, and the commercial party, which was more interested in exploiting trade routes and markets.

With the serial warmongering prosecuted by the Romans it was not long before the spoils of war began to insinuate themselves into the fledgling Roman economy in the shape of war booty and tribute. Land annexations and agreements with *socii* to provide military support in times of need made it a simple option for the Romans to just let the Greeks and Etruscans get on with the business of seaborne trade. In the fourth century BCE a divide emerged redefining the maritime commerce of the Mediterranean: the Aegean, Adriatic and Ionian Seas usually came under the control of the sea-board cities of the Greeks, whereas the western Mediterranean came under the aegis of the Carthaginians; the Tyrrhenian Sea was shared by Carthage with the Etruscans and the Greek colonies of southern Italy.

Four treaties were signed between the two states between 509 BCE and 279 BCE. And then came the three Punic Wars, after the first two of which further treaties were concluded in 241 and 201 BCE.

First Treaty 509 BCE
Having got rid of Lucius Tarquinius Superbus, the legendary seventh and last king of Rome, the newly established Roman Republic had an urgent need to secure its supplies, which were controlled largely by Greek and Etruscan merchants through Etruscan Caere and Pyrgi, its port. Rome looked to Carthage for support since they were already operating in and out of Caere, as evidenced by votive writings uncovered written in both Etruscan and Phoenician. Polybius (3, 22) tells us that the treaty stipulated that there 'shall be friendship between the Romans and their allies, and the Carthaginians and their allies'.

Second Treaty 348 BCE
After 150 years of relentless military campaigning, Rome had conquered much of Etruria, destroyed Veii and repelled the Gallic invasion of 390 BCE although, according to Livy (7,11, 2–11), it felt threatened by the second Gallic invasion of 360 BCE. Rome was also riven by internal strife, the Conflict of the Orders, not least between the patricians and the plebeians for rights to public office and to political involvement and the management of land and the spoils of the incessant wars. Rome was also fighting the Ernici, the Volsci, the Tiburtini and the Etruscans and was preparing to do battle with the Samnites, who were raiding rich Campania, which Rome also coveted.

The second treaty was in effect an iteration of the first treaty, with a few cities added. The Carthaginians added Tyre and Utica and promised not to attack the coastal cities of Latium that had allied themselves with Rome. Polybius records (3, 24) that as with the first treaty, the new treaty proclaimed that there 'shall be friendship between the Romans and their allies, and the Carthaginians, Tyrians, and [the] township of Utica' on the conditions listed, and that Romans be permitted to trade in the Carthaginian province of Sicily and in Carthage, and Carthaginians were allowed to reciprocate by trading in Rome.

Third Treaty 306 BCE

By now Rome dominated most of southern Etruria and Campania; it had been embroiled in its wars with the Samnites from 343 BCE, and would be for another fifty years or so. In 306 BCE, Rome had come to an agreement with Rhodes, another city in the throes of commercial expansion. In 303 BCE, Rome and Taranto concluded a treaty that pegged the limits of Roman navigation at the Lacine Promontory (Capo Colonna).

Polybius argued that the Third treaty was a fiction and a forgery by the pro-Carthaginian historian Philinus (Polybius 93.26), but research by John Serrati in 2006 suggests that the treaty did in fact exist.[1] Philinus said that Rome agreed not to enter Sicily and Carthage agreed not to encroach on the peninsula; while the stipulations on Carthage did not change, Rome was excluded from the Sicilian market.

Fourth Treaty 279 BCE

In 282 BCE, ten Roman ships appeared in Tarantine waters, violating the treaty referred to above, but they were either destroyed or forced to flee. A Roman delegation set sail to request restitution for the ships and the prisoners, but it was rejected, and war between the two states began in 281 BCE. The Tarantine attempt to form an anti-Roman league with the Italic nations came to nothing, and in 280 BCE they enlisted the assistance of Pyrrhus, the king of Greece, to lead the war against the Romans.

Pyrrhus showed up with an army of 25,000 men and 20 elephants in Taranto; his assault on Rome was proclaimed a success: the Battle of Heraclea in Lucania against the legions under Publius Valerius Laevinus owed its success to the deployment of elephants, weapons of mass destruction which the Romans had never set eyes on before. In 279 BCE, Pyrrhus saw the Battle of Asculum as a victory over the armies under consuls Publius Sulpicius Saverrio and Publius Decius Mus. That battle, however, was won at a heavy cost to the victor and inspired the term 'Pyrrhic victory'. Pyrrhus subsequently returned to Taranto.

Agathocles (Pyrrhus' new father-in-law) offered Pyrrhus the crown of Sicily in exchange for helping defeat the Carthaginians. Pyrrhus accepted, partly to avoid the Romans: he landed in Sicily and successfully pushed the Carthaginians back to Lilybaeum, on the western coast. This all prompted Carthage to sign the fourth treaty with Rome.

The Treaty of Lutatius 241 BCE, amended 237 BCE
The Treaty of Lutatius was signed between Carthage and Rome in 241 BCE (amended four years later), after the First Punic War and its twenty-three years of conflict. A draft treaty was rapidly agreed upon, but when it was referred to Rome for ratification the Romans rejected it.

Rome then despatched a ten-man legation to settle the matter, which agreed that: Carthage would hand over what it still held of Sicily; relinquish its occupation of groups of islands nearby; release all Roman prisoners without ransom, although ransom had to be paid to secure the release of prisoners held by the Romans; and pay an indemnity of 3,200 talents of silver – 82,000 kilograms – over 10 years. The treaty got its name from the victorious Gaius Lutatius Catulus, who was also the chief negotiator.

In 237 BCE, with Carthage recovering from a debilitating civil war, it set off to regain the island of Sardinia, which had been lost to rebels. To the cynical Romans this was tantamount to an act of war. Their peace terms were the surrendering of Sardinia and Corsica and the payment of an additional 1,200-talent indemnity. Laid low by thirty years of war, Carthage agreed rather than enter into another conflict with Rome; the additional payment and the ceding of Sardinia and Corsica were appended to the treaty.

Trade with Greece

Greece was not well-endowed with natural resources, so if they wanted to compete in an increasingly competitive market place around the Mediterranean basin they had to colonize to garner saleable resources. From the eighth century BCE, Greek travellers established colonies in Sicily and southern Italy, and there were others as far away from the motherland as southern France and Spain in the west and as far east as the Black Sea, where Socrates noted the settlers were like 'frogs around a pond'. These Greek colonists: 'were driven in part by curiosity. Real curiosity', the *National Geographic* informs us (https://factsanddetails.com/world/cat56/sub408/entry-6382.html): 'they wanted to know what lay on the other side of the sea'. Money and wealth were obviously other motivators but they also expanded abroad to 'ease tensions at home where rival city-states fought with one another over land and resources. Some Greeks became quite wealthy trading things like Etruscan metals and Black Sea grain'. In time, when Rome had discovered its sea legs, these colonies became important markets for Roman merchants.

In the early days of the Republic Rome was pre-occupied with suppressing and overcoming neighbouring tribes on the peninsula and then extending its reach further on all points of the compass. By the second century BCE, however, Rome had become an international power and, as regards Greece, Rome's victory over the city state of Corinth and its allies in the Achaean League at the Battle of Corinth (146 BCE) was decisive, marking the end of the Achaean War and the beginning of Roman domination over Greece. It is also notable for the subsequent erasing of Corinth by the Romans in much the same way as they had totally wiped out all meaningful traces of Carthage in 146 BCE at the end of the Third Punic War. Before Corinth, however, the Romans had been gradually gaining control of mainland Greece by defeating the Kingdom of Macedon in the Macedonian Wars. The Fourth Macedonian War had ended in 148 BCE with the defeat of the Macedonian Andriscus.

When in 88 BCE, Athens and other Greek city-states revolted against Rome they were ruthlessly subdued by Lucius Cornelius Sulla; they suffered badly too in the Roman civil wars when they were systematically and economically laid waste; that was until Augustus took control and organised the Greek peninsula into the province of Achaea in 27 BCE, after which the Greek economy steadily recovered under Roman administration.

We will cover the controversy relating to things Greek pervading in Rome in our chapter on *Romanitas* below: some Romans, such as the two Catos, Juvenal and Martial, loathed with a vengeance the influence Greek culture and society was having on Rome as it slowly percolated into the fabric of Roman life, while others, men and women, adored it and embraced it. Suffice for us here to quote Horace, who puts the dilemma well when he wittily writes: *Graecia capta ferum victorem cepit* ('Captive Greece has captured her wild conqueror').[2]

In the early empire, Rome saw the economic and cultural benefits of a thriving Roman Greece and invested heavily, bringing in resources and rebuilding the cities they had wrecked; ironically, they also established Corinth as the capital city of Achaea, while Athens was allowed to prosper again as a centre of philosophy, education, the arts, architecture and the pursuit of knowledge generally.

This was the beginning of the period called the Pax Romana; the time when for roughly 200 years Rome and many of its subject nations enjoyed and benefitted from something some have labelled a 'Golden Age of Roman Imperialism': relative peace and public order, prosperous stability, power, and limited regional expansion. All this helped open up opportunities for new markets and the importation of new crops, incense, exotic flavours and foods, textiles and jewels. It began with the accession of Augustus as emperor in 27 BCE and lasted until 180 CE on the death of Marcus Aurelius, the last of the so-called Five Good Emperors.

It was during this golden age that, as we have noted, the Roman Empire achieved its greatest territorial extent in 117 CE under Trajan, and its population grew to 70 million people, around one third of the known world's population. According to Cassius Dio, the dictatorial reign of Commodus, later followed by the Year of the Five Emperors and the Crisis of the Third Century, marked the descent 'from a kingdom of gold to one of iron and rust' (72, 36, 4).

There were many beneficiaries of this extraordinary period of relative peace and economic and social stability. Roman trade was obviously one of them and it grew significantly during the Pax Romana. Roman merchants now had the freedom to sail east, largely safe from the threat of enemy action and piracy. From the east they returned to Rome laden with cargoes of silks, precious stones, onyx and spices to sate the demand from an increasing number of wealthy, fashion-conscious Romans who craved the luxurious and opulent as a means of spending their growing wages and disposable income. Margins were high for the merchants, demand was seemingly inexhaustible, and all seemed well in the Roman empire for the rich minority.[3]

As the Pax Romana was largely contemporaneous to the Pax Sinica of the eastern world during the Han Dynasty, long-distance and far-reaching travel and trade in Eurasia was significantly stimulated during these eras.

* * *

To answer in part our curious Roman's wonderment described at the opening of this book regarding the provenance of all the goods laid out in the thronging markets and bustling shops, we can reveal the sources of supply for some of the commodities as the Roman Empire expanded and more and more nations fell under her sway:

> 'The fact that many goods were produced as regional specialities on often very large estates, for example, wine from Egypt or olive oil from southern Spain, only increased the inter-regional trade of goods. That such large estates could produce a massive surplus for trade is evidenced at archaeological sites across the empire: wine producers in southern France with cellars capable of storing 100,000 litres, an olive oil factory in Libya with 17 presses capable of producing 100,000 litres a year, or gold mines in Spain producing 9,000 kilos of gold a year. Although towns were generally centres of consumption rather than production, there were exceptions where workshops could produce impressive quantities of goods. These "factories" might have been limited to a maximum workforce of 30 but they were often collected together in extensive industrial zones in the

larger cities and harbours, and in the case of ceramics, also in rural areas close to essential raw materials (clay and wood for the kilns).'

Source: Mark Cartwright, https://www.worldhistory.org/article/638/trade-in-the-roman-world/

The heaving ports which processed the imports and exports included Gades, Ostia, Portus, Puteoli, Alexandria, and Antioch.

We can conclude that the Romans' trade in lands beyond her borders was an extension of what the Romans were doing within the confines of the empire, using much the same methods, logistics and techniques but with the added perils of security and jeopardy associated with longer lines of supply.

One of those perils was piracy, particularly in the western Mediterranean where Illyrian (modern-day Croatia) freebooters were a constant threat at the end of the third century BCE. Rome had to do something about it and so went to war.

Teuta – Pirate Queen

Teuta was the queen regent of the Ardiaei tribe in Illyria; she reigned from about 231 BCE to 227 BCE as she succeeded her alcoholic husband Agron (250 BCE–230 BCE), acting as regent for her young stepson Pinnes. Polybius, somewhat disparagingly, says that she ruled 'by women's reasoning'. The trouble started when Teuta backed the piratical raids carried out by her subjects against neighbouring states (Polybius 2, 4, 1).

Things began to escalate when Teuta captured and later fortified Dyrrachium and Phoenice; while off the coast of Onchesmos, her ships raided a flotilla of Roman merchant vessels. After this Teuta's forces extended their piratical operations further southward into the Ionian Sea, defeating the combined Achaean and Aetolian fleet in the Battle of Paxos and capturing the island of Corcyra. This enabled Teuta to attack the crucial trade routes between mainland Greece and the Greek cities in Magna Graecia. Teuta had now become the 'terror of the Adriatic Sea'.

This naturally exercised Rome, concerned as they were about their trade and the protection of that trade. In 230 BCE the Romans protested to Queen Teuta but she glibly told the ambassadors that, according to Illyrian law, piracy was a legal trade, that Rome had no right to interfere in what was effectively private enterprise, and that 'it was never the custom of royalty to prevent any advantage its subjects could get from the sea'. One of the envoys allegedly retorted that Rome would make it her business to introduce better law among the Illyrians as 'we Romans have an excellent custom of punishing private wrongs by public revenge'. Teuta then imprudently sanctioned the murder of one of the Roman envoys, Coruncanius, and imprisoned the other.

The Romans reacted on a massive scale when they mobilised and set sail with an army of 20,000 troops, 200 cavalry, and the entire Roman fleet of 200 ships, under the command of consuls Lucius Postumius Albinus and Gnaeus Fulvius Centumalus. This was the first time Roman armies had ventured across the Adriatic. This was the first time that Rome had gone to war with trade and trade protection as a *casus belli*.

Significantly, the Romans set up Demetrius of Pharos as a client king to challenge Teuta's power. Demetrius had previously enjoyed a similar position under Teuta, and was himself renowned as a pirate. The Romans took Corcyra, Apollonia, Epidamnus, and Pharos, and finally laid siege to Scodra, Teuta's capital city. She surrendered ignominiously in 227 BCE, and was subjected to restrictions on military and naval activity, most crucially not to sail into an exclusion zone south of Lissa, while her territory was confined to the region around Scodra. However, the Romans did not quash the Illyrians but set up a protectorate instead. This meant that the Illyrians, as *amici* (friends), remained free, unoccupied, and untaxed, but had a moral obligation to show gratitude to Rome in the shape of military support as required. The benefits of this diplomatic solution were far-reaching for all parties in the region, not least to traders in Greece and Magna Graecia. Corinth admitted Rome to the Isthmian Games – a sure indication of the goodwill generated in the region.

Our sources are, of course, written by male historians who are hostile to the Illyrians and to Teuta in particular. In his *Histories*, Polybius opens the story of the reign of Teuta as follows:

> '[Agron] was succeeded on the throne by his wife Teuta, who left the details of administration to friends on whom she relied. As, with a woman's natural myopia, she could see nothing but the recent success and had no eyes for what was going on elsewhere ...'
>
> *Polybius, 2010, 2:4:6–2:4:8*

Cassius Dio is no less misogynistic: he describes the queen as:

> 'Woman-like, in addition to her innate recklessness, she was puffed up with vanity because of the power that she possessed ... In a very short time, however, she demonstrated the weakness of the female sex, which quickly flies into a passion through lack of judgment, and quickly becomes terrified through cowardice.'
>
> *Cassius Dio 1914, 12*

According to legend Teuta ended her life in grief by throwing herself from the Orjen mountains at Lipci in modern Montenegro.[4]

Markets

As stated, we opened this book with a glimpse at the curious Roman in awe at the huge variety of goods laid before him or her, exotic or commonplace, in the teeming markets and thronging shops. The *Forum Cuppedinis* in Rome was a general goods, delicatessen-kind of market; there were, however, at least four other sizeable markets specializing in specific goods such as cattle, wine, fish, herbs and vegetables; a *forum venalium* was a meat market. These commercial *fora* were extensions of the Roman Forum.

In his *Politics*, a pragmatic Aristotle in the fourth century BCE proposed that a city should have both a free square in which 'no mechanic or farmer or anyone else like that may be admitted unless summoned by the authorities', and a marketplace 'where buying and selling are done ... in a separate place, conveniently situated for all goods sent up from the sea and brought in from the country'.

The Roman Forum was originally used for athletic games and trading of all kinds; however, the forum became a political and financial hub where bankers and brokers maintained their offices. The *forum civilium* (judicial) and *forum venalium* (mercantile) were built under the empire to cater for the growth of the city and the burgeoning provincial business.

Harold Whetstone Johnston in his *The Private Life of the Romans* (1903, rev 1932) tells us that:

> 'The streets of Rome were so narrow that wagons and carriages were not allowed in them at hours when they were likely to be thronged with people. Through many years of the Republic, and for at least two centuries afterwards, the streets were closed to all vehicles during the first ten hours of the day, with the exception of four classes only: market wagons, which brought produce into the city by night and were allowed to leave empty the next morning, transfer wagons (*plaustra*) conveying material for public buildings, the carriages used by the Vestals, *flamines*, and *rex sacrorum* in their priestly functions, and the chariots driven in the *pompa circensis* and in triumphal processions. Similar regulations were in force in almost all Italian towns.'

The smaller *fora venalia* that specialized by type of produce started up along the Tiber, near Portus Tibernius, with the *Suarium* at the foot of the Quirinal Hill towards the Campus Martius. These included the *Forum Boarium* for cattle, its situation near the Tiber between the Capitoline, the Palatine and Aventine hills. On the site of the original docks of Rome (Portus Tiberinus) and adjacent to the Pons Aemilius, the earliest stone bridge across the Tiber, the *Boarium* was always a frenetic place for commercial activity. The *Forum (H)olitorium* (cabbage market) sold all manner of vegetables, sandwiched between the cattle market and buildings located in the Circus Flaminius. The *Forum Suarium* was the place for pork, you went to the *Forum Piscarium* for fish which in 179 BCE was incorporated in the general *Macellum*, built by Marcus Fulvius Nobilior.[5] The *Forum Pistorium* catered for bread, and the *Forum Vinarium* for wine.[6]

But of course, it was the *Forum Romanum* which drew most of the traffic, human and otherwise. Cities across the empire, like Timgad in modern Algeria, were laid out deliberately according to an orthogonal grid plan which facilitated and expedited transportation, storage and commerce generally. Helpfully, these cities were connected by good roads and navigable rivers; some canals were also dug.

Peace as opposed to war was a key engine for the expansion of trade; the unpredictability of war and homeless populations were inimical to trade. To that end, all new settlements would be located in economically viable positions and defensible hilltop positions were the preference for smaller settlements; the scourge that was piracy rendered coastal settlements particularly vulnerable for all but the larger cities.

Trade by road

Despite the many benefits of well-built and functional Roman roads, most traffic – military and mercantile – animals, carts, pedestrians – moved decidedly slowly. Consequently, the journey of choice was by sea wherever possible. Where that was not an option, one of the empire's main arteries was the Via Salaria (Salt Road), named for the salt carried from the salt pans of Ostia to Rome. The Via Domitia connected Italy to Spain, the Via Egnatia linked Rome to Byzantium. An eastward branch of the Via Egnatia, the famous road to Damascus, ran across Turkey and southward to Beirut and Syria.

Roman army engineers built pontoon bridges to convey traffic across waterways and used horses to scout the enemy on reconnaissance operations. Trajan built a bridge across the Danube, an amazing achievement for the times, to facilitate his conquest of Dacia, but it was destroyed by Hadrian who felt that it might assist a barbarian attack on Rome. Merchants naturally availed themselves of these civil engineering feats to get from market to market.

They also made use of the over 53,000 miles of paved roads, stretching from Caledonia to East Europe and on to Mesopotamia in present-day Iraq, to North Africa. Until modern times it was the greatest highway system on the planet. John Keegan in his *History of Warfare* explains how Roman roads were built primarily to facilitate the movement of troops and supplies. Roman legionaries would not have been nearly as successful in their conquests if getting materiel to them was troublesome. The system was so well organised that commanders could accurately calculate how long it would take to get their armies from one place to another: from Cologne to Rome was 67 days, Rome to Brindisi 57 days, and Rome to Syria (including two days at sea), 124 days.

Despite that, given that Roman roads were designed more to suit feet or hooves rather than wheels – with most land trade moving by pack mule – roads were never an economically viable means of transport of goods over long distances.

In the twenty-first century CE with its ubiquitous potholes, endless *stau*, jams and congestion we gaze in awe at the viability and efficiency of the 2,000-year-old Roman road network – a network which could only have helped enormously both international as well as domestic trade, generating good service for customers, and amplifying local and national economies.

However, there were no real addresses to help get the goods to their final destination. Few streets had names and those that did were devoid of signs or numbers. One wonders what difficulties this caused delivery men. Harold Whetstone Johnston reveals that:

> 'Messengers could cover a distance of about 200 miles a day on main roads by changing horses every 10 miles or so, pony express-style. Travelling in this fashion it took only about six days to reach Britain from Rome (a record that was not improved upon until the invention of modern automobiles in the 20th century).'

Sea Trade

It was not just the domestic markets which specialised by commodity. By the first century CE there was considerable interchange in trade between the provinces of the Empire by sea routes. Clearly there was specialization, particularly in manufacturing, agriculture and mining. Some provinces focussed on certain types of goods, such as grain in Egypt and North Africa and wine and olive oil in Italy, Hispania, and Greece. Before the Punic Wars completely changed the complexion of commerce in the Mediterranean, the Republic, as described above, enjoyed important commercial relations with Carthage. As we shall see, the Roman Empire traded with India and the Chinese along the Silk Road.

Marine archaeology and manuscripts show evidence of the existence of large Roman commercial fleets in the form of the remains of harbours, moles, warehouses and lighthouses at ports such as Civitavecchia, Ostia, Portus, Leptis Magna and Caesarea Maritima. At Rome itself, Monte Testaccio is evidence of the scale of this commerce. As we have described, Roman ships were prey to pirates – a menace only partly mitigated by protective fleets of *liburna* galleys and triremes of the Roman navy. A *liburna* was a small and speedy galley suited for raiding and patrols.

On board, a trading vessel might be fitted out with a lookout post bristling with arms and, according to Athenaeus (*Deipnosophists*, 43), 'four young fully-armed men and two archers'; Pliny confirms this (*NH* 6,26): wooden palisades with iron fittings could be raised when under attack, with stones for the crew to hurl down on malevolent assailants (Thucydides, 4, 25, 6) – a legacy of the Greek navy, stones which might also be hauled up to the top of the masts for the riggers to bombard the pirates with. Some ships were issued with small catapults (*Sivakasindamani)* and grapples (ravens), designed to clench enemy craft and winch them into a vulnerable position (Athenaeus, *Deipnosophists*, 43). Athenaeus also tells us how 'dolphins' (torpedo-shaped lead ingots) were deployed to bomb enemy craft and shatter their timbers.

Sea transport was obviously the preferred method for bulky, low-value commodities like grain and construction materials, since, according to Keith Hopkins, the cost of sea transportation was sixty times lower than land.[7] Sea was also the fastest method of transport; a sound vessel could sweep through 1,000 nautical miles in nine days. On the other hand, weather was a hazard and storms were greatly feared; add to that those attacks by often murderous pirates, then a cargo voyage was never going to be a relaxing affair. The unpredictable weather also ensured that ships and merchant seamen often stayed in the safety of port between the stormy months from November to March. Staple goods and commodities like grain and cereals and papyrus scrolls for the all-important books were imported from Ptolemaic Egypt to Italy.

Mark Cartwright tells us that:

'From the analysis of over 900 shipwrecks from the Roman period the most typical size of merchant vessel had a capacity for 75 tons of goods or 1500 *amphorae* but there were bigger vessels capable of transporting up to 300 tons of goods. One interesting example is the 40s CE *Port Vendres II* wreck located in the Mediterranean off the Spanish-French border. The cargo was taken from at least 11 different merchants and contained olive oil, sweet wine, fish sauce, fine pottery, glass, and ingots of tin, copper, and lead.'

The trade across the Indian Ocean thrived in the first and second centuries CE. The sailors took advantage of the monsoon to cross the ocean from the ports of Berenike, Leukos Limen and Myos Hormos on the Red Sea coast of Roman Egypt to the ports of Muziris and Nelkynda on the Malabar Coast. The main trading partners in southern India were the Tamil dynasties of the Pandyas, Cholas and Cheras. As we shall see, many Roman artefacts have been found in India; for example, at the archaeological site of Arikamedu, in Puducherry. Detailed descriptions of the ports and items of trade around the Red Sea and the Indian Ocean will be found in our coverage of the *Periplus of the Erythraean Sea*.[8]

There were, as we know, deities for every aspect of Roman life and activity – from conception to life in the afterlife. Mercury started off as god of the *mercatores* and the grain trade, then had his portfolio extended and became the god of all who were involved in commercial activities. On the Mercuralia on 14 May, all Roman merchants would perform the proper rituals of devotion to Mercury and ask the god to cleanse from him and from his belongings the guilt and stain arising from all the cheating and extortion he had inflicted on his customers and suppliers in the past year.

The markets, obviously, reflect demand which is in turn dictated by diet and social convention. For a Roman, bread was a staple at every meal; we know of some fifty varieties being available. Breakfast, for example, was, for those who could afford it usually bread dipped in wine or oil with cheese, milk, eggs and olives. Meat was scarce and rarely eaten by the poor, who relied more on fish complemented by radishes, pulses, turnips, leaks and porridge. Further up the social ladder, or food chain, the better off and the social climbers could enjoy an extensive menu of exotic foods, some of which to modern palates are decidedly bizarre. Spices from as far away as China found their way into Roman dishes and onto Roman tables – used to flavour every kind of 'delicacy' from peacocks' brains to stuffed dormice, flamingo tongues and parrot livers. Salads and fruits were popular – not because of any healthy diet regime such as 'five a day', but on account of their relative inexpensiveness.

When it came to doing trade, theoretically at least Roman senators were subjected to restrictions under the *lex Claudia* of 218 BCE. Senators and sons of senators were not allowed to own a ship with a greater than 300 amphorae capacity (about seven tons). But they swerved round the legislation somehow and were still dabbling in trade in Cicero's time: he refers to this law in his attack on Verres, although he makes no attempt to charge him.[9]

Under the size restriction senators were still permitted to own and make use of ships. Cato the Elder (234–149 BCE),[10] when considering where to build a farm, specifically mentions that it needs to be built close to a river, road or port to facilitate and expedite transportation of goods; on the other hand, Livy was later to demonise profit made through trade by a senator.[11] Senators often utilized freedmen and enslaved agents as a loophole to legal restrictions, thereby allowing themselves to bolster and spread their sources of income.[12]

The reason why the senatorial class were allowed limited opportunities for trade in law lies probably in the financial risks involved: Cato the Elder was, as we have seen, a trader but he himself cautioned against it as it was a risky business;[13] part of the reasoning to keep senators excluded from the trade may well have been that if they had the misfortune to suffer a commercial disaster, they might fall below the financial threshold required for a senator, whereas land owning and agriculture were far safer and predicable investments. However, there is no reason to doubt that it was the wealthy senatorial class which invested most and benefitted most from the trading opportunities beyond the Empire's borders; for the most part they were the people who could afford to take the risk.

On the moral front, Polybius draws a comparison between the attitudes of Carthage and Rome towards profit from trade.[14] The feeling was that there is nothing wrong with large scale trade; on the contrary it was considered completely honourable and legitimate to import large quantities of a given product from around the world, especially if it happens to lead to a successful trader buying land and investing in Roman agriculture. Romans seem to have thought that what was dishonourable was trade on a small scale, which may have been considered by the senatorial aristocrats as somewhat grubby – in much the same way as British aristocrats in the early-twentieth century believed that 'trade' was beneath them. Small trade is considered vulgar by Tacitus when he describes the dabblings of Sempronius Gracchus in low level trade.[15]

Plutarch details Cato's involvement in trade; he was not impressed: 'He also used to lend money in what is surely the most disreputable form of speculation, that is the underwriting of ships' (Plutarch, *Cato the Elder* 21, 5–6).

Plutarch goes on to reveal how Cato would use a proxy (a freedman called Quintio) to run his business through a group of fifty other men – a consortium. The elder Cato was typical in his use of his most capable freedmen as agents, factors and merchants. In a fleet of fifty grain transports, his consortium underwrote the purchase and cost of a single ship and its grain complement. Any profit, or loss, was shared by all fifty investors.[16]

Members of the equestrian order, on the other hand, were free to partake. The important role of plebeians and freedmen who worked their shops or manned stalls at markets should not be underestimated, while legions of slaves did all the heavy lifting and the more unpleasant tasks. The slaves, of course, were themselves subject to commercial transactions and the trade in slaves was itself an important element of the Roman economy. Whatever, freedmen must have seen trading as an opportunity for upward social mobility as more and more enriched themselves on the commissions earned from import-export.

Trade, and traders, feature in Roman literature. One of the earliest references is the comedy *Mercator* by Plautus (251–184 BCE), in which Charinus, the son, explains how he entered trade on the death of his father and, after years of labouring on the family farm, he used his legacy to buy a boat of fifteen tons and marketed his cargoes of merchandise all over the place, thus making him very rich.

In his dialogue *Navigium* ('The Ship') Lucian describes Adimantus who visits a large corn freighter in the Piraeus and learns how lucrative owning a ship can be. But perhaps the most famous description of the benefits of life in trade comes from Trimalchio, who hosts a luxury dinner party in the novel by Petronius written during the reign of Nero:

> 'Then, as the Gods willed, I became the real master of the house … and came into an estate fit for a senator. But no one is satisfied with nothing. I conceived a passion for business. I will explain now – I built five ships, got a cargo of wine – which was worth its weight in gold at the time – and sent them to Rome. You may think it was a put-up job; every one was wrecked, truth and no fairy-tales. Neptune gulped down thirty million in one day. Do you think I lost heart? Lord! no, I no more tasted my loss than if nothing had happened. I built some more, bigger, better and more expensive ships, so that no one could say I was not a brave man. You know, a huge ship has a certain security about her. I got another cargo of wine, bacon, beans, perfumes, and slaves. Fortunata [his wife] did a noble thing at that time; she sold all her jewellery and all her clothes, and put a hundred gold pieces into my hand. They were the leaven of my fortune. What God wishes soon happens. I made a clear ten million sesterces on one voyage [£77,662.75]. I at once bought up all the estates which had belonged to my patron. I built a house, and bought slaves and cattle; whatever I touched grew like a honey-comb. When I came to have more than the whole revenues of my own country, I threw up the game: I retired from active work and began to finance freedmen.'
>
> *Petronius,* Satyricon; *trans. Michael Heseltine, Ed (1913)*

Petronius shows us clearly how conspicuous wealth, extravagance and exotic consumption were all *de riguer* amongst the Romans who were rolling in new money, comparable to the wealth of the old senatorial aristocracy. Around this time Rome was importing thousands of gallons of essential products like wine and olive oil from the provinces: Gaul, Spain and North Africa, supplemented with goods from beyond the empire. Indeed, this tsunami of imports caused Rome a major recycling problem in that little of it was actually recycled and so formed mountains, literally, of discarded pottery, the largest of which was Monte Testaccio.

Monte Testaccio

Monte Testaccio (or Monte dei Cocci, 'Mount of Shards') is a huge artificial mound, a kind of ceramics slag heap in Rome composed almost entirely of *testae* – shards of broken Roman pottery, mostly discarded *amphorae*, some of which were labelled with *tituli picti*. These are painted or stamped inscriptions which record invaluable detailed information such as the weight of the oil contained in the vessel, the names of the people who weighed and documented the oil and the name of the district where the oil was originally bottled. Again, it was many centuries before such enlightened labelling came again into its own. Archaeologists can thus establish that the oil in the vessels was imported under state authority and was earmarked for the *annona Urbis* or the *annona militaris*.

David Stone Potter says that:

'The *tituli picti* on the Monte Testaccio amphorae tend to follow a standard pattern and indicate a rigorous system of inspection to control trade and deter fraud. An amphora was first weighed while empty, and its weight was marked on the outside of the vessel. The name of the export merchant was then noted, followed by a line giving the weight of the oil contained in the amphora (subtracting the previously determined weight of the vessel itself). Those responsible for carrying out and monitoring the weighing then signed their names on the amphora and the location of the farm from which the oil originated was also noted. The maker of the amphora was often identified by a stamp on the vessel's handle.'[17]

We can also glean more important information from the *tituli picti* relating to the social history of the trade in oil: many of the inscriptions list more than one name, such as 'the two Aurelii Heraclae, father and son', 'the Fadii', 'Cutius Celsianus and Fabius Galaticus', 'the two Junii, Melissus and Melissa', 'the partners Hyacinthus, Isidore and Pollio', 'L. Marius Phoebus and the Vibii, Viator and Retitutus'. From this we can assume that 'many of those involved were members of joint enterprises, perhaps small workshops involving business partners, father-son teams and skilled freedmen.[18]

Amanda Claridge adds more detail in her 1998 *Rome: An Oxford Archaeological Guide*, stating that Monte Testaccio is one of the largest spoil heaps found anywhere in the ancient world, covering an area of nearly five acres at its base and with a volume of approximately 580,000 cubic metres. It is estimated by Bryan Ward-Perkins (2005) that it contains the remains of 53 million olive oil *amphorae*, in which some 1.3 billion imperial gallons of oil had been imported.[19] The mountain boasted a circumference of nearly 0.6 miles, standing 115 ft high, though it was surely much higher in ancient times. It was close to the east bank of the River Tiber and its wharves, near the Horrea Galbae warehouses where the state-controlled reserve of olive oil was stored in the late-second century CE as described by Lynne C. Lancaster.[20] So awesome was it that the mound later took on religious, social and military significance.

Most of the *amphorae*, and therefore the imported oil, came from Baetica (the Guadalquivir region of modern Spain), and smaller quantities of two types of *amphorae* from Tripolitania (Libya) and Byzacena (Tunisia). Today they are known as Dressel 20 types. Julian Bennett adds that:[21]

> 'Studies of the hill's composition suggest that Rome's imports of olive oil reached a peak towards the end of the 2nd century AD, when as many as 130,000 amphorae were being deposited on the site each year. The vast majority of those vessels had a capacity of some 15 imp gal; from this it has been estimated that Rome was importing at least 1.6 million imperial gal. of olive oil annually. As the vessels found at Monte Testaccio appear to represent mainly state-sponsored olive oil imports, it is very likely that considerable additional quantities of olive oil were imported privately.'

But the ceramics mountain was not just some random graveyard for used oil jugs: Amanda Claridge explains how it was a highly organised and carefully engineered edifice, presumably managed by a state administrative authority. She reveals how excavations in 1991 taught us that the mound had been raised as a series of level terraces with retaining walls made of nearly intact amphorae filled with sherds to anchor them in place. Empty amphorae were probably carried up the mound intact on the backs of donkeys or mules and then broken up on the spot, with the sherds painstakingly cut in half to nestle into one another. Lime appears to have been sprinkled over the broken pots to neutralise the smell of rancid oil.

Most archaeologists, including Claridge, Peña and Lancaster, agree that Dressel 20s may have been unusually difficult to recycle, unlike other types of *amphorae* which could be re-used for transporting the same product or repurposed for a different use – for instance, as drain pipes or flower pots. Fragmentary amphorae could be pounded into chips to use in *opus signinum*, a type of concrete widely used as a building material, or could simply be used as landfill. The Dressel 20 amphora, however, stubbornly broke into large curved fragments that could not readily be reduced down to small shards. It is likely that the difficulty of reusing or repurposing the Dressel 20s meant that it was more economical just to discard them.

Monte Testaccio stopped growing around 260 CE when the city's quays moved away. But there was still a need to rid Rome of the endless river of *amphorae* and archaeologists have discovered nine places around Rome where the shards were used in construction work. One such place was the Circus Maxentius, constructed between 308 and 312 CE at the third mile of the Via Appia: at least 6,000 and probably as many as 10,000 *amphorae* were used in this project. Theodore Peña tells us that directing these vessels:

> 'Toward state-sponsored construction projects for use as space-fillers in concrete vaulting, the *praefectura annonae* could have succeeded in disposing of substantial numbers of highly cumbersome and otherwise useless oil containers, while at the same time reducing the amount of lime, sand and rubble that would have been required to complete these initiatives.'[22]

José Remesal of the University of Barcelona, co-director of the Monte Testaccio excavations, told *Archaeology Magazine* (2023) that the main challenge archaeologists and economic historians generally face is the lack of 'serial documentation', that is, documents for consecutive years that reflect a true chronology. On the other hand, this is what makes Monte Testaccio a unique record of Roman commerce and provides a vast amount of datable evidence in a clear and unambiguous sequence. 'There's no other place where you can study economic history, food production and distribution, and how the state controlled the transport of a product', Remesal says. 'It's really remarkable.'[23]

Maritime Insurance

Insuring and financing voyages were big business in ancient Rome. We have noted how ancient sea transport was much more efficient than the pack animal and cart method using the ox-drawn cart. After a certain distance, about 25 miles, oxen and horses eat more grain than they can carry, so merchants preferred to head towards the sea, despite the manifold risks and dangers – storms, pirates, mutinies – and it was much cheaper for Rome to import grain by sea from Egypt, for example, than to haul it around over land. Getting enough food to feed the largest city in the known world and the military scattered around the empire was an existentialist issue: without efficient trade Rome was simply unsustainable.

So getting the maritime insurance right was of cardinal importance. Dan Wang, in his *How Maritime Insurance Helped Build Ancient Rome* (2016) tells us:

> 'Instead of paying a fee to insure cargo, merchants took out loans. These loans had very high interest rates and carried special terms: if the borrower couldn't pay back the loan, then the creditor was able to seize the ship; in addition, if the ship sank, then the borrower didn't have to pay back the creditor. The practice dates back to the Ancient Babylon of 1800 BCE. It's known as 'bottomry': the owner of a ship borrows money on the 'bottom' of the ship, so that if the borrower doesn't pay back interest given a safe voyage, then he'd forfeit the ship.'

Wang continues by informing us that historians record that merchants and creditors thought of high interest rates explicitly as compensation for taking risk. Romans copied the practice of bottomry from the Greeks, and they also equated high interest rates with paying for risk. While Roman law capped interest rates at 12 per cent, it sanctioned higher interest rates explicitly for maritime voyages because 'the price is for the peril'.

Peter Temin has estimated that it would have taken 2,000 to 4,000 ship voyages each year to feed Rome at its peak. It was a sophisticated process, with Roman agricultural products processed by machines, packed in *amphorae*, shipped in cargo boats, and distributed by inland waterways or roads.

Wang adds:

> 'Such a large trading system required a financial ecosystem to fund and insure each voyage. Every voyage was a feat of financial engineering, with multiple financial interests at play. Creditors emerged as a class of financial intermediaries to provide bottomry loans. Not every lender operated on a large scale. Surviving records of maritime loans indicate that a ship was typically insured by more than one lender. Modern scholarship broadly agrees that the shipping industry – and by extension, ancient cities – depended on these bottomry loans. These loans were so common that Romans developed a standard boilerplate that parties could copy for each voyage.'

Weights and Measures and Accounting

As for weights and measures and invoicing, the accounting of Roman trade was conducted with counting boards and the Roman abacus, which was ideally suited to the counting of Roman currency and tallying of Roman measures. The Roman abacus was of course the Roman equivalent to the modern calculator and computer; it was the first portable calculating device available for engineers, merchants, and tax collectors. It greatly reduced the time needed to perform the basic operations of commercial arithmetic using Roman numerals.

Volume

Both liquid and dry volume measurements were based on the sextarius, defined as 1/48 of a cubic foot, known as an *amphora quadrantal*. A sextarius would theoretically measure about 95 per cent of an imperial pint (568.26125 ml). A standard *amphora*, the *amphora capitolina*, was kept in the temple of Jupiter on the Capitoline Hill in Rome, so that others could be compared to it.

Weight

Units of weight or mass were usually based on factors of twelve. Modern estimates of the *libra* range from 322 to 329g (11.4 to 11.6oz), with 5076 grains or 328.9g (11.60oz) an accepted figure. The *as* was reduced from twelve ounces to two after the First Punic War, to one during the Second Punic War, and to half an ounce by the 131 BCE *lex Papiria*.

Money

As we shall see, the state monopolised much of the trade in and out of Rome to ensure the lines of supply to a hungry Italy – the *Cura Annona* and the grain dole. Of course, much trade was also carried out independently from the state, though, assisted by the development of banking. Cartwright tells us that although banking and money-lending generally remained a local affair there are records of merchants taking out a loan in one port and paying it off in another once the goods were delivered and sold on. And, which interests us most, there is also abundant evidence of a free-trade economy beyond the reaches of the empire and independent of the larger cities and army garrisons.

What we would describe as coinage was only introduced by the republican government around c.300 BCE. Well before that the great cities of the Magna Graecia region in southern Italy such as Neapolis (now Naples), Syrakousai (Syracuse), Akragas (Agrigento), Taras (Taranto), Rhegion (Reggio Calabria), Kroton (Crotone), Sybaris (Sibari), and several other Italian cities, already had a long tradition of using coinage by this time and produced them in large quantities during the fourth century BCE to pay for their wars against Italian foes encroaching on their territory. And for commercial transactions. So, the Romans would certainly have been familiar with coinage systems long before their official introduction by the government. Eventually, the economic conditions caused by the Second Punic War made the Romans fully adopt a coinage system.

The Traders

In what was a sophisticated set up, the *negotiatores* were bankers since they lent money on interest. They also bought and sold staples in bulk and acted as wholesalers. The *argentarii* acted as agents in public or private auctions, held deposits of money for individuals, cashed 'cheques' (*prescriptiones*) and served as moneychangers. The *argentarii* occasionally did the same work as the *mensarii*, who were public bankers appointed by the state. They kept strict books, called *tabulae*, which were treated in disputes as legal proof by the courts.

The *mercatores* were most often plebeians or freedmen and could be found in all the open-air markets or covered shops, selling from stalls or flogging goods by the roadsides. They also set up stalls near Roman fortresses in the *vici* and *canabae*, and around military camps during campaigns selling food, drink and clothing to the soldiers and paying cash for war booty.[24]

We have information on the economy of Roman Palestine from Jewish sources of around the third century CE where itinerant pedlars (*rochel*) took spices and perfumes to the rural population.[25] This suggests that the economic benefits of the Empire did reach the upper levels of the lower orders at least.

John Haywood summarises the economic situation well:[26]

'The empire's commercial classes remained small and enjoyed neither wealth nor the status of the landowning aristocracy ... most production in the empire was small scale and under-capitalized, the rich preferring to invest in land. It is in any case doubtful, in view of the poverty of most of the empire's population, whether the markets existed to support a greater degree of industrial production. This is probably one of the factors behind the surprising lack of technological innovation in the empire ... The ready availability of cheap slave labor may also have deterred investment in expensive machinery ... But most of the west was too poor and under-populated to support this level of urbanization and towns remained primarily administrative or military centers.'

Merchant Ships

On Greek ships we learn that:

'Early large Greek merchant ships of the Kerkouros type with combined rowing and sailing capacity seem to have been in use between 500 BC and 100 BC according to Arnaud (2012). They could carry an average of 250 tons of cargo, up to 500 tons. Their average dimensions may have been 21 x 3m, with 1:7 beam over length ratio, up to 50 x 7m for the larger ones. It may be noted also that Kerkouros ships usually docked stern first, while later ships also docked bow first as shown on the Torlonia relief. Alongside docking was required if heavy cargo (live animals, barrels) was to be lifted by cranes.'

https://www.ancientportsantiques.com/ancient-ships/merchant-ships/

The Tiber, as noted, was Rome's main trading artery in the early days of the Republic; indeed, the banks of the river were apparently dotted with quays and berths (*navalia*) to service that trade and constant military requirements. The *Navalia* itself was a military port of Rome which may also have included a naval dockyard. It is thought to have been sited on the left bank of the River Tiber to the south of the Campus Martius and is sometimes called the '*Navalia superiora*' to distinguish it from another military port further down the Tiber near the *Forum Boarium* (the '*Navalia inferiora*'). These buildings were also used to detain hostages and circus animals when silting meant navigation on the upper Tiber had become difficult.

Livy talks about 'the docks at Rome' (26, 51, 8) which existed perhaps from the mid-fourth century BCE, the earliest mentions we have. We can assume they were operational throughout the republican period, with its peak between 146 and 135 BCE. According to Cicero (*De Oratore* 1,62) their importance is testified by an expansion project in the second century BCE that attracted the prominent Cypriot architect Hermodorus of Salamis, then actively involved in several of Rome's prestigious buildings.

As Rome's expansion on the peninsula increased, so did its need to provision the towns and cities that were growing along with their burgeoning populations; add to this the expansion of the Roman army and the legionaries which all needed feeding and watering and we have a Republic that started to rely increasingly heavily on trade. Some of this was satisfied as the Romans came into frequent contact with other cultures, notably in the south of Italy: the Etruscans, the Greek cities of Magna Graecia and the Carthaginians – already seasoned maritime traders and explorers of new markets overseas.

Rome obviously had to develop her maritime capabilities, both militarily and commercially. The allied Greek cities of southern Italy, the *socii navales*, helped out with ships and crews, but the Roman fleet was embarrassingly small at twenty vessels primarily engaged in naval river patrols and deterring pirates on the high seas.

Things started to change when in 267 BCE four *praetores classici* were appointed to oversee maritime affairs, naval and commercial. Treaties were struck but, as we know, it was the First Punic War (264–241 BCE) that changed all of that when it expedited Roman naval prowess, leading to the conquest and destruction of Carthage in 146 BCE. Greece succumbed too and Rome was then able to enjoy naval superiority in the Mediterranean region (Rome's *Mare Nostrum*) by the time of the civil wars in the first century BCE, accelerating the extinguishing of the threat from predatory pirates and paving the way for the establishment of the Roman empire under Augustus.

As international trade and naval activity increased, so it followed that many types of transport ships were used to carry foodstuffs or other trade goods around the Mediterranean, many of which, especially *naves onerariae* according to Michael Charles (2005 p. 289), were often pressed into service as warships or troop transports in times of conflict, as, for example, when Scipio Africanus transported troops to North Africa in the Second Punic War in 204 BCE in 400 *naves onerariae* (Livy (29.26.3; 29.24, 9)).

The Romans named their ships specifically according to their appearance, function or cargo – usually as a compound with *navis*: and so we have *navis tecta* (covered ship), important to keep cargoes dry; *navis mercatoria* (merchant ship), or *navis praedatoria* (booty ship); *navis frumentaria* (grain), *navis lapidaria* (precious stones), and *navis vivaria* (live fish). The stunning Althiburos mosaic in the Bardo in Tunis shows a veritable catalogue of ships. In 1998 during works near the Pisa San Rossore train station, 'an impressive series of shipwrecks emerged in an exceptional state of preservation, with their cargoes of commercial products and evidence of life lived on board'. The exhibition at the Arsenali Medicei in Pisa's Museum of the Ancient Ships describe the sailors' life: clothing, luggage, lighting, how they cooked and ate, cults and superstitions, and games to pass the time during long crossings (https://www.navidipisa.it/en/).

Other finds include:

A trading ship dated to 200 BCE which was 100 feet long and had cargo holds in the fore and aft. It carried two lead anchors, bronze vessels and eight types of amphora.

First century CE ships have been found with cargos of granite stones, columns and a large anchor and amphorae carrying wine and oil. A fifth century CE ship has been found with iron anchors, hand-operated mill, a lamp from Carthage and Roman coins. Normal-size sea vessels held about 3,000 *amphorae* while large freighters held as many as 10,000.

In 2012, archaeologists found an almost intact Roman ship in the sea off the town of Varazze, some eighteen miles from Genova. Rossella Lorenz wrote in discovery.com:

'The ship, a navis oneraria, or merchant vessel, was located at a depth of about 200 feet thanks to a remotely operated vehicle (ROV) following tips from fishermen who had caught some jars in their nets. The ship sank about 2,000 years ago on her trade route between Spain and central Italy with a full cargo of more than 200 amphorae.'

Rossella Lorenz, discovery.com, August 20, 2012

Tests on some of the recovered jars revealed they contained pickled fish, grain, wine and oil. The foodstuffs were traded in Spain for other goods. 'There are some broken jars around the wreck, but we believe that most of the amphorae inside the ship are still sealed and food filled', Lieutenant Colonel Francesco Schilardi, who led the Carabinieri Subacquei, said.

In 2010, marine archaeologists using sonar scanners have discovered four ancient shipwrecks off the island of Zannone, with intact cargos of wine and oil.

'The remains of the trading vessels, dating from the first century BCE to the 5th-7th century AD, are up to 165 metres underwater. The vessels, up to 18 metres long, had been carrying amphorae containing wine from Italy, and cargo from North Africa and Spain including olive oil, fruit and garum. Another ship, as yet undated, appeared to have been carrying building bricks. It is unclear how the vessels sank and no human remains have been found. The vessels are the second 'fleet' of ships to be discovered in recent years near the Pontine Islands, an archipelago off Italy's west coast believed to have been a key junction for ships bringing supplies to the vast warehouses of Rome.

Annalisa Zarattini, archaeological services section of the Italian culture ministry. [Source: Gulfnews.com, August 23, 2010 by Ancientfoods]

Actuaria

An *actuaria* was a merchant galley used mainly for trade and transportation throughout the Roman Empire; the *actuaria* was powered with sails and oars. It was used where speed and reliability were of the essence and was consequently more expensive to operate or hire than standard merchant sailing ships. According to Casson (1991, 119–123), *actuariae* could carry both passengers and commodities such as honey, cheese, meat, and even live animals intended for gladiator combat.

Navis Oneraria

Naves onerariae were Roman merchant ships typically displacing 80–150 tons, used to carry such commodities as *garum* and grain from Egypt to Rome. They could have up to three square-rigged masts. They were totally dependent on the wind and were unable to leave port on oar power alone. Charles (2005, pp. 291–292) tells us that Claudian in *De Bello Gildonico* states that *naves onerariae* were in use until late antiquity.

Images of two *naves onerariae* are featured in the celebrated mosaic floor discovered in Lod, Israel in 1996. Haddad and Avissar suggest that it may have been commissioned as a kind of *ex-voto*, an offering in fulfilment of a vow made upon being delivered from grave danger, in this case, shipwreck. We see torn ropes, a broken mast and damaged steering oars; the wrecked ship takes centre stage apparently about to be swallowed up by a giant fish – a graphic artist's impression of the all too common disaster at sea.

Corbita

Corbitae were grain ships which have their origin with Greeks of the fifth century BCE; they could carry loads of around 150 tons. In the first century BCE they could transport as much as 1300 tons of grain and liquids; the latter in large *amphorae*. The hulls of the Roman *corbitae* were large, with high sides. Steering was provided courtesy of twin steering oars. The oars could be boxed in to the hull with reinforced planking for added protection.

The crew

Some cargo ships carried a sailor who looked after the cargo, a kind of naval quartermaster. The captain was the *naukleros*, responsible for all on board, including the merchants. Then there were the subordinate officers, a squad of pilots, lookouts, medical staff and specialist lookouts, carpenters, sailmakers and riggers – all according to Strabo (2,99), Philostratus (*Life of Apollonius of Tyana* 3, 35) and *Coptos Tariff* 674.

The Muziris Papyrus

The Muziris Papyrus (ca. 150 CE) is a fragmentary document found in 1985. On its verso, it provides a fascinating and detailed shipping cargo manifest which has been reconstructed as follows; at the same time, it illustrates how Roman customs officials taxed inbound eastern cargoes:

> '544 tons of pepper, 76 tons of malabathron (cinnamomum tamala leaves), 3 tons of ivory tusks and 0.5 ton of ivory fragments, 2 tons of tortoise shell, and 80 boxes of Gangetic nard (possibly 1 or 2 tons).'

That is a payload of ca. 628 tons, requiring a very large Roman ship (this one was called the *Hermapollon*). The total value of this cargo reaches a stunning amount of 9.2 million Roman sesterces, which is around 90 million modern Euros (https://www.ancientportsantiques.com/ancient-ships/merchant-ships/) The tax bill was 2.2 million sesterces (24 per cent). The 120 ships in the merchant fleet mentioned above were, according to Strabo (2,5,12), probably shipping over 1 billion sesterces of Indian goods per annum. The *Hermapollon* was returning from a trade journey to Tamil India.

This confirms that much of our knowledge of merchant shipping and their cargoes derives from shipwrecks. Wrecks tell us that *amphorae* were sensibly stowed vertically, cushioned by bales of straw and secured with ropes. Copper and tin ingots were stowed at the bottom of the hold, doubling as ballast. It is believed that wheat was carried in sacks of one *artaba* (ca. 30kg) for easy loading/unloading.

Portus, the Port

Portus is twenty miles southwest of Rome, considered by some as one of the Romans' greatest engineering achievements. Taking nearly twenty years to complete, the new port was almost a mile wide, spanned 170 acres, and included two sea walls and a lighthouse. Archaeologist Simon Keay says (*Archaeology* March 2015: https://www.archaeology.org/issues/168-1503/features/2971-rome-portus-rise-of-empire): 'The fortunes of the city [Rome] are inextricably tied to it [Portus]. It's quite hard to overestimate'. Portus solved the problem of Rome's lengthy search for an efficient deep-water harbour. Finally, the Romans just got on with it and dug one. In 1999, ABC Science reported: 'A detailed picture of the huge, vital and complex trade regimes in ancient Rome has been revealed by English and Italian archaeologists working on the remains of Portus, an ancient trading port'. The investigation was led by Professor Simon Keay and Professor Martin Millett, University of Southampton in collaboration with Dr Helen Patterson, British School at Rome and Dr Anna Gallina Zevi and Dr Lidia Paroli.

'Portus is the largest maritime infrastructure of the ancient world, created to guarantee the food supply of the population of Rome whose inhabitants numbered almost one million in the Imperial period,' said Soprintendente Archeologo di Ostia, Dr Anna Gallina Zevi. 'Portus is therefore central to understanding one of the fundamental mechanisms of the economic life of Rome.' Zevi continues:

> 'Portus was first built by Claudius (r. 41–54 CE), and was later enlarged by the Emperor Trajan (r. 98–117 CE). It was a major port which handled all the trade and tribute destined for Rome, as well as the supplies for its provinces. Although the site has been known since the sixteenth century,

excavation has been extremely limited, and little was previously known about the internal organization of Portus or about its links to the River Tiber and to Rome.'

Claudius boasts on his inscriptional plaque in 46 CE that he had saved Rome from future flooding, but Tacitus asserts that 200 or so grain ships were sunk in the harbour in a severe storm in 62 CE. Around 103 CE Trajan extended Portus, carving out another ninety-seven acres in a distinctive hexagonal shape, connected to the outer Claudian Basin and the sea; it was also linked to the Tiber by a canal. Portus could now handle up to as many as 350 ships at any one time.

'Concentrating on the harbour of Trajan – a large hexagon linked to the sea and to the River Tiber – the archaeological team has discovered rows of warehouses and a colonnaded square along the eastern side of the hexagon. Even more significant are discoveries on flat land between the hexagon and the Tiber. Here the geophysics clearly reveal the line of the late Roman wall which defined the limits of the harbour area on its landward side. Also visible is a major canal, around 40m wide, which linked the Trajanic harbour to the river; this was lined with buildings in which pottery containers and marble from around the Mediterranean were unloaded. Running parallel to the canal are an aqueduct, the road to Rome, and a number of mausolea.'

Soprintendenza Archeologica di Ostia.
[Source: ABC Science, November 29, 1999]

The NASA website informs us that:

'The ancient port has been the subject of intense study since 2007. Researchers from the University of Southampton, the British School at Rome, the Soprintendenza Speciale per i Beni Archeologici di Roma, and the University of Cambridge have brought everything from geophysical mapping tools and computer modelling together with old-fashioned archaeological digging to learn more about the ancient port. Recently, the effort yielded evidence of a great canal connecting Portus to the other famous Roman port at Ostia.'

Ostia

There was obviously an impact on Ostia with the opening of Portus. Ostia was Rome's principal port and was located at the mouth of the Tiber. It is fifteen miles southwest of Rome. An inscription seems to confirm the establishment of the old *castrum* of Ostia as Rome's first colony in the seventh century BCE but the oldest archaeological remains so far discovered are from the fourth century BCE:

> 'Ancus Marcius, the fourth of the kings from Romulus after the founding of the city [Rome] founded this first colony.'

Ostia had considerable strategic value – separate it from Rome and you have a major problem feeding Rome. So, as Appian says, Ostia saw fighting during the civil wars in 87 BCE when Marius attacked the city to cut off trade to Rome, supported by his generals Cinna, Carbo and Sertorius; they captured the city and plundered it. It also played a part in Pompey's eradication of the pirate threat endured by Rome: in 68 BCE Ostia was sacked by pirates and set on fire; the war fleet was destroyed, and two prominent senators were kidnapped. Result: panic in Rome, causing Pompey to arrange for the tribune Aulus Gabinius to pass a law, the *lex Gabinia*, which permitted Pompey to raise an army. Within a year, the pirates had been defeated. Michael White (1997) tells us that the cult of Mithras was especially popular in Ostia, as shown by the discovery of eighteen Mithraea. Ostia was also home to the Ostia Synagogue, the earliest synagogue yet to be discovered in Europe.

There were other major ports at Civitavecchia, Leptis Magna and Caesarea Maritima. Civitavecchia is thirty-seven miles north-west of Rome on the Tyrrhenian Sea. The harbour comprises two piers and a breakwater, on which a lighthouse stands. The harbour was greatly extended by Trajan and thenceforth known as Centum Cellae due to the many vaulted 'cells' forming the harbour wall, some of which can still be seen today.

Some colonists were sent to Leptis Magna in Libya with a small garrison to take control of the city. The city prospered and it was not long before Italian merchants settled there and started a profitable trade with the Libyan interior. Olive-presses have been excavated and by 46 BCE its olive oil production was such that the city was able to provide three million pounds of oil annually to Julius Caesar in tax. We learn from Charles Gates (2011) that 'Leptis prospered through trans-Saharan trade in various lucrative commodities, including ivory, wild animals for the gladiatorial arena, gold dust, carbuncle gemstones, precious woods like ebony, and ostrich feathers.'

State Control and the Corn Dole

Keeping the citizens of Rome and other Roman populations sufficiently fed and happy was of cardinal importance, so it comes as no surprise that the state took over the sourcing, provision and distribution of grain with which to bake bread for the people. The corn dole was known as the *Cura Annonae*, and the prodigious distribution of *panem* by the second century CE kept up to one million inhabitants of Rome fed and, along with Juvenal's *circenses*, relatively sated and satisfied with life.

The enormity of the operation of getting grain to Rome would have had an impact on all maritime activity in the vicinity: shipbuilding, shipping to all and any destination, portage, and supply of ships and crews in the entire Mediterranean basin.

We know that it was 'cheaper to ship grain from one end of the Mediterranean to the other' than 'to cart it by land some 75 miles'.[27]

Thousands of vessels were pressed into service on the daily grain transport run to Rome's ports. Some ships had a capacity of 50,000 *modii* (350 tonnes) or more. The ships involved in the grain trade were, though, not state owned; rather they were privately owned and contracted to the state. To stimulate this business model, the government offered subsidies and tax breaks to encourage shipbuilding for the grain trade and bore the significant risk of shipping itself by providing a form of insurance to ship owners who delivered grain all year round, especially during the winter when the risks of shipwreck were highest and the seas were largely a no-go area.[28]

Inevitably, in the early Empire, especially under Claudius in the 40s CE, ship owners and the grain trade increasingly came under Imperial control and were identified with the emperor personally.[29]

It is not difficult to see why, commissions apart, they offered a range of privileges, including the granting of citizenship and exemption from import and harbour duties, to ship-owners willing to contract vessels of at least 10,000 *modii* into the grain trade.[30]

Interestingly, Kesler and Temin calculated that Rome's grain supply at the time required 2,000 to 3,000 merchant voyages annually, with each vessel laden with an average of 70,000kg, sometimes a lot more.[31]

Some provinces were almost entirely given over to the growing, harvesting and shipping of grain for the Romans; the most important sources of bread grain, mostly durum wheat, were Roman Egypt, Libya, Tunisia, Algeria, Morocco, and Sicily. Egypt alone contributed 29,000 tons of the total 80,000 (36.25 per cent) to about 200,000 of Rome's adult male citizens.

Tiberius publicly acknowledged the *Cura Annonae* as a personal and imperial duty, which if neglected or compromised would cause 'the utter ruin of the state'.[32] Indeed, the shipping lanes between Rome and its centres of grain supply assumed key strategic and military importance, because whoever controlled the grain supply had a measure of control over the city and the government of

Rome, which depended on timely arrivals of all that imported grain. After most winters, Rome's state grain stores were severely depleted so there were obvious commercial and social advantages in stockpiling several years' worth of harvest to create substantial grain surpluses and keep prices low, thus keeping the people fed and happy. The *Historia Augusta* claims that Severus left '7 years' worth of grain tribute' to the Roman people.[33] Rickman tells us that the same strategy was used to very different effect by civilian corn-traders, who stockpiled grain supplies to simulate and stimulate shortages and amplify grain prices on the open market.[34]

Now, there was a state merchant fleet to assist in replacing the system which had prevailed during the Republic of paying subsidies (*vecturae*) to attract private ship owners. There was also a dedicated official in charge of the grain supply (the *praefectus annonae*) who regulated the various ship-owner associations (*collegia navicularii*). The state controlled many local markets (*nundinae*) – often held once a week – as the establishment of a market by a large land-owner had to be approved by the Senate or emperor.[35]

* * *

We see evidence of state control in all those goods which were stamped or carried markings indicating their origin or manufacturer and in some cases guaranteeing their weight, purity and that they were the real thing – not fakes. Pottery, amphorae, bricks, glass, metal ingots for coinage, tiles, marble and wooden barrels were usually stamped and general goods for transportation carried metal tags or lead seals. Of course, this all helped to control trade, provide product guarantees and minimise fraud. Labelling inscriptions on olive oil *amphorae* were particularly detailed, and, as with the *tituli picti* on Monte Testaccio, they indicated the weight of the vessel empty and of the oil added, the place of production, the name of the merchant transporting them and the names and signatures of the officials who carried out these controls.

Roman fortresses, of course, would have generated much trade and necessitated port facilities, particularly imports – to feed and sustain not only the soldiers garrisoned there but also the hangers-on and the bustling *vici* and *canabae* which inevitably grew up around the fortress.

As an example, an important trading link with York was the Rhine estuary where the merchant L. Viducius Placidus from Rouen plied his trade. His dedication stone to Nehalennia – a goddess with a responsibility for ensuring the safety of cargoes – was dredged up from the Rhine estuary in 1970 and lost. York Archaeological Trust, during their Clementhorpe excavations in 1976, found it again, over-inscribed with a new dedication, this time from 221 CE to the Spirit of the place and the divinities of the emperors.[36]

The Impact of the Antonine Plague

Roman trade – within and without the borders of the empire – started its inexorable decline from the second century CE due to a number of factors: political and military turmoil, currency devaluation, rampant inflation, and the Antonine Plague (165–180 CE). 'The Antonine Plague was the first of three cataclysmic pandemics, the others being the Plague of Cyprian (249–262 CE) and the Justinian Plague (541–542 CE), which rocked the Roman Empire to the core due to their high mortality rates'.[37] As I have said in my 2021 book, 'it seems that the Antonine Plague found its way to the Roman empire along the Silk Road from China, festering in Ctesiphon, Seleucia and other urban centres, and on trading vessels sailing from the east'. Rafe de Crespigny speculates that the plague may have also broken out in Eastern Han China before 166 because of notices of plagues in Chinese records.[38]

> 'The Antonine Plague, or the Plague of Galen, which was probably smallpox, took hold during the golden reign of Marcus Aurelius (r. AD 161-AD 180), devastated the Roman army and may have killed over 5 million people in the Roman empire after the army came home from the war in Parthia (161–166). It has even been suggested that a quarter to a third of the entire population of the empire perished, estimated at 60–70 million. It was in fact the western flank of the pandemic which originated in China's Han dynasty in AD 200 and precipitated that empire's decline and fall.'

The plague killed up to 30 per cent of the Roman population, helped on its lethal way by troop movements and, of course, trade, with ships and their crews plying between ports and offloading infected goods for local distribution and vectors such as rats and fleas. Trade was, in effect, a super-spreader. This prodigious death toll severely reduced the number of people paying tax and contributing to the state's coffers, so government revenues plummeted. It diminished recruits for the army, candidates for public office, businessmen and farmers. Production on the farms fell as fewer farmers meant that so much more land was uncultivated with a further adverse effect on tax revenues. Crop shortages led to inflation and steep price increases in conjunction with decreasing food supplies. Fewer craftsmen and artisans also meant a downturn in productivity generally, which impacted local economies. Workforce shortages led to higher wages for those who survived the epidemic and fewer businessmen, merchants, traders and financiers caused serious interruptions in domestic and international trade. In short Rome, in every way, suffered a global disaster on a huge scale.

The pandemic first emerged as a Roman public health problem during the siege of Seleucia in Mesopotamia as prosecuted by the Romans in the winter of 165–166. All sources agree that Verus' troops imported disease back west with them on their victorious return. The spread of the contagion through the armed forces would have been accelerated by soldiers and sailors who had been on leave returning to active duty and infecting other legionaries and crews. Twenty-eight legions, totalling approximately 150,000 highly and expensively trained men were exposed to the virus: many succumbed.

Raoul McLaughlin writes that the Roman embassy visiting the Han Chinese court in 166 CE could have ushered in a new era of Roman Far East trade, but it was also a 'harbinger of something much more ominous'. McLaughlin argues that the origins of the plague lay in Central Asia, from some isolated population group, which then spread to the Chinese and the Roman worlds. The plague caused 'irreparable' damage to the Roman maritime trade in the Indian Ocean as proven by the archaeological record spanning from Egypt to India as well as significantly decreased Roman commercial activity in Southeast Asia.[39]

Chapter 3

The Borders of Empire (*Limes*)

imes is one of those Latin words which has acquired a more extensive meaning in modern times than its original meaning to the Romans; most often it now denotes the Germanic border in defence of Rome, defining the limits of the Roman Empire in Europe. The term also refers to the frontier defences in other parts of the empire, such as in the east and in Africa, but it was not used by the Romans with that meaning. Epigraphical evidence from Germany and Africa tells us that the Romans preferred *fines* when describing a boundary. *Limes* too is the word for a land boundary and not, initially at least, for a frontier. As the literary and inscriptional evidence confirms, if a river is involved then *ripa* is the word. *Limes* was initially used to denote a balk between fields; a road or path, and then only by the early-second century, a boundary of the empire and, later still, a frontier region as in, for example, *limes Tripolitanus*. The term was also commonly used after the third century CE to indicate a military district under the command of a *dux limitis*. The two major frontier constructs in Britannia, Hadrian's Wall and the Antonine Wall, are simply referred to as *vallum* in inscriptions and *murus* in literature.[1]

The frontier of the Roman Empire, at its widest extent, stretched for more than 3,100 miles from the Atlantic coast of northern Britain, through Europe to the Black Sea, and from there down to the Red Sea and across the coastal regions of North Africa and into Egypt, Nubia and the sub-Saharan world, before arriving back at the Atlantic coast. What remains of the *limites* today coincides with what is left of walls, ditches, forts, fortresses, and civilian settlements, some of which have been excavated, some reconstructed, and some destroyed. The two sections of *limes* in Germany are 340 miles long from the north-west to the Danube in the south-east. The seventy-four-mile long Hadrian's Wall was started in c.122 CE, while the Antonine Wall, a thirty-seven-mile long turf wall stretching from the Firth of Clyde to the Firth of Forth, was instigated by Antoninus Pius in 142 CE as a first line of defence against the 'barbarians' of the north[2] and stands as the most north-western section of the Roman *Limes*.

Anything outside the *limes* were described as *barbarica* – as in the forts mentioned in the *Notitia Dignitatum*, from around 400 CE.

Here are some of the Roman frontiers:

- Hadrian's Wall – *Limes Britannicus*
- Antonine Wall
- Saxon Shore, late Roman *limes* in South-East England
- *Limes Germanicus*, with the Upper Germanic & Rhaetian *Limes*
- *Limes Arabicus*, the frontier of the Roman province of Arabia Petraea facing the desert
- *Limes Tripolitanus*, the frontier in modern Libya facing the Sahara
- *Limes Alutanus*, the eastern border of the Roman province of Dacia
- *Limes Transalutanus*, the frontier on the lower Danube
- *Limes Moesiae*, the frontier of the Roman province of Moesia, from Singidunum in Serbia along the Danube to Moldavia
- *Limes Norici*, the frontier of the Roman province of Noricum, from the River Inn along the Danube to Cannabiaca (Zeiselmauer-Wolfpassing) in Austria
- *Limes Pannonicus*, the frontier of the Roman province of Pannonia, along the Danube from Klosterneuburg Austria to Taurunum in Serbia
- *Fossatum Africae*, the southern frontier of the Roman Empire, extending south of the Roman province of Africa in north Africa

Soldiers stationed on the *limes* were called *limitanei* and were usually recruited locally, were paid less than legionaries, and were somewhat less prestigious, their role being to deflect and deter minor raiders.

The *limes* itself is a basic construction. On the outside, the soldiers dug a ditch, the earth from which was used to build a mound. Stakes were affixed to the top of the mound. On several parts of the *limes*, instead of stakes, there might be a stone wall or mound, behind which there might be wood or stone control towers, each within plain sight of the next one, and usually able also to signal to the forts several miles to the rear.

It was possible to pass through the *limes* at points close to the watch towers. Here traders would be able to access the territories outside the empire and return from beyond the *limes*. The purpose of the *limes* with regard to trade was to monitor and control commercial traffic: the garrison would always be able to see the comings and goings from the towers. These crossing points acted as customs posts where goods would be examined and any taxes paid.[3] It could also act as a check on immigration, monitoring traffic, and may have discouraged smuggling; moreover, it was a powerful, visible symbol of the might of Rome.

In Syria an elaborate *limes* system was established, not only to control the itinerant native population and the caravan trade routes but also for defence against Parthian and Sasanian attacks.

Chapter 4

Communications – Getting Goods to and from Market

How did the Romans manage to get their goods for export to the various markets and how did they get their goods for importation back to the domestic markets within the empire? Successful trade – and repeat business – depends heavily on efficient logistics management.[1]

The established means of communicating information was through what might loosely be called 'the post', or, more precisely, the *cursus publicus* – the official Roman communication network. During the republic, the post was carried and delivered by *tabellarii* – slaves or freedmen employed as couriers by the state, by private organizations, and by private citizens who had important correspondence to send. To lower costs the service might be shared by friends or a number of companies. Julius Caesar is known to have used *tabellarii* to keep him up to speed with events in Rome while he was in Gaul; likewise, Cicero may have kept in touch by *tabellarii* when in exile through correspondence exchanged with his wife Terentia and his daughter. A first rate *tabellarius* could cover up to sixty miles in one day.

Augustus formalised all the official communication when he established the *cursus publicus*, a state-run courier and logistics service which lasted into the Byzantine Empire in the sixth century. It was used to send official messages, records and documents, actual officials, and tax revenues between the provinces along the roads to and from Rome. Apart from the general post the *cursus* gave the legions the opportunity to summon reinforcements, triage casualties and issue status reports before any situation got out of control; slaves were also sent through the system. The post was not established on all the public roads, but only on those that led to the busiest cities or ports. As for the ports, 'the *cursus* was extended over sea by the *naves publicae*, which the naval boards *(navicularii)* placed at the service of imperial messages or transports'. There is no doubt that this would have been used by merchants to communicate with customers over the borders and to report back to colleagues within the borders to ensure that demand was met by supply, to increase or decrease production as necessary and to get orders back to headquarters in a timely manner and thus expedite order fulfilment.

Transportation

The animals used in the postal service are generally described as *animalia publica* and included horses, mules, asses, oxen, and camels. The *carpentum*, like the *reda fiscalis*, had at first two, and later four, wheels, and was suited for large and heavy burdens. Later the state used it to provision the army wherever it be – for the supply of food, the vital *annona*, the system supplying Rome, the armies, and some other cities with grain and other foodstuffs, as with Septimius Severus' *cursus clabularis*, and for troop movements. The *cursus clabularis* was a heavy freight transport service mainly designed for the conveyance of such commodities as food and baggage, especially soldiers' kit. It can best be seen in the *Tabula Peutingeriana*,[2] a map of the Roman road network dated from around 400 CE. An example of the military use of the *cursus clabularis* is provided by the *Arad Corpus*.[3] This was uncovered in 2016 by researchers at Tel Aviv University, dating back some 2,600 years to around 580 BCE.

The 'service' was variable throughout the empire up to the borders; for example, there was only one *cursus* in Egypt and one in Asia Minor, as Pliny's letters to Trajan tell us. The large vehicles (*clabulae*) employed in this branch of the *cursus* had four wheels, were uncovered, built robustly, and drawn by mules or oxen. Their maximum load was 1,500 Roman pounds. The Romans modelled the *cursus* on the ancient Hellenistic network of royal mounted couriers, the *angarium*: the riders, slaves, or freedmen (*iuvenes*, *stratores*, or *tabellarii*) would be stationed along the road a day's ride apart, and the documents and packages would be handed from one courier to the next. Augustus initially followed the Persian relay method but soon switched to a system where one man made the entire journey.

The movement of goods was expensive.[4] The sender of a package, for example, engaged and supplied the courier, while the stations were financed by the local areas through which the roads passed. One day's journey usually involved the maintenance and provisioning of six or eight different stables, each of which had to keep a total of forty animals, including horses, mules and donkeys. The shipper was also obliged to supply and maintain the teams, and to keep the stables in repair; they had to secure the services of muleteers (*muliones*), mule doctors (*mulomedici*), wheelwrights (*carpentarii*), grooms (*hippocomi*), and security (*vehicularii*). This levy was naturally considered burdensome and was always vexatious, as attested by inscriptions from along the *cursus*.

Use of the *cursus* required a licence in the form of a diploma *(diplomata)* or certificate issued by the emperor himself. The system is known to have been abused by governors and their staff when they employed it for themselves and their families for free transport; *diplomata*, valuable documents in themselves, were sometimes forged and stolen.⁵ The usually punctilious Pliny the Younger was one of the offenders, allowing his wife to make free use of the system.⁶ Dedicated officials, a *vehiculis* or *praefectus vehiculorum*, were appointed to relieve the bureaucratic burden but seem not to have helped, nor did the imperial contractors, the *mancipes*.⁷

Diocletian and Constantine I reformed the service, introducing an express service, so to speak: the *cursus velox* using light carriages called *rhedae*, to run alongside the regular *cursus clabularis*. This fast lane provided horses (*veredi*, 'saddle-horses', and *parhippi*, 'pack-horses') and mules, while the regular service only offered oxen with two-wheeled carts (*birolae*). The *cursus velox* would have been vital for those urgent orders.

Procopius gives us the best description of the system:⁸

> 'The earlier Emperors, in order to obtain information as quickly as possible regarding the movements of the enemy in any quarter, sedition, unforeseen accidents in individual cities, and the actions of the governors or other persons in all parts of the Empire, and also in order that the annual tributes might be sent up without danger or delay, had established a rapid service of public couriers throughout their dominion according to the following system. As a day's journey for an active man they fixed eight 'stages,' or sometimes fewer, but as a general rule not less than five. In every stage there were forty horses and a number of grooms in proportion. The couriers appointed for the work, by making use of relays of excellent horses, when engaged in the duties I have mentioned, often covered in a single day, by this means, as great a distance as they would otherwise have covered in ten.'

All of this, of course, relies on good roads, and navigable rivers. https://paulbuddehistory.com/europe/on-the-roman-limes/ tells us that:

> 'The Roman army is still the single largest civil engineering organization that has ever existed. Their road building activities started in 312 BCE (Via Appia). Their all-weather road system remained in place until well into modern times. It was not until the Napoleonic era that road building on any significant scale was restarted again. In all over 85,000 km of road *(viae)* was built by the Romans and extended into Turkey, Romania, Jordan, Spain, North Africa, Britain and Germania.'

Paul Budde adds that roads were designed by architects and surveyed by *agrimensores*, a ditch (*fossa*) was dug out and filled with layers of rubble and sand and finally with gravel or paving. They also used concrete. All roads were between 2.4 (minimum) and 9 metres wide, and some had extensive shoulders and/or drains. Timber bridges carried the roads over waterways while ferries transported goods across rivers.

There were places for civilians to stay in *tabernae* (hostels), *cauponae* (inns), *mutationes* (horse relay stations, complete with blacksmith, vets and cartwrights) and post offices. Merchants would be amongst the many who took advantage of these resting places as they travelled back and forth in and out the lands beyond the empire's boundaries. Rivers such as the Scheldt, Rhine and Meuse played an even more important role as major military and trading routes, getting the goods for export to the borders or back into the empire as imports. It has been estimated that transport by ship was ten times cheaper than transport over land.

Chapter 5

The Romans' Attitude to Foreigners: Roman-ness and *Romanitas*, Xenophobia and Barbarians

Before we go into detail about the individual regions the Romans visited and dealt with outside the established borders of empire, it will be instructive to establish how the Roman both regarded himself and those nations and peoples he came into contact with. What might have been the Roman merchant's attitude to the foreign traders he came across in his voyages to lands beyond the empire, how did he deal with these *barbaroi*? His attitude and behaviour will have informed the Roman's dealings with strangers abroad, and how he conducted himself in these foreign, non-Roman parts of the known world.

From the very foundation of Rome in 753 BCE Rome was characterised by its ability and willingness to assimilate and integrate other peoples and their cultures: Romanization, acculturation, integration and adoption and, in religion, syncretism, of newly incorporated, liminal populations was boosted, in part, by the city's foundation myths, with Rome being founded as something like a political sanctuary by Romulus; the abduction of the Sabine women demonstrated how different tribes and peoples had commingled since the very beginnings of the city and how, in the case of the Sabine women, these newcomers performed a valuable political and diplomatic role for Rome once the early dust had settled.[1] Dionysius of Halicarnassus, a Greek historian who lived in Roman times, amplified the multicultural origin of the Romans when he wrote that Romans had since the foundation of Rome welcomed innumerable immigrants not only from the rest of Italy, but from the entire world, whose cultures blended with theirs.

The Romans were, for the most part, unconcerned about anything like our modern notions of race or ethnicity: skin colour or physical appearance were of no consequence. Dench tells us that terms such as 'Aethiop', which Romans used for black people, carried no social implications or stigmas, and though there was certainly stereotyping in Ancient Rome, inherited physical characteristics were usually not relevant to social status;[2] people who looked different from the typical Mediterranean populace, such as black people, were generally not excluded from any profession or discriminated against and there are no records of stigmas or biases against 'mixed race' relationships.[3] Inclusivity was very much the order of the day. The main factor in divisive social issues in ancient Rome had little to do with physical features or the colour of your skin, but rather on differences in class or rank. Romans, of course, used slavery extensively, but slaves were slaves not because of any ethnic affiliation; they were slaves because they were prisoners of war, criminals or victims of some other such misfortune or accident of fate. Dench concludes that it was 'notoriously difficult to detect slaves by their appearance'.[4]

What do we know about 'Roman-ness' and what being a Roman actually meant and involved? This idea of 'Roman-ness' dictated much of what Romans did in their daily life and how they went about it. Romans at the dawn of empire would also have been acutely conscious that the empire was an unimaginably big place; it had evolved over 800 years and it was made up of people from all over the known world. Romans were everywhere and they came from everywhere. But because of this diversity, there was no such thing as a Roman, as an identifiable entity or concept. The Roman man and woman was forever changing and evolving, he and she was a moving target, in place and in time. The Roman back in fourth-century BCE Italy was very different from, and quite unrecognisable to, for example, the Romans in first-century CE Eboracum, York.

We can identify certain qualities which have commonly and consistently been attributed to Romans, wherever and whenever they were. Those qualities fall conveniently under the term *'Romanitas'*, a word that was never actually uttered by the Romans themselves until the third century CE Roman writer, Tertullian.[5] Tertullian's use is pejorative, to acidly describe his fellow Carthaginians who aped Roman ways. Juvenal had said much the same not long before, vilifying his fellow Romans who were slaves to the ways of Greeks and to all things Greek; to Juvenal Greece was polluting, and diluted what he would have called *'Romanitas'*:

> 'What is more sickening than this: no woman thinks herself beautiful unless she's changed from being a Tuscan to a little Greek bit ... Everything has gone Greek: however, it's even more grotesque when Romans have no Latin. They show their fear, their anger, their joys and their worries in Greek; they pour out every secret of their souls in this tongue ... You might allow this in a young girl, but will you still be Greeking it when you're pushing eighty-six? Such a way of speaking is surely not right for a little old lady.'
>
> *Juvenal 6, 184–191*

Martial agreed:

> 'Laelia, you don't live in Greek Ephesus, or Rhodes, or Mitylene, but in a house in a posh part of Rome; and although your mother was a dusky Etruscan who never wore make-up; and although your father was a hard man from Aricia, you, and I'm ashamed to say it, are a citizen of Roman Hersilia and Egeria – yet you keep bombarding me in Greek.'
>
> Martial 10, 68

The concept of *'Romanitas'* took on an air of respectability, sophistication and nobility, chiming with the 'grandeur that was Rome'; it came to mean quintessential 'Roman-ness' – what it means to be a Roman and how the Romans regarded themselves; it defined a true Roman; it encapsulated the Roman ideal.

As we have seen with Juvenal and Martial, the manifold foreign influences engendered an element of xenophobia; Cato the Elder and Cato the Younger and many others beside exhibit a conservatism and traditionalism running down the collective backbone of the Roman people. This mutated over time into a national character which had its roots in the early humble, agricultural days and was characterised as demonstrating hard-work, honesty, exuding *gravitas* (dignified, serious or solemn conduct) and being diligent in every way. Moreover, the true Roman lived by and respected the *mos maiorum*, the way the ancestors had gone about things. He, or she, was expected to be dutiful, to exhibit *pietas* in every sphere of life: towards family, friends, country, fellow citizens, comrades in arms and gods. *'Romanitas'*, *gravitas* and *pietas* certainly defined the Roman.

But there was always a difficult line to be drawn between espousing diversity and exhibiting xenophobia – fear and suspicion of foreigners. The arch-conservative Cato the Elder (234–149 BCE) became a symbol of this. As champion of the *mos maiorum* and despiser of things Greek, Cato spoke out sternly against what he saw as a period of moral decline and the erosion of the sturdy principles on which Rome had lain her foundations.[6] Among other things, he identified the growing independence of the women of Rome as an ominous ingredient in this.[7] The defeat of Hannibal at Zama in 202 BCE, the victory over the Macedonians at Pydna in 168 BCE and the final extinguishing of the Carthaginian threat in 146 BCE all allowed Rome to relax more and encouraged an unprecedented influx of Greek and eastern influences and luxuries into a receptive Rome.[8] In 191 BCE Cato defiantly addressed a Greek audience in Athens in Latin.[9]

Cicero too was a stickler for *'Romanitas'*.[10] The Latin language, or rather to possess a facility for speaking it, and the practice of Roman law were equally potent badges of Roman-ness. Here is Cicero championing and advocating the use of Latin by traders beyond Rome's borders:

> 'Ordinary men, born in obscurity, go to sea and they go to places which they have never seen before; places where they can neither be known to the men among whom they have arrived, nor where they can always find a lawyer. However, due to this singular faith in their Roman citizenship, they think that they will be safe, not only among our own magistrates, who are constrained by fear of the law and of public opinion, but also with our fellow citizens who are joined with them, among many other things, by a common language and laws; but wherever they come they think that this will protect them.'
>
> Cicero, in Verrem 2, 5, 167

In the *Brutus*, 37, 140, he is even more explicit, declaring that it is a matter of shame not to know Latin; a facility for Latin was for Cicero a mark of the good Roman citizen. Suetonius tells us that the emperor Tiberius believed it important that soldiers in the Roman army be able to speak Latin from an incident when he refused a Greek soldier permission to reply in Greek when summonsed to give evidence.[11] The conquering Roman army was the prime vehicle for and deliverer of 'Romanization' when it consolidated the lands into the Roman empire: speaking Latin was a key element in that 'Romanization'. There is good evidence that foreign troops and mercenaries in the Roman army learned Latin. As Cicero demonstrates above, international trade came a close second as one of the key ways in which Roman practices and values were spread abroad to the conquered, annexed and those with whom Rome desired or needed to do business.

Wills had to be written in Latin; tombstones for Roman soldiers, be they Roman or foreign, throughout the empire are always in Latin, except for Roman Egypt where Greek is used. To the Romans, Latin was the only language of any significance; it would not have occurred to them to learn a 'barbarian' tongue – Latin symbolized civilization. In about 30 CE the historian Valerius Maximus reported how Roman magistrates throughout the Roman world used Latin as a weapon in upholding Roman *maiestas*, greatness, when they insisted that court proceedings be in Latin and that the Greeks use interpreters to translate into Latin.[12] Speaking Latin inculcated respect for Roman power and symbolised Roman-ness. Who knows, it may have given the Romans an edge in doing business in some markets when negotiations would usually have to be conducted through interpreters. Latin was an enduring emblem of '*Romanitas*', 'Roman-ness'.

It is tempting to think that Rome's equanimity towards foreigners and their eagerness to take the best things these outsiders had to offer would indeed have been a distinct asset in their trade negotiations. Romans were confident and could be arrogant; they had military clout in spades and they had much to offer their neighbours when it came to bringing goods to market. But at the same time throughout the Empire emperors never lost sight of the existentialist importance of military and diplomatic success. Roman emperors displayed anti-barbarian imagery on their coinage, and barbarians were frequently depicted cowed and cowering on countless triumphal arches and columns – the Arch of Constantine and Trajan's Column being just two famous examples. Romans viewed themselves as superior over foreigners, but, as Rubel argues, 'this stemmed not from perceived biological differences, but rather from what they perceived as a superior way of life. 'Barbarian' was as such a cultural, rather than biological, term. It was not impossible for a barbarian to become a Roman; the Roman state was itself seen as having the duty to conquer and transform, to civilise, barbarian peoples.'[13]

Chapter 6

The Celts and the Germani

First, some definitions:

- Mac Cana & Dillon. 'The Celts, an ancient Indo-European people, reached the apogee of their influence and territorial expansion during the fourth century BC, extending across the length of Europe from Britain to Asia Minor.'
- Puhvel, Fee & Leeming 2003, p. 67. '[T]he Celts, were Indo-Europeans, a fact that explains a certain compatibility between Celtic, Roman, and Germanic mythology.'
- Riché 2005, p. 150. 'The Celts and Germans were two Indo-European groups whose civilizations had some common characteristics.'
- Todd 1975, p. 42. 'Celts and Germans were of course derived from the same Indo-European stock.'
- Encyclopedia Britannica, *Celt.* 'Celt, also spelled Kelt, Latin Celta, plural Celtae, a member of an early Indo-European people who from the second millennium BCE to the first century BCE spread over much of Europe.'
- Drinkwater 2012, p. 295. 'Celts, a name applied by ancient writers to a population group occupying lands mainly north of the Mediterranean region from Galicia in the west to Galatia in the east. (Its application to the Welsh, the Scots, and the Irish is modern.) Their unity is recognizable by common speech and common artistic traditions.'
- Waldman & Mason 2006, p. 144. 'Celts, in its modern usage, is an encompassing term referring to all Celtic-speaking peoples.'

To the expansionist Romans it must have seemed that the Celts turned up everywhere they went – from Britannia in the west, through western Europe, Spain and Italy and the Danube countries, from the Black Forest to the Black Sea and into Anatolia. Indeed, they were probably the most numerous and widespread people in Europe.

Under Gallic Brennus they sacked Rome in 387 BCE after the Roman disaster at the Battle of Allia; they persistently harried Julius Caesar in Gaul and on the borders of Germania; they were there, menacingly, at the lethal revolt of

Boudica, and they were behind the incursions from north of Hadrian's great wall; they populated Roman Iberia and Lusitania; and they were waiting there in Galatia, central Anatolia, when the Romans came.

Who exactly were they? They were a group of tribes which originated around the headwaters of the River Danube in central Europe and were united by a more-or-less common language, religious beliefs, traditions and culture. The Celts first came onto the scene around 1200 BCE, spreading in migratory waves through Ireland, Britain, western Europe, northern Spain and Portugal, France and Germany and then on to the Black Sea coasts and what is roughly modern Turkey.

We start our Celtic story around 700 BCE in Hallstatt, Austria, near Salzburg where excavated graves of chieftains reveal one of the first Iron Age cultures in Europe. These Celts were clearly economically sophisticated and, from Bavaria to Bohemia, got rich by trading their ironware for Greek luxuries made from bronze, and pottery vessels. They controlled key trade routes along the Rhône, Seine, Rhine, and Danube and were key players in Celtic unification. Moving west, the 'Hallstatt' warriors overran other Celtic peoples, introducing the use of iron, which of course explains their own military success.

Historical evidence

Herodotus (490–425 CE) relates (4, 152) that in 640 BCE a silver merchant called Colaeus from Samos was trading on the north African coast when he was driven off course by tides and gales and ended up at Tartessos (modern Guadalquivir in southern Spain). Colaeus found there a tribe of Keltoi mining the rich silver deposits. Current thinking has it that the storm was a fabrication by Colaeus to conceal his trade route from his competitors and defend the revenues from this previously untapped source of silver. Colaeus' voyage was profitable enough for him to devote one tenth of his earnings to Hera.

In the same paragraph Herodotus tells us that Sostratos of Aegina was a famous merchant and made 'the biggest profit any Greek trader we have reliable information about has ever made from his cargo'. Indeed, Sostratos has only recently emerged from the shadows, having received increasing validation from modern archaeology when a stone anchor dedicated to Apollo at Gravisca (the port of the Etruscan city of Tarquinii) is thought to have been dedicated by Sostratos: it can now be seen at the museum there. Around 600 BCE some merchants from central Greece made a treaty with Celts to trade their goods for silver; the king of the Celts in question was Arganthonius whose name derives from the Celtic word for silver – *argento*.

The Greek historian Ephorus of Cyme produced the world's first known universal history in the fourth century BCE; he believed the Celts originated from the islands at the mouth of the Rhine and were 'driven from their homes by the frequency of wars and the violent rising of the sea'. Polybius in about 150 BCE describes the Gauls of Italy and their conflict with Rome. Pausanias in the second century CE reports that the Gauls, 'originally called Celts', 'live on the remotest region of Europe on the coast of an enormous tidal sea'. Posidonius described the southern Gauls about 100 BCE; although the work is lost, later writers such as Strabo used Posidonius. Strabo, writing in the early first century CE, covers Britain and Gaul as well as Hispania, Italy and Galatia. Caesar wrote extensively about his Gallic Wars in 58–51 BCE, but he gives no archaeological evidence for commerce in perishable goods of plant or animal matter. However, Caesar mentions that Gauls 'take the greatest pleasure' in working cattle and therefore are willing to pay an exorbitant fee for them.[1]

Diodorus Siculus in the first century CE tells us about the Celts of Gaul and Britain. Diodorus Siculus and Strabo both suggest that the homeland of the people they call Celts was in southern Gaul. Diodorus says that the Gauls were located to the north of the Celts, but that the Romans referred to both as Gauls; linguistically the Gauls were certainly Celts.

By the mid-fifth century BCE the La Tène culture, with its abstract geometric designs and stylized bird and animal forms, found a home among the Celts of the middle Rhine. Here, trade with the Etruscans gradually replaced Greek trade; between the fifth and first centuries BCE the La Tène culture travelled with the ever migrating Celts into eastern Europe and westward into the British Isles. The Celts were essentially an agricultural economy, but trade generally flourished due in large part to their advanced transport systems and road building prowess. Irrigation systems in the Po valley also helped sustain commerce. Celtic commodities paid for those Mediterranean luxury items so much in demand: indeed, the Celts were generally more affluent than classical writers give them credit for.

But before that bands of Celts had penetrated northern Italy in 400 BCE during the great invasion of migrating Celtic tribes: these tribes included the Insubres, Boii, Senones, and Lingones. As noted, Rome was sacked by Celts in 387 BCE: hostilities opened when the Senones and others attacked the Etruscan city of Clusium, which came to Rome seeking military support. Matters were not helped when the Gauls protested at the murder of some of their ambassadors by the Romans, and marched south from Clusium into the Tiber valley. The Roman army was beaten at the Battle of the River Allia, thence fleeing to Veii. A defenceless Rome was largely abandoned and fell to the Senones, and according to Polybius, was occupied by them for seven months. They eventually returned north homewards to defend their homeland from the Veneti.

Rome was never likely to forget this humiliation and set about constructing the Servian Wall around Rome, which was put to the test around 357 BCE when again the Gauls appeared outside the gates of Rome, this time to be defeated by the Roman army. The Po valley was now firmly 'Cisalpine Gaul' ('Gaul on this side of the Alps'), but as Rome steadily expanded in central and southern Italy, the alarmed Etruscans, Samnites and Gauls, plus Sabines and Umbrians, formed a coalition against Rome. An eight-year war saw Rome prevail. Rome now sought to secure the Tiber valley and attacked the Senones in 285 BCE, completing their conquest and driving them out by 282 BCE. Their former territory became Roman 'Public Land', the *Ager Gallicus*.

Meanwhile, marauding bands roamed belligerently around the whole length and breadth of the peninsula as far south as Sicily. These warlike peoples were to remain an ever-constant thorn in the side for Rome until their defeat at Telamon in Etruria in 225 BCE.

Things had been going relatively well with the Celts and Romans in northern Italy for more than a decade; the tribes of Cisalpine Gaul, notably the Boii, had even repelled a force of Celts from Transalpine Gaul in 230 BCE on behalf of the Romans. The Romans, however, did nothing to reward their allies. On the contrary, Rome pursued their relentless expansionism. In 232 BCE, Gaius Flaminius, a plebeian tribune, swerved round the Senate and partitioned the *Ager Gallicus* into small lots for Roman citizens, much to the displeasure of the allies, for the public land really belonged to the Federation, and the Roman senatorial magnates who were used to leasing large portions of it. The Gauls feared further encroachment, but bided their time, working on alliances and negotiating with their Transalpine brothers.

After Telamon the Romans were intent on ridding Italy of the Gauls and subduing northern Italy, a feat which they achieved at Clastridium (222 BCE). One of the key reasons given was that they were anxious to protect trade in the region. State-sanctioned piracy was a major problem and continued to be so until the late-first century BCE when Pompey did much to rid the seas of this curse. In the third century BCE it was the Illyrians who represented the biggest problem, with their domination of the coastline from Dalmatia southwards. As we have seen, in 230 BCE, in what was Rome's first significant political contact with Greece, the Romans had strongly protested to Queen Teuta (r. 231–227 BCE) about the piracy which she openly condoned. The queen was having none of it – obviously with a wary eye on her treasury: she told the Roman ambassadors that royalty never prevented its subjects from gaining an advantage from the sea.

Celtic independence, and their conflict with Rome, finally came to an end in Gallia Transalpina with Germanic tribes pushing west toward and across the Rhine, and Roman armies moving to the south. The Germanic onslaught came in the form of the Cimbri in Bohemia, the land of the Boii, and in Noricum, a Celtic kingdom in the eastern Alps. A Roman army sent to the relief of Noricum in 113 BCE was defeated, allowing the Cimbri, now joined by the Teutoni, to deprecate Transalpine Gaul, overcoming all Gallic and Roman resistance. But when they tried to enter Italy, these German marauders were finally routed by Roman armies in 102 and 101 BC.

Proto-Celtic cultures in western and central Europe had already established trade links with various Mediterranean populations, and this continued with the Celts: tin from Britain, amber from the Baltic, and horses from eastern Europe and the Balkans were also imported for domestic use or passed on southwards. In addition, the Celts could offer, for example, slaves, iron, gold, wool cloth, and furs. These goods were exchanged for copious quantities of wine, silver, luxury manufactured goods such bronze flagons, fine Greek pottery, Etruscan bronze kraters, silk, and precious materials for use in *objets d'art* and jewellery.

The discovery of archaeological artefacts supports this: from the first half of the second century BCE, Roman merchants began to penetrate deeper into central Europe providing opportunities to Celtic peoples to engage in regular and profitable trade. Evidence comes from digs at Kelheim, Manching and Hascherkeller, but we can also see it by considering the number and nature of shipwrecks during the Late Iron Age. P.S. Wells (1987)[2] invites us to:

'Consider the number of shipwrecks as a comparative device against the overall 'volume of shipping' for a time, then a direct link can be made to intensified shipping during the period 150–100 BCE based on the increased number of shipwrecks along the southern coast of Gaul. Explorations of wrecked ships along the southern coastline may be able to produce physical examples of the cargo those ships once carried.'

Becki VandenBoom takes up the story:[3]

'The physical evidence of settlement and community discovered at trading centres may provide the best overall view of Celtic trade in Gaul. Termed *Oppida* by Caesar, and characterised by their likeness to Roman towns, Late Iron Age settlements like La Pegue, Vienne and Saone at Chalon have yielded solid evidence of trade with the wider Mediterranean, through archaeological excavations.[4] Each of these settlements was located along the Rhone River trade route and Saone at Chalon sat at an easy distance to the Aeduin capital of Bibracte. They have all produced amphorae dated to the Late Iron Age ...[5]

'Celtic coins would have been minted of bronze, silver or gold. Excavations at the *oppidum* of Essalois in the Sequani territory of Gaul have yielded a number of coins representative of the Aedui and Sequani tribes and also coins of Massalia.'[6]

VandenBoom adds that given the proximity of the tribes of northern France (Gaul) and southern Britain it is not surprising to find allusions to and physical evidence of trans-Atlantic trade relations. Diodorus Siculus claimed to know of sources for people participating in a British tin trade which began in Belerium (Land's End) and from which smelted tin was transported via boat to an island apparently known as Ictis [Isle of Wight]. From Ictis Diodorus Siculus says it was shipped across the channel to Gaul and then transported on foot, via a thirty-day journey to the 'mouth' of the Rhone river. VandenBoom suggests that 'it does not seem to be a big stretch to imagine that tin and other British exports ended up in the Greek trading port of Massalia'.

Cunliffe writes that:

'Following the surge of trade through Gaul in the late-second century BC, so called Roman entrepreneurs set out to extend their influence to incorporate trade with Britain. All over Southern Britain farmsteads and hillforts were being abandoned as the major focus shifted to controlling the 'movement of commodities'. New settlements began to rise up along the common trade routes. Hengistbury Head would have provided an excellent collection base and place from which to ship the metals, corn, hides and slaves that were much sought after by Rome.'[7]

Strabo lists British exports as metals such as gold, silver and iron as well as grain, cattle, dogs, hides and slaves.[8]

Coinage

We now believe that the notion that the Celtic monetary system consisted solely of barter is something of a myth, although we still do not understand it fully. The absence of large numbers of coins leads us to assume that 'proto-money' was used and included bronze items made from the early La Tène period and beyond, often in the shape of axe heads, rings, or bells. A large number of these have been found in some burials, and it is thought they had a relatively high monetary value, and were probably used for everyday transactions.

In most Celtic populated areas of the continent and in south-east Britain before any Roman conquest of these lands, low grade coinages of potin, a bronze alloy with high tin content, were minted. Higher-value coinages, viable for exchange and barter in trade, were minted in gold, silver, and good quality bronze. Initially, gold coinage was much more common than silver coinage but as Roman commerce blossomed with the Celtic world, silver and bronze coinage became more common, coinciding with a significant increase in gold extraction in Celtic areas to meet the Roman demand.

Gallo-Roman culture

Trade, of course, brings with it secondary, cultural and sociological consequences and influences. Ideas in art, religion, and technology espoused by the Romans percolated into the Celtic way of life. The Roman invasion of Gaul naturally brought a great number of Celtic peoples into the Roman Empire and with them came the Gallic experience of life, habits, values and practices. Gallo-Roman culture emerged as a by-product of the Romanization of the Gauls under the dominion of the Roman Empire. It was characterized by the Gaulish adoption, absorption or adaptation of Roman culture, language, morals and way of life dressed up in a uniquely Gaulish context.[9]

Later, the barbarian invasions began in earnest in the late-third century CE and exerted fundamental changes in politics, economics and military organization on Gallo-Roman culture.

Interpretatio romana offered Roman names for Gaulish deities such as the smith-god Gobannus,[10] but of the Celtic deities, only the horse-patroness Epona percolated down into Romanized cultures beyond the confines of Gaul.[11]

Inse Jones tells how Roman influence led to many changes in Celtic religion, the most noticeable of which was the diminishing of the druid class. Romano-Celtic deities also began to emerge, sharing both Roman and Celtic attributes when they combined the names of Roman and Celtic deities, or included couples with one Roman and one Celtic deity. Other changes included the adaptation of the Jupiter Column, a sacred column set up in many Celtic regions of the empire, primarily in northern and eastern Gaul. Another major change in religious practice was the use of stone monuments to represent gods and goddesses. The Celts had probably only created wooden cult images (including monuments carved into trees, which were known as sacred poles) before the Roman conquest.[12]

For example, Celts adopted flat grave burials and minted their own coins. It was a catalyst for competition between Celtic tribes to acquire the resources needed to pay or barter for trade. The Celtic world was extending its horizons and an ever-growing rich elite was becoming part of the social and political fabric with consequences for the wider continent as the Celtic gaze began to focus on their rich trading partners. The feeling was mutual.

Celtic Britain

Up to the invasion of Claudius in 43 CE and the subsequent construction of Hadrian's Wall and the Antonine Wall in the early-second century CE, Britain qualifies as a land beyond Roman power and suzerainty.

What did Britain look like to the Romans when they made their first tentative and wary steps towards occupation in 55 BCE with Julius Caesar? The island – as far north as the Forth-Clyde estuaries – was home to numerous Britonnic tribes; a society in which largely independent tribes held sway over smaller autonomous tribes or communities. But, unlike the Romans, they had no centralized national government, and, more importantly, no cohesion binding them: neither military, political, commercial, religious nor social. Many of the tribes appear to have made the crossing from the continent over to Britannia, especially the Belgae, in the first century BCE, probably to exploit the potential for trade and the need for *lebensraum* as the Romans occupied more and more of what is now France, Belgium, the Netherlands and Germany. We will meet a number of these tribes when dealing with the Roman occupation. They include:

Cantii (Kent) – these were *Belgae* who made the crossing with other *Belgae* in the first century BCE and were the Romans' first experience of native Britons on British soil. Agriculture was one of the priorities on the agenda for these Celts: we know from Caesar that they presided over many farms and lots of cattle, while their lands provided the plundering, living-off-the-land Romans with rations when they were marooned by a destructive storm in the 55 BCE expedition. Settling in and marking out their new territory came at a price: the Cantii obviously had to displace previous native incumbents, something which they appear to have managed with their superiority in arms, until eventually wiped out in the Claudian invasion some ninety years later.

Belgae (Wiltshire and Hampshire) – also originally from the near continent.

Atrebates – a Belgic tribe settled around today's Berkshire. Related to or a branch of the Atrebates who lived in Gallia Belgica.

Catuvellauni (Hertfordshire) – a Belgic tribe, neighbours of the Iceni whose famous rebellion they joined in. May have been related to the Catalauni.

Trinovantes/Trinobantes (Essex) – neighbours of the Iceni.

Regnenses/Regni – a Belgic tribe, in today's East Hampshire, Sussex and Surrey.

Parisi (East Riding of Yorkshire around modern Hull)

Brigantes – a confederacy of troublesome tribes spread over most of northern England

Corieltauvi/Coritani (East Midlands including Leicester)

Cornovii (Midlands)

Damnonii (Southwestern Scotland)

Iceni (East Anglia) – under Boudica they rebelled against Roman rule

Ordovices (Gwynedd, Wales)

Silures (south Wales) – resisted the Romans in present-day south Wales

Caesar got it about right when he wrote in his record of the Gallic Wars:

'The inland part of Britain is inhabited by tribes ... indigenous to the island, the coastal part by tribes that migrated in earlier times from Belgium to procure booty by invasion. Nearly all of these are called after the names of the states from which they originated when they went to Britain; and after the invasion they settled there and began to till the fields. The population is huge; the farm-buildings are found very close together, being very like those of the Gauls; and there are many cattle. They use either bronze or gold coins, or instead of coined money tallies of iron, of a certain weight. In the midland districts of Britain tin is produced, in the maritime iron, but not much; the bronze they use is imported. There is timber of every kind, as in Gaul, except beech and pine. To them it is wrong to eat hare, fowl, and goose; but they do keep them as pets or for pleasure. The climate is more temperate than in Gaul, the cold seasons more moderate.

The most civilized of all these nations live in Kent, which is entirely coastal, nor do they differ much from the Gallic customs. Most of the inland inhabitants do not sow corn, but live on milk and meat, and are clad with skins. All the Britons, indeed, dye themselves with woad, which gives off a bluish colour, and make them look more terrible in combat. They wear their hair long, and shave every part of their body except their head and upper lip. They have ten and even twelve wives common to them, even brothers sharing with brothers, and parents with their children; but if there are any children by these wives, they are said to be the children of those who they married when still a virgin.'

Caesar, De Bello Gallico 5, 14

We cannot know with any accuracy the population of Britain in the first century BCE; however, best estimates give 4–5 million spread over a wide area and concentrated in the *oppida* (key towns); guesswork also prevails over the ratio of the sexes. War, such as that in Britain during and after the invasion of Claudius, may indeed have led to a dip in population amongst menfolk, particularly amongst the Welsh tribes and the Brigantes. The Boudican revolt may well have redressed the disparity when many women and girls were slaughtered at Camulodunum, Verulamium and London. Warfare leaves a terrible legacy of widows and unmarried girls; moreover, the occupation itself would have affected the ratio as thousands of largely unmarried or at least unaccompanied male legionaries and support personnel poured onto the island. The Trentholme Drive cemetery in fortress York supports this with four male skeletons to every one female – similar to Cirencester (5:2) but very different from Lamyatt Beacon near Glastonbury (1:11).

Mysterious Britannia, then, would have been very much part of the Roman national discourse and a prominent feature of the political and military landscape. For Julius Caesar treading water in nearby Gaul it was but a short step away geographically, politically and militarily.

British communities were not the only peoples to be influenced and changed by Roman trade incursions into Gaul. The proximity of German tribes made it inevitable that some interaction was going to occur.

Caesar gives us our first reference to the Germani, albeit to those within sixty or so miles from the River Rhine.[13]

The Germani

Germania also went by the names Magna Germania, Germania Libera or Germanic Barbaricum (southern Scandinavia) which distinguish it from the Roman province of the same name. Roughly speaking it extended from the Middle and Lower Rhine in the west to the Vistula in the east; as far south as the Upper and Middle Danube and Pannonia, and to what was known of southern Scandinavia in the north.

The Gallic Wars of the first century BCE brought Julius Caesar up against peoples originating from beyond the Rhine, which he referred to as 'Germani' and their lands beyond the Rhine as 'Germania'. In the empire, Augustus had ambitions to expand eastwards across the Rhine towards the Elbe, but this all came to nought when his armies were catastrophically defeated, first in 16 BCE in the *Clades Lolliana* when the consul Marcus Lollius was defeated by the Sicambri, Tencteri and Usipetes, Germanic tribes who had crossed the Rhine; and then by Arminius at the catastrophic Battle of the Teutoburger Wald, with the loss of three legions in 9 CE.[14]

Tacitus in his *Germania* provides an invaluable source for the region. The prosperous Roman provinces of Germania Superior (modern western Switzerland, the French Jura and Alsace regions, and south-western Germany) and Germania Inferior ('Roman Germania': modern-day Luxembourg, the southern Netherlands, part of Belgium, and part of North Rhine-Westphalia in Germany, west of the Rhine) were subsequently formally established in c. 85 CE, despite being occupied since Augustus' reign, while those territories east of the Rhine remained outside Roman control.

Both Caesar and Tacitus see fit to mention wine in a commercial and militaristic context.[15] Caesar tells that:

> 'Merchants had no access to them and they banned the importation of wine and other things smacking of luxury; because, they thought that by their use the mind is dulled and courage impaired: they were a savage people and of great bravery.'

While Tacitus records:

> 'A liquor for drinking is made out of barley or other grain, and fermented to make something resembling wine. Those living near the river Rhine also buy wine ... In quenching their thirst they are not equally moderate. If you indulge their love of drinking by giving them as much as they want, they will be overcome by their own vices as easily as enemy action.'

Indeed, Roman wine vessels have been excavated in the Jutland Peninsula with traces of a fermented drink concocted from malt and berry juice, a bit like cranberry juice, according to Mortimer Wheeler, mixed with honey and myrtle.[16]

Dio tells us of the potential dangers of speculative trade when a number of Germans were killed after they had held up a delegation of Romans intent on doing trade and then murdered them.[17] Pliny the Elder has the story of a pioneering Roman who, during the reign of Nero, set out for the Baltic as agent for one Julianus, to call on *commercia* (agents), whence he returned loaded with amber, hitherto a trade monopolized by local tribes.[18] The Hermunduri (who lived north of the Upper Danube as far as Thuringia) enjoyed something of an exclusive agreement with the Romans,[19] while in 173 CE Marcus Aurelius put things on a sound footing when he fixed the trading days and the places for conducting trade.[20]

Transportation

Beresford Ellis points out that 'the high preponderance of Celtic words in Latin at so early a stage is indicative of Celtic pre-eminence in the field of road ways and transport in their early contacts with Rome'.[21] As examples he cites the following:

> '*Carpentum* from the Celtic *carbanto*, a two-wheeled carriage later used for a baggage wagon and a vehicle built specifically for women.
> '*Carrucac*, a four-wheeled goods wagon.
> '*Covinus* and then *covinarius*, introduced by Martial (an Iberian Celt) as a travelling cart from the Celtic *covignus*, a shared transport.
> '*Plaustrum* and *ploxenum*, used by the Celts of Cisalpine Gaul: Catullus, Cato, Varro and Virgil all use it as a heavy duty wagon drawn by oxen, asses or mules, with disc wheels and iron tyres'.

The Celts also built river craft to access markets along the rivers Danube, Rhine, Rhône, Seine, Loire and Po. Ship building must have occurred to allow the migrations of the Iberian Celts and the Belgae. Caesar reports that:

> 'These Veneti exercise by far the most extensive authority over all the seacoast in those districts, for they have numerous ships, in which it is their custom to sail to Britain [to trade], and they excel the rest in the theory and practice of navigation. As the sea is very rough, and open, with but a few harbours here and there which they command themselves, they have as tax payers almost all those who usually sail that sea.'
> *Caesar,* Gallic Wars *3, 8; adapted from Loeb 1917*

The Veneti were a Gallic seafaring tribe located in Armorica, in the northern part of Brittany, during the Roman period. The Veneti exerted a strong influence on south-western Brittonic culture through trading relations with Britain. After they were defeated by Junius Brutus Albinus in a naval battle in 56 BCE, their maritime commerce gradually declined under the Roman Empire.

In 56 BCE, the Veneti took prisoner the envoys Rome had sent to demand grain supplies in the winter of 57–56, in order to use them as bargaining chips to secure the release of the hostages they had previously surrendered to Caesar. Hearing of the developing revolt, all the coastal Gaulish tribes bound themselves by oath to act together. This is what Caesar tells us is the reason for the war. Levick points out that this version is contradicted by Strabo, who contends that the Veneti aimed to stop Caesar's planned invasion of Britain, which would have threatened their trade relations with the British islands.[22] Strabo's claim appears to be confirmed by the participation in the war of other Gallic tribes involved in trade with Britain, and by the involvement of Britons themselves.[23]

Caesar gives us more detail about the suitability of the Venetian ships to the local turbulent seas in comparison to his less adaptable vessels:

'Not so the ships of the Gauls, for they were built and equipped in the following fashion. Their keels were considerably more flat than those of our own ships, that they might more easily weather shoals and ebbtide. Their prows were very high, and their sterns were similarly adapted to meet the force of waves and storms. The ships were made entirely of oak, to endure any violence and buffeting. The cross-pieces were beams a foot thick, fastened with iron nails as thick as a thumb. The anchors were attached by iron chains instead of cables. Skins and pieces of leather finely finished were used instead of sails, either because the natives had no supply of flax and no knowledge of its use, or, more probably, because they thought that the mighty ocean-storms and hurricanes could not be ridden out, nor the mighty burden of their ships conveniently controlled, by means of sails. When our own fleet encountered these ships it proved its superiority only in speed and oarsman per ship; in all other respects, having regard to the locality and the force of the tempests, the others were more suitable and adaptable. For our ships could not damage them with the ram (they were so stoutly built), nor, because of their height, was it easy to hurl a pike, and for the same reason they were less readily gripped by grapnels. Moreover, when the wind began to rage and they ran before it, they endured the storm more easily, and rested in shoals more safely, with no fear of rocks or crags if left by the tide; whereas our own vessels could only dread the possibility of all these chances.'

Caesar, Gallic Wars 3, 13; *adapted from Loeb 1917*

There is little archaeological evidence for this Celtic mastery of shipbuilding, but we do have two important finds: the Hasholme logboat is a Late Iron Age boat (750–390 BCE) discovered at Hasholme near Holme-on-Spalding-Moor in the East Riding of Yorkshire, now on display in the Hull and East Riding Museum in Hull. It is very similar to Caesar's description. And then there is

St Orlan's Stone – a Pictish cross-slab dating to the 700s or early 800s CE on which is carved the only representation of a boat from this era in Scotland. It too bears close resemblance to Caesar's description 800 years earlier. For detail we go to Canmore: National Record of the Historic Environment: https://canmore.org.uk/event/1033666:

> 'The lowest panel contains a rowing boat above two quadrupeds. There are six people in the boat: a steersman at the back holding the rudder, a small figure in front of him, then a larger oarsman facing towards the back of the boat, another small figure facing front, another backward-facing oarsman and, in the prow, a particularly large figure.'

Kelheim

Both the Iron Age settlements of Kelheim and Manching would have been found on the borders of Celtic and German territory. Kelheim was an *oppidum* from the La Tène period and has been identified with the Celtic city of Alcimoennis by Ptolemy in his *Geography*.

According to Wells, excavations at Kelheim revealed evidence of something approaching an industrial society with artefacts typical of those supporting mining, smelting, and casting of iron all found in the same place.[24] As well as the iron-working evidence were finds of associated tools such as 'chisels, knives … nails and keys' along with domestic items such as imported jewellery, including glass beads and domestic pottery, suggesting that workers' homes coexisted in the same area.[25]

The site has also yielded bronze casting and evidence of coin minting; four coins of 'central European appearance' have also been found.[26]

Chapter 7

Rome and the Nordic Countries

In Scandinavia the period when the Roman Empire dominated Europe is called The Roman Iron Age, covering the years 0 to 400 CE. After this comes the Germanic Iron Age (400–800 CE) and then the Viking Age (800–1050 CE). North Germanic peoples, usually called Scandinavians, Nordic peoples and in later medieval times Norsemen, were a Germanic linguistic group originating from the Scandinavian Peninsula.

The North Germanic peoples emerged as a distinct people in what is now southern Sweden in the early centuries CE. Several North Germanic tribes are mentioned by classical writers in antiquity, in particular the Swedes, Danes, Geats, Gutes and Rugii.

During the Iron Age Scandinavians exported slaves and amber to the Roman Empire in return for prestige goods, as attested by grave goods in the shape of artefacts of gold and silver. These have been excavated at wealthy, high status burials from the period, such as the graves at Himlingøje, or from the war booty sacrifices.

It seems likely that North Germanic tribes, Swedes mainly, operated as middlemen in the slave trade along the Baltic coast between Balts and Slavs and the Roman Empire. Waldman and Mason tell us that the North Germanic tribes at the time were skilled metal and leather workers, who supplemented their trade in iron and amber.[1] In his *Germania*, Tacitus mentions the Swedes (Suiones) as being governed by powerful rulers and excelling at seafaring. From a very early time, Germanic tribes are thought to have interacted with and possibly settled in the Baltic states, on which they would leave a profound influence, particularly on the ancient Estonians.[2]

The most tangible, visible evidence for communication between Rome and the Nordic countries results from the significant import of goods such as coins, vessels, bronze images, glass beakers, enamelled buckles and weapons; generally the style of metal objects and clay vessels was distinctly Roman. Roman artefacts from the imperial period have been found all over Scandinavia, in Norway, Sweden and especially Denmark. More than 11,000 Roman coins have been unearthed in the region, as well as bronze vessels, pots and pans, terra sigillata, glass and much more. Practically no local cultural museum in Southern

Scandinavia does not project a wealth of Roman artefacts. All show a living contact with the Empire, through trade and perhaps also through alliances, as client states or providing auxiliary support to the Roman armies.[3]

There have been many bog bodies from this time found in Denmark, Schleswig and southern Sweden. Notable bogs include Vimose in the vicinity of Odense, Illerup Ådal and Alken Enge near Skanderborg, which demonstrate proof of armies fighting – often equipped with Roman weapons. Military activity influenced by the Romans also comes in the form of large rampart buildings in Jutland such as the Olgerdiget, Vendersvold and Kong Knaps Dige – clearly copied from Roman *Limes* fortifications. Two sacrificial wagons, exactly like the one described in Tacitus, were found in Dejbjerg in Jutland in 1881 and 1883. Further evidence of military forays into the Scandinavian region comes with a Roman dagger – a *pugio* – and several other parts of what may have been a Roman centurion's uniform found near Horsens, including a high quality riveted Gallo Roman *hamata* – a suit of mail armour. In Vimose a horde of Roman artefacts was found in the mid-nineteenth century, including several Roman first- and second-century *gladii* and a griffon from a gladiator's helmet.

It may come as a surprise to learn that what is today Denmark has yielded the largest collection of Roman weapons in the world outside Italy. Particularly fruitful have been the Illerup Aadal excavations from 1950–56 and 1975–85, with discoveries of bog offerings after major battles in the third century, the earliest from 200 CE, probably between a Norwegian-Swedish and a Danish army. More than 100 swords and other materiel from this battle between 400 combatants have Roman fabrication stamps on them.

Members of many different Germanic tribes would have served with the Roman legions as auxiliaries. Germanic chieftains who fought with the Romans were Romanized to the extent that they clearly tried to adapt to and adopt Roman culture, and they sought to ingratiate themselves with the Roman nobility. In exchange for military service they were gifted Roman objects, although not Roman weapons, as Roman legislation prohibited the exporting of arms to Germanic tribes. To compensate though, Germanic tribes who fought against the Romans would have seized weapons and armour as war booty.

The bogs also reveal much more evidence in the form of grave goods: there are weapons, household wares and woollen clothes. While the principal burial tradition was cremation, the third century and thereafter saw an increase in inhumation. It seems that things Roman were distinctly *à la mode* in the wealthier societies. Apparently women wore dresses Roman style, men wielded Roman weapons, and in the town of Tjoerring in Jutland a chieftain even laid out his farm along the lines of a Roman *villa rustica*. Tacitus records that the general Caius Silius took command of the Upper Rhine Army between 14–21 CE, succeeding the ill-starred Quintillius Varus. One of his assignments was to find new allies in Germania who might help him find the legions from the Teutoburger Wald debacle. In 1920 in Hoby on the isle of Falster in Denmark a fine collection of Roman dishes and silver drinking cups with the name 'SILIUS' stamped on the bottom was found in a nobleman's grave. In the same region, parts of a Roman *cline* – a Roman couch – have also been excavated.

Many of the Roman objects found in Scandinavia surely got there via trade networks from the Mediterranean, through Germanic chieftains. Dina Dobson argues that these trade networks may pre-date the Roman Empire and suggest a complex and advanced social structure and organization among the Germanic tribes and societies. Scandinavian amber has been found as far away as Mycene, in Greece.[4]

Throughout the fifth and sixth centuries, gold and silver become increasingly common as a result of the depredation of the Roman Empire by Germanic tribes, after which many Scandinavians returned home laden with looted gold and silver. We have fine works in gold from this period not least in the manufacture of scabbard mountings and bracteates.

One of the most tangible markers of Roman socio-cultural influence in the Nordic countries are the gold medallions minted in Scandinavia in the fourth and fifth centuries. The inspiration came from the weighty gold coins presented as gifts by the emperor of the day which the Scandinavians copied: for public relations and propaganda purposes the image of the Roman emperor was replaced with a depiction of a local chieftain wearing full native regalia – usually the imperial crown and a cape with a large buckle on his shoulder. Anderrson tells us that 'On one such Scandinavian medallion from Tunalund in Uppland, central Sweden, the reverse side shows a rider with a person in front. This is a Scandinavian interpretation of a Roman motif depicting the triumph of the emperor over a defeated enemy'. The Upplandic medallion has been given an unmistakably Scandinavian makeover showing the defeated enemy skiing – the Nordic people did not slavishly copy the motifs of the Roman medallions, but, exhibiting their own cultural identity and independence, repurposed them to chime with Scandinavianism.

Along with the medallions there is from the mid-fifth century CE, another object clearly based on Roman models: it is a gold pendant stamped on one side only, called a bracteates;[5] as with the medallions, the bracteates were clearly inspired by Roman coins. The inspiration for the Scandinavian pendants were coins that were about one hundred years old, minted during the reign of Constantine and his nearest successors. The Scandinavian pendants depict ancient Norse gods such as Odin, Balder and Tyr. Many details on the pictures originate in Roman culture, among them the circlet worn by Odin.

Animal ornamentation, or Style 1, prevalent in the fifth and sixth centuries, likewise feature motifs by the Romans, such as images that have been interpreted as sphinxes or the emperor raising his hand to speak.

Green's book, *'Trade, Gift-Giving and Romanitas'*[6] is interesting in that it compares the purpose and impact of goods imported into western Britain and Scandinavia:

> 'Whilst the nature of the artefacts, their origin, the chronology of the importation, and the contexts in which they are discovered are significantly different, the two regions seem fundamentally similar. Both see continuous directed trading from the Roman Empire to some of the least Romanized areas of western Europe, involving goods that are clearly luxuries for the cultures in which they are found. This trade and its imports were securely in the control of the highest elites in the respective regions, who were consciously trying to appear Roman in their usage of these items (thus securing their position in society) ... Outside of their area, the local elites seem to have redistributed the items to other elites, probably via elite exchange and again with the aim of securing their position.'

Green concludes that 'the presence, distribution and use of these items in Western Britain and southern Scandinavia can be taken as evidence for the influence of the Roman Empire on barbarian societies and their concepts of kingship; for the existence of what might be described as early kingdoms in these regions, based ultimately around gift-exchange for which the imports were used ... and for the presence of a healthy economy that could clearly produce sufficient surplus to make long trips by Roman traders worthwhile'. He adds that the cargo ships would have held around forty tons of Cornish tin, (Campbell 1996a, 81) – combined with a sufficiently well organized political system that allowed imports to be collected at a single centre (or possibly a number of centres) for trading.

Depictions of hunting using trained birds of prey are also evident and significant. This type of hunting was popular in Scandinavia as early as the Late Iron Age (c. 520/530–1050 CE): different types of birds of prey used for hunting are present in aristocratic burials from this period. The depiction of hunting with trained birds of prey has been uncovered on an Upplandic rune stone and a bronze pendant from Grimsta, near Stockholm.

Female costumes also show traces of Roman influence. Extensive bead settings, worn in several rows in the Vendel Period (c. 520/30–750 CE), may also be an indication of influence from the beads worn at the Byzantine court. Much of the silk found in richly equipped graves in Viking Age Birka originated in Byzantium. A few examples of silk from China appear in the Birka material.

Religion and Society

However, as well as the importation, adapting and copying of physical objects, Rome brought to bear a significant influence on Scandinavian religion and society. For example, the peoples of the north created their own alphabet – the runic alphabet – based on Roman letters. They also named the days of the week according to the Roman way and began counting days rather than nights, which was the old traditional method. Domestic systems of weights and measures were developed based on Roman measuring systems.

As David Parker says in the abstract to his thesis *Vestiges of Roman Cult Religion and Household Deities in the Northern Barbaricum*:[7]

> 'Military alliances with the tribal societies of the northern Barbaricum resulted in Celtic mercenaries returning with a multitude of Roman prestige goods. Among these goods were objects associated with the Roman cults, particularly in relation to the concept of private cult worship and domestic religion.'

More evidence of religious syncretism comes from David Parker, from whom we learn that the Öland statuette of a woman has been interpreted as either a Roman deity, such as Venus or Juno, or possibly a Roman empress.

Genetic studies play a part too in establishing connections between Scandinavia and Rome. Maria Hofstaetter, a historian at the University of Copenhagen, tells us that during the Roman Iron Age (400 BCE–400 CE), the populations of Scandinavia saw a significant influx of genetic material from the Roman Empire. 'This was a period of intense trade and cultural exchange between the Roman Empire and the Scandinavian region. There is evidence of Roman coins, jewellery, and other artefacts being found in Scandinavia, which suggests that there was a significant amount of contact between these two regions'. The genetic impact of this period of contact can still be seen in the modern populations of Scandinavia, according to Dr Hofstaetter. 'Genetic studies have shown that there is a significant Roman contribution to the genetic makeup of modern-day Scandinavians.'[8]

Norway[9]

The King of the Great Mound (Storhaug)
In the summer of 779, a powerful king was buried in a large ship at Avaldsnes. He was buried with a smaller boat, a sleigh, a horse, weapons, a gold bracelet

and many other rich burial gifts. The 'King of the Great Mound' (*Storhaug*) had made Avaldsnes the centre of a kingdom in Western Norway.

The mound and its contents post-date the Roman period in the west but there is nothing to say the objects were from much earlier times, preserved as heirlooms by the king and his ancestors, from earlier trading with the Romans.

Marit Synnøve Vea, Director at the Avaldsnes Project Stavanger, tells us that people came from afar to join in the essential rituals connected with the burial of a king.[10] It may have been weeks or months before the grave in the Great Mound was closed when, finally, a huge burial mound was built over the king and his ship. The mound was raised over three cone-shaped layers of approximately 75,000 stacked logs from 30,000 trees, on which were heaped some 80,000 cubic metres of sand taken from trenches around the mound, clay and soil. The first dig at the site was by amateur archaeologist Anders Lund Lorange (1847–1888) during the years 1869–70. He reached the bottom of the mound but although unsuccessful in finding a burial chamber did find the remains of a horse. He considerately left a letter to future archaeologists in a sealed bottle in his second shaft, together with silver coins and two bottles of beer.[11]

Vea continues:

'Ships' graves are always aristocratic graves and only 14 such graves have been found in Northwest Europe. The magnificent burial of this king with his ship, horse and gold ring in the Great Mound was a cult ritual which was intended to show that the dead king was descended from the gods. The burial was also carried out to ensure that the blessing of the gods was transferred to the next ruler.'

The ship in the Great Mound was made of oak and sturdily built. The keel was about 22 m, which means that the ship must originally have been at least 27 m long. The gunnels were sturdy and unusually thick: 6 cm. Vea is correct when she says: 'This must therefore have been a seagoing vessel built to withstand rough waters'; a ship more than fit for trading? A smaller boat and a horse were buried with the king. Shetelig writes that there were also the remains of a sleigh in the grave. The ship, boat, horse and sleigh were placed there to help the deceased king to reach the world of the dead.

Paul Mercer opens his fascinating article on evidence of the Roman impact and influence in Norway by setting the scene, telling us that during the third century CE, a powerful prince was buried in what is called the Flag Mound at Avaldsnes, on Karmøy, a large island on the west coast between Stavanger and Bergen. In 1835, the secrets of the Flag Mound were revealed, and despite the crude and often destructive excavation methods used, during which much was lost (not least by a farmer who used part of the ship for winter fuel) both during and after the excavation, we still have enough information to be able to describe the 'Prince of the Flag Mound' in some detail.

Thor Lanesskog of *Thornews.com* (March 6 2025) adds that:

> 'The Prince was buried in a large mound which measured 141 ft in diameter and was 16.4 ft high. It contained a chamber made of slate slabs with the Prince lying in an oak coffin … The grave contained more gold than found in any other Scandinavian grave dating back to the Late Roman Empire Period (c.200–400 CE) including four Roman gold rings.'

Mercer continues:

> 'It was intended that the Prince of the Flag Mound should not be bored or lack anything he needed for his personal care while in his grave. A board game with 31 pieces of blue and black glass was found, along with a tin-plated bronze mirror, a bronze pair of scales, a complete set of bronze vases and platters, a silver cup, a silver fitting for a drinking horn and a bronze wine sieve. These objects are some of the best evidence we have of trade and communication with Roman lands. The same applies to the prince's weapons.'

However, the most striking object in the Flag Mound was 'a magnificent, double-edged *spatha* sword.'[12] Its grip was adorned with a silver button and the leather-bound sheath was richly decorated with gilded plates of silver'. Swords of this quality belonged to the Roman army, so, Mercer asks: 'how did the Prince of the Flag Mound come to possess one? Was he one of the Germanic chieftains who fought against the Romans further south in Europe? If so, the sword could be booty taken from a fallen enemy. Or was this man perhaps one of the Germanic chieftains who were in the service of the Romans?' He provides more detail:

> *In the primary burial chamber:*
> - A double-edged sword with a silver button and sheath made of two plates of wood. Possibly a Roman gladius: a one-handed, light-weight stabbing weapon – a standard weapon for soldiers in the Roman army up until ca. 300 AD. The pieces of wood in the sheath were joined together at the edges by small silver fastenings and then covered with leather decorated on the outside with bronze plating and ornamental plates of beaten silver, partially gilded with round ferrules. Similar tin silver ornamentation was found on a sheath fastening at Illerup, Jutland.

- 31 game pieces of glass from two sets of board games – one with counters made of amber and the other with counters of blue and yellow glass. Roman or from a Roman province, perhaps from the Rhinelands in Gaul.
- Hanging bowl with lion's head. Provincial Roman. A type of bronze vessel used for hand washing at the Roman table. Unique, no known equivalents. Something similar may be found at Thüringen. Could come from the Danube area or from Italy.
- Vase ('Hemmorspann') of bronze with silver inlay. Unique object due to its decoration and small size: provincial Roman: from Gaul, lower Rhinelands. A close counterpart was found at Barnsdorf, Hanover.
- Bronze sieve. Provincial Roman/Gaul, lower Rhinelands. An important piece of equipment at Roman banquets.
- Drinking horn covered with silver at its opening. Nordic.

Boathouses at Ferkingstad
At Ferkingstad (on the western shore of the island of Karmøy), there are slipways, quays and boathouses big enough to accommodate boats up to 30 m long. The boathouses date from the Roman period. The ships moored here were large enough to cross the Skagerrak. Mercer wonders whether the ships were loaded with goods to sell and were bound for the south (towards the borders of the Roman empire), or were they full of aggressive warriors like the ones who fell at Illerup?

The Warrior Prince who became the King of Peace

> 'There are many theories about the Prince of the Flag Mound: he may have been a leader of an immigrant ethnic group or he may have been an officer in the Roman army who was subsequently given the right to trade with the Romans etc.'

Mercer concludes that there must have been trade between the Roman Empire and Western Norway at this time. Some products from Norway may have been important for equipping the Roman forces, which at their height comprised 650,000 men. The Prince of the Flag Mound may have been given the power to oversee this trade and, if so, this would have been a weighty privilege indeed. It would have meant that the Prince had to establish a network of allies, both with other princes on the Continent and with chieftains in neighbouring areas of Norway. Peace was necessary to secure the trade along the coast. The Prince of War became the King of Peace.

A Roman cultural hub at Avaldsnes
Mercer's theories are supported by Professor Haakon Shetelig:[13]

> 'I wish in particular to mention one centre for foreign trade during the first centuries AD: Avaldsnes at Karmøy ... Roman imported goods are found both in the northern and southern parts of Western Norway, but there is no other place with such dense concentrations of findings than at Karmsund. Avaldsnes ... can almost be regarded as a hub for all cultural dissemination along the west coast of Norway.'

Finland

With the Romans came an inpouring of imported iron and other artefacts into Finland; for example, Roman wine glasses as well as various coins of the Empire. Most of the gold found in Finland dates back to the Roman period.

The Fenni get their first reference in Tacitus' *Germania* in 98 CE, although he does not specify exactly where they were located: 'The Venedi overrun in their predatory excursions all the woody and mountainous tracts between the Peucini and the Fenni'.[14] Ptolemy, who published his *Geographia* in ca. 150 CE, refers to a people called the *Phinnoi* (Φιννοι), generally believed to be the Fenni. He locates them in two different places : a northern group in northern *Scandia* (Scandinavia); and a southern group, to the East of the upper Vistula river in south-east Poland.[15]

This is what Tacitus has to say about the Fenni:

> 'The Fenni are astonishingly savage and disgustingly poor. They have no proper weapons, no horses, no homes. They eat wild herbs, dress in skins, and sleep on the ground. Their only hope of getting better fare lies in their arrows, which, for lack of iron, they tip with bone. The women support themselves by hunting, exactly like the men; they accompany them everywhere and insist on taking their share in bringing down the game. The only way they have of protecting their children from wild beasts or bad weather is to hide them under a makeshift covering of interlaced branches [tents?]. Such is the shelter to which the young folk go back and in which the old must lie. Yet they count their lot happier than that of others who groan over field labour, sweat over house building, or hazard their own and other men's fortunes in the hope of profit and the fear of loss. Unafraid of anything man or god can do to them, they have reached

a state that few human beings can attain: for these men are so well content that they do not even have to pray for anything.'
Tacitus, The Agricola and the Germania, *Trans. Harold Mattingly, Harmondsworth 1970*

Whitaker (1980) cautions that:

'This brief section appears at the very end of the Germania, and it has been suggested that the inclusion of these three paragraphs serves to provide a literary contrast with the Germans, compared with whom the Fenni seem half-animals. It is clearly an account based on one or more eyewitnesses, but instead of his usual literary sources Tacitus had to rely on such informants as traders,[16] who would perhaps have visited these tracts to obtain furs from the inhabitants.'

It is significant that some of the students of Tacitus who are not concerned with minute ethnographic description have dismissed this section as *fabulosa* (fantasies),[17] although J.G. Anderson also adds:

'The description of the Fenni, despite its rhetorical traits, is not an imaginary idealization of a primitive people. The style expresses the writer's feeling of marvel at the existence of such extreme barbarism. The facts were probably drawn from the report of a traveller [or merchant] who had spent some time in the amber country of the Baltic and had gathered information about the tribe.'
A textual note to Cornelii Taciti De origine et situ Germanorum, *Oxford, 1958, 217 e.*

We have to wait until the mid-sixth century for our next reference to the Fenni/Finni, which appears in the *Getica* of bureaucrat and historian Jordanes. In his description of the island of *Scandza* (Scandinavia), he mentions three groups with names similar to Ptolemy's *Phinnoi*: the *Screrefennae, Finnaithae* and *Mitissimi Finni* ('softest Finns').[18] '*Screrefennae*' is believed to mean the 'skiing Finns' and they are generally identified with Ptolemy's northern *Phinnoi* and today's Finns.[19] The *Finnaithae* have been identified with the Finnveden of southern Sweden.

Roman coins have been discovered in Finland dating from the first and second centuries CE, although it is difficult to say when exactly they reached Finnish shores. Ancient and early medieval coins were often used as pendants and other jewellery but these obviously were not:

- KM 4653, Sääminki – 79–81 CE, txt: DIVO AUG(usto)T(ito) DIVI VESP(asianus)F(ilo) VESPASIAN(o)S(enatus)C(onsultum)
- KM 8078, Pernaja – a worn-out coin with image of emperor Nero, KM: 7594: Saarijärvi – 98–117, Imp Caes Nervae Traiano Aug Ger Doe PM TR P Cos VPP
- KM 7188, Uusikaarlepyy – a badly-burned coin depicting emperor Hadrian. Reverse is almost totally destroyed by fire
- KM 7326: Lempäälä – AVRELIVUS CAE – SAR AVG (asti) PII FIL(ius),

Source: National Board of Antiquities – Musketti

Chapter 8

Eastern Europe; the Amber Road

This chapter examines the extent of trade with Rome in the countries outside the Empire in what we term eastern Europe.

Sarmatia and its Culture

There is disagreement amongst both ancient and modern writers as to the precise extent and borders of Sarmatia in relation to modern geography, but for our purposes we can define it as centring on the Black Sea and Caspian Sea regions extending east to the Vistula, encompassing parts of the modern Russian Federation, Ukraine, the Baltic States, Central Asian nations and extending into central European countries such as Romania and Poland. The ancients further divided it into Sarmatia Europea, which included East Central Europe, and Sarmatia Asiatica, the homelands of ancient Iranian peoples who were closely related to the Scythians. European Sarmatia largely corresponded to what was later known as the Grand Duchy of Lithuania. Herodotus describes the *Sauromatae* as the descendants of Scythian fathers and Amazon mothers.[1] He refers to Scylax of Caryanda, a Carian sailor in Persian service under Darius and author of a *periplus*, who made a reconnaissance expedition along the shores of the Indian Ocean (c.515 BCE) as one of his sources. Scylax positions the Sarmatians west of the Don, as evidenced by richly-stocked Sarmatian tombs.

Ptolemy, in Book 3, 5 deals with the location of Sarmatia at some length. The Sarmatians were a people of Iranian stock who migrated from Central Asia to around the Ural Mountains between the sixth and fourth century BCE, and eventually settled in most of southern European Russia and the eastern Balkans.

Strabo identifies four main tribes within the Sarmatian confederacy:

- The Iazyges lived in the south, on the shores of the Sea of Azov. A contingent of 5,000 auxiliary Iazyge cavalrymen was sent to Britain by Marcus Aurelius to guard Hadrian's Wall (after 175 CE).
- The Urgi in the north on the banks of the Dnieper, modern Kiev.

- An ancient Scythian tribe, the Royal Scythians, was still living in the east of Ukraine and had become the most important member of the Sarmatian coalition. They and the Urgi became known as *the* Sarmatians.
- The Roxolani moving to the west.

Incessant eastern migrations brought the Sarmatians into contact with the Greeks: they were sufficiently powerful to demand tribute from the Greek towns on the northern shores of the Black Sea. However, there was some cordiality when the Greeks traded with the Sarmatians and sometimes joined forces with these tribes when they felt threatened by the Scythians, eventually leading to their downfall; the Scythians more or less disappear from history, their country becoming known as Sarmatia.

Like the Scythians, the Sarmatians had honed excellent skills in horsemanship, particularly in equestrian warfare. They also had a reputation for administrative aptitude, which went a long way to explaining their widespread influence. By the fifth century BCE the Sarmatians controlled the land between the Urals and the river Don. In the fourth century they crossed the quietly flowing Don and subdued the Scythians, replacing them as rulers of almost all of southern Russia by the second century.

Sarmatia and Mithridates (135–63 BCE)

Relations between Rome and Sarmatia reached a low when in the early first century BCE the Sarmatians struck an alliance with Mithridates VI Eupator, the ruler of the Kingdom of Pontus in northern Anatolia from 120 to 63 BCE, one of the Roman Republic's most formidable and dangerous foes. His single-minded objective was to dominate Asia Minor and the Black Sea region. In pursuit of this his forces waged several hard-fought but ultimately unsuccessful wars (the Mithridatic Wars) in an attempt to break Roman hegemony over Asia and the Hellenic world.[2] He is also remembered for cultivating an immunity to poisons by regularly ingesting sub-lethal doses; this practice, *'mithridatism'*, is named after him.[3] In 66 BCE, he was defeated by Pompey the Great and expelled from Asia Minor. Not to be outdone, Mithridates continued his war from the Crimea, still supported by the Sarmatians, but was ultimately forced to commit suicide. The Sarmatians continued the anti-Roman alliance with his son Pharnaces, who was defeated in 47 BCE by Julius Caesar at the Battle of Zela (of 'I came, I saw, I conquered' fame).

* * *

The Roman province of Lower Moesia (roughly Bulgaria) was invaded during Nero's rule, (r.54–68 CE), and an alliance which the Sarmatians formed with neighbouring Germanic tribes continued to pose a critical threat to the Romans during the first century CE. Later, the Sarmatians, in the form of the Iazyges, invaded Dacia (Romania) and the lower Danube region before moving on to what is modern Hungary. Dacia was a Roman province from 106 to 271–275 CE on the borders of the empire, only to be overwhelmed by the Goths during the third century CE, though many Sarmatians signed up with their conquerors in the Gothic invasion of western Europe. The Roxolani had settled on the lower reaches of the Danube, but were forestalled by the Roman Legion III Gallica in 68/69. The Romans were happy with these movements, because it weakened Dacia.

Towards the end of the first century, however, Dacia re-emerged as a force to be reckoned with, and allied with the Sarmatians. One Roman legion, XXI Rapax, was annihilated in 92 CE with the result that, in order to defend their empire, the Romans were forced to consolidate by conquering territories on the north bank of the Danube between 102 and 106, when Trajan subdued the Iazyges, Dacians, and Roxolani. Hadrian kept control of Dacia while the Iazyges and Roxolani, on the other hand, received their independence again and allied with the Roman empire.

During the reign of Marcus Aurelius, the Sarmatians became troublesome once more. They were bolstered by other tribes which had joined the federation, such as the Alans from around the Caspian Sea, requiring the Romans to fight costly wars against the Sarmatians and their allies, the Marcomanni.

Sarmatia did not survive the great migration of Huns after 370 CE into southern Russia. Those surviving became assimilated or escaped to the West to fight the Huns and the last of the Goths. By the sixth century they had disappeared from the historical record.

We have noted the historical similarities between Scythian and Sarmatian. Similarities there were, but there were also differences. Scythian women were somewhat reclusive and led a domestic life much like Greek women.[4] However, unmarried Sarmatian females were much more dominant in their society and even, especially in the society's early years, took up arms with their menfolk, leading to the association pedalled by many authors that Sarmatian female warriors were in fact the Amazons.[5]

However, this early matriarchal society was later supplanted by a system of male chieftains and eventually by a male monarchy. The transition may well have stemmed from the rapid development of horsemanship and a male cavalry corps which in turn spawned the invention of the metal stirrup and the spur – innovations of huge importance in equine military history and a key factor in their military successes, influencing the way in which the Romans prosecuted their battles and wars and formulated their tactics.[6]

The significance of this half-century-long belligerence towards Rome lies in the increasingly opulent graves left by the Sarmatians. Were the grave goods buried with the deceased's war booty acquired during the Mithridatic and other wars, or were they the result of trade with the Roman empire over time? Oleksandr V. Symonenko believes that 'The objects, somehow related to the Near East, came to the Sarmatians in two main ways – as military trophies and as traded merchandise. Spoils of war included helmets of Montefortino and Pilos types seized by Sarmatians in Asia Minor during the Mithridates wars.' Other trophies were the 'silver Parthian and Persian bowls and Achaemenid *phialai* with Parthian and Chorasmian inscriptions found in the graves of rich nomads in the Ural and Western Siberia regions which arrived possibly through Iran to Graeco-Bactria, robbed by Sarmatians in the late-second century BC'.

He adds that:

'Some jewellery, eye-decorated, trace-decorated and mosaic beads from Sarmatian graves were made in the Near East. The Egyptian origin can be determined for amulets of 'Egyptian' faience in the shapes of scarabs, lions, frogs, amphorae, tiny altars, double cylinders. Some glass vessels from Sarmatian graves were made in the Near East: the moulded and cut Achaemenid calix, moulded glass kantharoi, millefiori vessels, faceted beaker of Eggers type 187 and some types of balsamarii, red-slip pottery of Eastern sigillata type.'[7]

The helmets of Montefortino type are from Sarmatian sites of the late-second – early-first century BCE; they have their closest parallels in Spain but those helmets came to the Sarmatians from Asia Minor in an unusual way, says Symonenko.

In 89 BCE when Mithridates instigated a war against Rome, according to Appian, among Mithridates' allies were the Galatians of Asia Minor and the Sarmatian tribes.[8] In 75 BCE, Mithridates concluded an alliance with a mutinous praetor of Spain, Quintus Sertorius. According to the terms of their agreement, Sertorius transferred his officers from Spain to the Pontic kingdom to train and re-equip the army of Mithridates in the Roman way. Apparently, the Spanish Montefortino helmets first came to Mithridates' Galatian soldiers and from them they were issued to the Sarmatians. Symonenko concludes that 'As there were no other contacts between the Sarmatians and the owners of such helmets (Romans, Iberians or Celts), this is the sole way these objects came to be in Sarmatian graves'. They arrived there then through an unusual, circuitous form of trade.[9]

The seizing of war booty explains the remains of Roman armour of the *lorica plumata* type found in the north Caucasus in Sarmatian graves of the first century BCE. Similar scales have been unearthed in Masada which, according to Symonenko, 'were made and repaired in a Roman camp'. We know that the Sarmatians were involved in a war in that part of the Roman empire and at the Battle of Zela against Julius Caesar as allies to Mithridates' son, Pharnaces in 47 BCE and presumably they appropriated the armour from one or another of the battlefields.[10]

The Balts

To Herodotus they were the Neuri – a race which seemingly enjoyed the ability to turn themselves into wolves. We call that lycanthropy. They are descended from a group of Indo-European tribes who originated from the Pontic-Caspian Steppe, near the Black and Caspian Seas, and later settled the area between the lower Vistula and the southeast shore of the Baltic Sea and the upper Daugava and Dnieper rivers. The name Balt, coined in the nineteenth century, is derived from the Baltic Sea; Tacitus called them 'hardworking *Aestiorum Gentes*': farmers and amber gatherers, and located them vaguely somewhere east of the *Suiones* (Swedes).[11] Extensive tracts of modern Russia, Belarus, Latvia, Lithuania, and northern Poland were settled by Balts. During the Bronze Age, roughly 1250 BCE, the western part of this Baltic region became known in the civilized areas of the Mediterranean basin as the 'land of amber'.

As E.V. Bunkśe says in the introduction to *Baltic Peoples, Baltic Culture and Europe*, the Balts are among the most ancient people in Europe. They have lived in these territories for perhaps four millennia. Their amber-sun culture may have inspired ancient Roman religious beliefs. Their folk culture certainly inspired Johann Gottfried Herder (1744–1803) to promulgate the Enlightenment idea that the culture and history of ordinary people, including women, is as worthy of study and attention as that of dukes, kings, and great thinkers and artists.[12]

Between 600 and 500 BCE the Lusatian culture still persisted, and a healthy amber trade continued while the Lusatians continued to be mediators between the Baltic and Germanic amber gatherers and the Hallstatt culture in the eastern Alpine area and, from the seventh century BCE, the Etruscans in Italy.

Between the second and fifth centuries CE the material standards of the Baltic culture rise tremendously, due to intensive amber trade with the provinces of the Roman empire. The eastern Baltic area became a strong cultural centre, and its influences extended across north-eastern Europe. This is the Baltic culture's 'golden age', according to Marija Gimbutas.

It is this amber trade with Rome that interests us.

The Amber Road

Graciela Gestoso Singer describes the Amber Road as an ancient trade route for the transfer of amber from coastal areas of the North Sea and the Baltic Sea to the Mediterranean Sea.[13] Prehistoric trade routes between Northern and Southern Europe were defined by the amber trade. This, 'the gold of the north', had been transported from the North Sea and Baltic Sea coasts overland by way of the Vistula and Dnieper rivers to Italy, Greece, the Black Sea, Syria and Egypt for thousands of years.

The ubiquity of amber through time and place is staggering: the breast ornament of Tutankhamen (c. 1333–1324 BCE) comprises large Baltic amber beads.[14] Schliemann found Sicilian amber beads at Mycenae, as shown by spectroscopic investigation. The quantity of amber in the Royal Tomb of Qatna, Syria, is unparalleled for known second-millennium BCE sites in the Levant and the Ancient Near East.[15] Amber was sent from the North Sea to the Temple of Apollo at Delphi as an offering.

During the Roman empire, the main route ran south from modern Lithuania, the entire north–south length of modern-day Poland, through the land of the Boii (modern Czech Republic and Slovakia) to the Adriatic Sea (Aquileia by today's Gulf of Venice). But it was not just amber which was exported to Rome: animal fur and skin, honey, and wax, in exchange for Roman glass, brass, gold, and non-ferrous metals like tin and copper were imported into the early Baltic region.[16] So vital was this lucrative trade route connecting the Baltic to the Mediterranean that the Romans built military fortifications along the route to protect merchants and traders from Germanic raids.

As Lundgren (2018, p.9) points out:

> 'There are no guarantees that amber found in Rome is of Baltic origin, but based on the ancient sources, which do not mention it being gathered in the Empire to any noteworthy extent, combined with the fact that to this day 80 per cent of the world's amber comes from Samland, it is safe to assume that amber found in ancient Rome generally is of Baltic origin.'

Samland, or the Kaliningrad Peninsula, is in the Kaliningrad Oblast of Russia.

Before that, whatever amber managed to reach Italy came by sea, or as trade through the Celts. It also came from the east:

> 'For a long period it, like tin, was carried by sea through the Gates of Hercules; Phoenicians were likely the main transporters. The Adriatic appears to have been the main destination for amber intended for the

markets of the Italian peninsula. Once at the Adriatic, amber must have been moved by water along the Italian coast, finding its way inland along river valleys and mountain passes.'[17]

There was an obvious economic need to cut out these fractious Celtic middle men.

Pliny the Elder (*NH* 37,11) tells us all that he knows about amber, even though he seems to use it as an opportunity for some Greek bashing:

'Next in rank among the objects of luxury, we have amber; an article which, for the present, however, is in request among women only. All these three last-mentioned substances hold the same rank, no doubt, as precious stones; the two former for certain fair reasons; crystal, because it is adapted for taking cool drinks, and murrhine vessels, for taking drinks that are either hot or cold. But as for amber, luxury has not been able, as yet, to devise any justification for the use of it. This is a subject which affords us an excellent opportunity of exposing some of the frivolities and falsehoods of the Greeks; and I beg that my readers will only have patience with me while I do so, it being really worthwhile, for our own practical improvement, to become acquainted with the marvellous stories which they have promulgated respecting amber.'

Pliny the Elder, The Natural History, *trans. John Bostock*

He continues by elaborating on its provenance, the market amongst women, and its alleged health benefits:

'Amber is imported by the Germans into Pannonia, more particularly; from whence the Veneti, by the Greeks called Eneti, first brought it into general notice, a people in the vicinity of Pannonia, and dwelling on the shores of the Adriatic Sea. From this it is evident how the story which connects it with the Padus first originated; and at the present day we see the female peasantry in the countries that lie beyond that river wearing necklaces of amber, principally as an ornament, no doubt, but on account of its remedial virtues as well; for amber, it is generally believed, is good for affections of the tonsillary glands and fauces, the various kinds of water in the vicinity of the Alps being apt to produce disease in the human throat [such as goitre].'

He then informs us how the newly-learned fact that the distance from Carnuntum in Pannonia back up to the coasts of Germany from which the amber is brought, is a distance of about six hundred miles, and there is still living a member of the equestrian order who was sent there by Julianus, the manager of the gladiatorial exhibitions for Nero, to procure a supply of amber. The Amber Road was fully operational by this time. After visiting the various markets, he brought back amber in such vast quantities that there was enough to allow the nets, which are used for protecting the podium against the wild beasts, to be studded with amber. The arms too, the litters, and all the other equipment, were, on one day, decorated with nothing but amber, a change of display being made each day for each of the spectacles. The largest piece of amber that this *eques* brought to Rome weighed thirteen pounds.

More than half the route was through Celtic territory which led the Romans on the expedition to report that the amber coast was too far away, and the routes through the pathless forests would be impossible to control.[18] Better, then, to work at a distance, by proxy and federations, *foederati*.

The Romans were also anxious to control the regions beyond the *limes*. Characteristically, they divided and ruled, forming alliances, fighting battles and establishing buffer states in the changing pattern of alliances and conflicts. The Marcomanni were particularly troublesome, adept as they were as border guards, merchants (including of amber) and commodity brokers. Theirs was:

> 'A kind of protection racket in no man's land and [they] might demand tributes from both the Romans, who needed them as guarantors of border security, and from the original inhabitants, who very much wanted access to the Roman luxury goods, and in addition very much wanted to avoid being exported to the south as slaves. Those who could not pay the protection money were of course sold to the Roman slave traders. In this matter, the Marcomanni had basically no scruples; human-trafficking was perhaps the most important border trade. The Romans showered the cooperative bosses of the frontier trade with honors; made them dependent. But every now and then these *foederati* became so wealthy and influential that they became a threat to Rome.'[19]

To facilitate trade generally the old rough and ready routes and paths south of the Danube were now incorporated into the Roman road network. The *limes* did not stop the north-south trade; on the contrary, the trade in fact intensified. Carnuntum, in a celebrated wine-growing region, was a Roman legionary fortress and headquarters of the Pannonian fleet from 50 CE. After the first century, it was capital of the province of Pannonia Superior and became a large city of 50,000 inhabitants. It can be thought of as a trade crossroads, an entrepôt, 'a place of trans-shipment, where Northern Europeans exchanged their loads of amber for Roman wines or luxury items such as bronze vessels or glass; Roman trading operations and 'forwarding agents' took over the amber business. Anders Hammarlund records in *Baltic Worlds*:

> 'From Carnuntum, which was in the province of Pannonia Superior, a route ran south through what today is the border region between Austria and Hungary, passed the citadel of Scarbantia (Sopron) and the Roman colony of Savaria (Szombathely), then turned off to the southwest and, via Emona (Ljubljana), reached the Adriatic Sea at Aquileia.'

As Aelium Carnuntum, the capital of Pannonia Superior, it was made a *municipium* by Hadrian. Its importance is indicated by the fact that Marcus Aurelius lived here from 172–175 CE during the war against the Marcomanni, and wrote part of his *Meditations* there. Also, Septimius Severus, at that time governor of Pannonia, was proclaimed emperor at Carnuntum by his soldiers (193), to replace Emperor Pertinax, who had been murdered. During the Severan dynasty (193–235) Carnuntum experienced an economic boom, the *canabae* reaching their maximum size.

According to Kristian Kristiansen, in Scandinavia the amber road probably gave rise to the thriving Nordic Bronze Age culture, bringing influences from the Mediterranean Sea to the northernmost countries of Europe.[20]

Kaliningrad Oblast is sometimes referred to in Russian as Янтарный край, which means 'the amber region'.

Amber

What was it that attracted the Romans, and many before and after, to amber? Obviously, its beautiful colour and magical-seeming properties: it could burn and evaporate; rubbing it gives off a pleasant aromatic scent, and makes it negatively electrically charged, giving it the ability to attract light objects such as human hair and pieces of paper. In ancient Syria, amber was referred to as '*harpax*' – a word which meant 'to drag'. This was on account of the electrostatic properties of amber. Syrian women noticed that when rubbed with cloth, amber drew light objects such as hair, fibres or leaves in spite of opposing gravitational forces pulling them down. Amber was used to make the whorls of spinning spindles, as it attracted the chafed fibres away from the fabrics, keeping the equipment clear. It came to be known by the Persians as *kahruba* or 'straw-robber' for these powers of frictional electricity. The word *electricity* derives from the Greek name for amber, *élektron*.

Amber oil and succinic acid were extracted from the stones, which were believed to have medicinal properties. Pliny the Elder wrote extensively about the healing properties of amber: 'in a pendant around the neck, it will heal fever and illnesses, crushed and mixed in honey and rose oil it will help against earache, and mixed with Attic honey it will also cure weakened eyesight'. The Romans would have been very impressed by this endorsement, passionate as they were about complementary medicine. That amber sometimes contained remarkably well-preserved encapsulated insects and plants simply trapped over many millennia only added to the fascination. One of the first materials used for ritual offering and ornamentation, the placement of amber alongside the deceased, in ritualistic formations indicates the extent to which prehistoric peoples revered the material. Roman cemeteries often contained what appear to be offerings of amber beads, particularly with child burials.[21]

Consequently, it became a medium of barter and a lucrative commodity, which soon found a market in the Mediterranean region. That large quantity of gems found in the royal tombs at Mycenae have been chemically determined to be Baltic amber, or succinit, which is the scientific name, from the Latin *succinum* (succinic acid is thus 'acid of amber'). In Imperial Rome a huge demand grew and grew; people craved *succinum* for health-giving and as attractive jewellery, as well as for its decorative qualities in temple and palace interiors. Tacitus reminds us, however, that as placatory gifts, or bribes for barbarians who were potential allies or enemies, amber failed to impress; Lundgren (2018) puts it well:

'According to Tacitus, the Germans had a very different concept of wealth than the Romans.[22] Even though the Germans had silver vessels that they had received as gifts, they did not treat them as more valuable than simple pottery. They also lacked appreciation for amber. There are Roman accounts that let us know that amber was nothing more than toys for the barbarian children who casually picked it from the river banks until the Romans taught them its value.[23] Tacitus writes that the Germans were amazed that anyone would pay them for the amber that they considered useless.[24] These Roman accounts are only the Romans' opinions on the matter. The Germans' side of the story was never recorded. However, the Romans' claims fit the archaeological material. The use of amber amongst the Baltic communities was sparse during the first and second centuries AD.[25] Despite this, according to Pliny, the markets of Rome were flooded with imported amber every single day.'[26]

But as Lundgren goes on to point out (p.13), 'The Germans must have been shrewder than the Romans let on. They were capable of providing Rome with enough amber to supply an entire industry and they would not have done it for free'. Strong's catalogue contains a variety of amber items consisting of what one might expect to find in a Roman grave assemblage. The sixteen items listed as being Roman consist of figurines, finger-rings, pendants, various beads, a die and perfume vessels.[27]

Aquileia (at the head of the Adriatic) was the Roman centre for distribution and the refining of amber. There jewellery, toilet articles, figurines, boxes and other trinkets were manufactured. The city had a near monopoly on amber carving as well as a taste for amber figurines that was so great that most of these figurines never got as far as the city gates.

Anders Hammarlund tells us that Kalisia (Kalisz) is mentioned by Ptolemy – it is here that two vital trade routes intersect: one is the Amber Road, the other goes from the southeast to the northwest and conveys salt; 'the salt came from the salt lands of Halychyna (Galicia), to salt-poor North-western Europe; and amber, to succinum-thirsty Rome'.[28]

Hammarland speculates, interestingly, that salt revenues may have bankrolled the amber trade:

'Kurlansky (2003) points out that the Gauls were "masters of salt".[28] The Gauls were thus "the salt people". Place names throughout Europe speak volumes about the history of salt mining and extraction that the Gauls controlled; the German cities of Halle and Schwäbisch Hall arose around ancient salt sources. The Austrian name Hallein means "salt works", the nearby Hallstatt "salt place". And not far from them there is even Salzburg. And then of course we have the important provinces of Galicia in Poland/Ukraine (in Polish: *Galicja*, Ukrainian: *Halychyna*) and Galicia in northern Spain. These Gauls should perhaps be thought of as a cosmopolitan salt trading aristocracy ... it is the salt men that are thought to have provided the trade and transport along the Amber Road during antiquity with its efficient organization.'

Pliny (*NH* 37, 30; 37, 50–51) explains that amber was liked and coveted only by women since it was a useless luxury. You can't even fashion it into something to drink out of he exclaims. But some men of Rome were also taken by the beauty of amber, even if their indulgence was more discreet. Nero described his wife's hair as amber-coloured in a poem that inspired many respectable women of Rome to dye their hair. Pliny was especially taken with Falernian amber:

'The most highly esteemed amber is that known as the "Falernian", from its resemblance to the colour of Falernian wine; it is perfectly transparent, and has a softened, transparent, brightness. Other kinds, again, are valued for their mellowed tints, like the colour of boiled honey in appearance. It

> ought to be known, however, that any colour can be imparted to amber that may be desired, it being sometimes stained with kid-suet and root of alkanet; indeed, at the present day, amber is dyed purple even.'
>
> Pliny, NH 37, 12; trans. John Bostock

Lundgren refers to a paper by Ellen Swift in which she investigates the appearance of a certain kind of amber beads of German design in Germania and Rome. Swift asserts that there were no amber beads in any adult male graves within the Roman Empire; instead they have been found in the graves of women and children in the Roman world. Beyond the frontier they occurred more frequently in women's graves rather than children's, and only a small amount of the amber beads comes from the graves of men.[29]

Lundgren points out that it was thought important for babies to wear amulets of amber, but Pliny writes that Callistratus claims that amber is good for people of any age for a variety of medicinal purposes. A person can receive these benefits both by wearing it as an amulet or by consuming it in liquid form.[30]

The Romans' predilection for amber, particularly among rich Roman ladies, lasted until the end of the second century CE when amber dropped out of fashion. By the second century there was considerable unrest in Germania and the reason for the abrupt end to its fashionability is most likely linked to the dangers and difficulties of obtaining amber from the Baltic Sea.

Chapter 9

Britannia

This chapter is concerned with trade in, to and from Britain before it became a Roman province, Britannia, after the invasion by Claudius in 43 CE.

What did the ancients know about Britain and what was it they saw here or heard about which attracted them?

In the beginning, before about 6,500 BCE, the islands we know as Britain were populated by peoples who had moved west in a series of migrations across Europe in the early Stone Age when there was no Channel to impede them and they just walked across. In time melting glaciers, rising sea levels and sinking land caused Britain to be cut adrift, marooning these immigrants so that they became islanders and, effectively, British. Naturally, they brought with them their religious beliefs and skills to construct the megalithic stone burial chambers we see at Avebury and Stonehenge; just as significant is the fact that they were adept at metallurgy, which touched all aspects of prehistoric life and our history, for it was bronze and iron which they fashioned into weaponry and agricultural tools replacing the crude stone and flint of earlier civilizations. The result was, of course, not only armed conflict and agriculture, but also some basic commerce and economics when the natives initiated and developed a trade in luxurious and desirable objects bartered with visitors from or visits to tribes on the European mainland and further east. Inevitably, their more sophisticated weapons enabled subsequent waves of invaders and the more powerful indigenous tribes to dominate the weaker, less advanced natives and establish themselves on the productive, most fertile lands, relegating their previous occupants to the unforgiving and unproductive moors, marshes and weather beaten uplands.

This was, in reality, the origin of what is now called the north-south divide, where disparities in the socio-economics of the north and south still bedevil us today. Soon, an obvious division emerged between the more workable and productive regions of much of the south and east and the comparatively barren northern and western areas; by the time the Romans arrived, this geographical dichotomy naturally created an economic and social divide which was to manifest itself in relative affluence and stability for the one and discontent and comparative poverty for the other. The northerners were more inclined to foment opposition against the Roman way and against Roman rule which was to hamper and harass the Romans for many years of their occupation.

Pytheas of Massalia

The earliest name of the archipelago which we now know as the British Isles was current some 2,000 years ago when classical geographers described our island group, from about the fourth century to around 50 BCE, using variations of the word 'Prettanikē'.

Indeed, our first record comes from the fourth-century BCE Greek explorer and geographer Pytheas of Massalia (Marseilles), who in 325 BCE circumnavigated and visited much of modern-day Great Britain and Ireland, referring vaguely to Prettanikē or Brettaniai as a group of islands off the coast of North-Western Europe – an ancient Greek transliteration of the original Brittonic term in a non-extant work by Pytheas based on his extensive travels and discoveries. According to Strabo (63 BCE–c. 24 CE), Pytheas referred to Britain as Bretannikē, which is a feminine noun. Bretannikē may derive from a Celtic word meaning 'the painted ones' or 'the tattooed people' in a reference to the local predilection for body art and the use of woad. Other early records of the word can be found in the *peripli* by later authors, and those in Strabo's *Geographica*, Pliny's *Natural History* and Diodorus Siculus' *Bibliotheca Historica*. Pliny the Elder (23–79 CE) says of Britain: 'Its former name was Albion; but at a later period, all the islands … were included under the name of Britanniae'. He mentions many things related to Britain, including the long days, the tides recorded by Pytheas, local magic, the daubing of natives with warlike woad, the wild geese, oysters, coracles, and trade opportunities in pearls, the cherry tree, amber, tin and lead.

Pliny was the first known scientist to see and describe the Arctic, polar ice, Thule (Iceland or Orkney or Norway?) and the Celtic and Germanic tribes. He is also the first one record to describe the midnight sun. Strabo tells us that Pytheas 'travelled over the whole of Britain that was accessible' (*Geographica* 2, 4, 1). Ptolemy (c. 100 – c. 170) the Greek-Egyptian mathematician, astronomer, geographer and astrologer later gives more information between 127 CE and 141 CE based on the work of Marinus of Tyre from around 100 CE.

Marcian of Heraclea (fl. c. fourth century CE), in his *Periplus Maris Exteri*, described the island group as αἱ Πρεττανικαὶ νῆσοι (the Prettanic Isles). Marcian was a minor Greek geographer; his known works include *A Periplus of the Outer Sea* which introduces us to places stretching from the Atlantic Ocean to China.

Diodorus Siculus (fl. first century BCE)

In the first century BCE, Diodorus Siculus in his *Bibliotheca Historica* of 36 BCE mentioned Pretannia, a version of the indigenous name for the Pretani people whom the Greeks believed to inhabit the British Isles. This is his description:

> 'Britain is triangular in shape, very much like Sicily, but its sides are not equal. This island stretches obliquely along the coast of Europe, and the point where it is least distant from the mainland, we are told, is the promontory which men call Cantium [Kent] and this is about one hundred stades [eleven miles] from the land, at the place where the sea has its outlet, whereas the second promontory, known as Belerium [Cornwall] is said to be a voyage of four days from the mainland, and the last, writers tell us, extends out into the open sea and is named Orca [Orkney] ... And Britain, we are told, is inhabited by native tribes and preserve in their ways of living the ancient manner of life ... Their way of living is modest, since they are far from the luxury which comes with wealth. The island is also heavily populated ... It is controlled by many kings and potentates, who for the most part live at peace among themselves.'
> *Diodorus Siculus*, Bibliotheca Historica 21, 3–6

Not many trade opportunities there then according to Diodorus.

Diodorus goes on to tell us about a cold and frosty place where the people live in thatched cottages, store their grain underground and bake bread. When they fight they do so from chariots, just like the Greeks did in the Trojan War. It was, however, a place shrouded in mystery and dread. According to Plutarch:

> 'The island was incredibly big, and caused so much controversy amongst many a writer, some of whom swore that its name and story had been made up, since it had never existed and did not exist then.'[1]

Or maybe it was just a figment of the imagination, according to Strabo, *Geography* 2,4, 1, written soon after Caesar. Polybius, *Histories* 34.5, is less than convinced, although his rubbishing of Pytheas may have been to amplify his own more modest Atlantic expedition.

At first the Romans referred to *Insulae Britannicae* in the plural, a place consisting of Albion (Great Britain), Hibernia (Ireland), Thule and many smaller islands. However, when the Romans wanted to describe the place in later times they used the Latin name 'Britannia'. Britannia is a Latinization of the native Brittonic word for the island, Pretanī, which also gave that Greek form Prettanike or Brettaniai. Brittonic was an ancient Celtic language spoken in Britain.

Our earliest reference for Great Britain, Albion (Ἀλβιών) or *insula Albionum*, is either from the Latin *albus* meaning 'white' – a reference to the white cliffs of Dover, the first you see of us from the continent – or meaning the 'island of the Albiones'? Pseudo-Aristotle gives us our earliest mention of Great Britain:

'... ἐν τούτῳ γε μὴν νῆσοι μέγιστοι τυγχάνουσιν οὖσαι δύο, Βρεττανικαὶ λεγόμεναι, Ἀλβίων καὶ Ἰέρνη.'

'There are two very large islands in it, called the British Isles, Albion and Ierne.'

Aristotle, On the Cosmos *393b*

Ptolemy referred to the larger island as Great Britain (μεγάλη Βρεττανία) and to Ireland as Little Britain (μικρὰ Βρεττανία) in his *Almagest* (147–148 CE). In his later work, *Geography* (c. 150 CE), he gave the islands the names Alwion, Iwernia, and Mona (the Isle of Man), suggesting these may have been the names of the individual islands not known to him when he wrote *Almagest*. The name Albion appears to have fallen out of use sometime after the Roman conquest of Britain, after which Britannia became the more usual name.

Tin Islands

It was tin that first attracted serious attention from outsiders when the Greeks, Phoenicians and Carthaginians – all experienced travellers and traders – began buying and exporting tin back to their various homes. The Greeks then began to call Britain (specifically Cornwall and the Scillies), amongst other north Atlantic places, the *Cassiterides*, or 'tin islands'. A rather sceptical Herodotus in the fifth century BCE vaguely located these lucrative mines somewhere off the west coast of Europe. He declares no real evidence for this, though, but concedes that they must exist if only because the Greeks must get their tin from somewhere, probably from 'the ends of the earth'.[2] He prefers this explanation to the mythical story that tin comes from the one-eyed Arimaspians who steal it from the griffins who are responsible for guarding it. The Arimaspians were a legendary tribe of one-eyed people of northern Scythia.

The Cassiterides were reputedly known first to Phoenician traders or Carthaginians from Gades (Cadiz). Pliny reports that a Greek named Midacritus (c.600 BCE) imported tin from Cassiteris island).[3] The Carthaginians kept their tin routes secret; hence Herodotus's doubts about the existence of the Cassiterides. Pytheas visited the miners of Belerium (Land's End) and their tin depot at Ictis;

but it was a Roman, probably Publius Licinius Crassus, governor in Spain around 95 BCE, who revealed the tin routes: Strabo refers to a (non-extant) treatise on the Cassiterides written by Publius Crassus, grandson of Licinius. Several scholars of the nineteenth and early-twentieth centuries, including Mommsen and Rice Holmes, believed the source of this to be founded on an expedition during Publius' posting in Armorica (Brittany). More recently, historians assign authorship to the elder Publius, compiled during his proconsulship in Spain in the 90s BCE, in which case the grandson's Armorican foray may have been prompted in part by commercial interests to capitalize on the survey of resources established earlier.

Diodorus, tells how 'tin is brought in large quantities also from the island of Britain to Gaul opposite, where it is taken by merchants on horses through the interior of Celtica both to the Massalians and to the city of Narbo [Narbonne], as it is called'.[4]

Himilco

Himilco was a Carthaginian navigator and explorer of the late-sixth or early-fifth century BCE, at a time when Carthage dominated the region. He is the first known explorer from the Mediterranean to reach the northwestern shores of Europe. The oldest reference to Himilco's account of his voyage is a brief mention in Pliny's *Natural History*;[5] he was referenced three times by Rufus Festus Avienus, who wrote *Ora Maritima* (the *Sea Shore*), a poetical geographical account in the fourth century CE.

Himilco sailed along the Atlantic coast from the Iberian Peninsula to the British Isles. He travelled to northwestern France specifically to trade for tin (to be used for making bronze) and other metals. Records of the voyages of Himilco also mention the islands of Albion and Ierne.

To enhance his reputation, no doubt, as an intrepid voyager and to deter and frighten superstitious Greek rivals from following his trade routes, Himilco embroidered his journeys with sensational tales of sea monsters and seaweed.

Avienus also tells us that the Tartessians – native Iron Age Andalusians – visited the Oestrumnidan Isles to trade with the inhabitants; later, Carthaginian tradesmen travelled along the same route. But where were the Oestrumnidan Isles? Avienus says they were two days' sailing distance from Ireland, and they 'were rich in the mining of tin and lead. A vigorous tribe lives here, proud spirited, energetic and skillful. On every ridge trade is carried on'. All things considered it seems that Avienus meant ore-rich Brittany and the small islands off the coast rather than Cornwall or the Scilly Isles – the other two possibilities – although the Tartessians traded not just with the inhabitants of Brittany, but beyond – Cornwall, Wales and Ireland.

Between the time of Julius Caesar and Claudius Britain would have been very much on the Romans' radar, so to speak, with references in libraries from a number of extant and non-extant historians, geographers, travellers and encyclopaedists. These sources would have been readily available for those with a mind to look.

Britannia

By the first century BCE 'Britannia' was synonymous with and came to be used for what we have for centuries known as Great Britain. After the conquest by Claudius from 43 CE, Britannia *was* Roman Britain, a province covering the island south of Caledonia (roughly today's mid- to southern-Scotland), walled off by Hadrian's famous construction. Indigenous people living in Britannia were called *Britanni*, or Britons.

Britannia was sufficiently well enough known amongst the learned and literate, even during the turbulent years of the first century BCE before Caesar's reconnaissance visits. The Epicurean poet Lucretius (99 BCE–55 BCE) uses the adjective *Britannus* as a metaphor and an example of a 'region far from fatherland and home' in his *De Rerum Natura*.[6] In a poem that can be confidently dated after Caesar's first invasion and before the death of Caesar's daughter Julia, the neoteric and rebellious poet Catullus (c. 84–c. 54 BCE) refers to the place three times in poem 29 where he rails against Mamurra in an invective against triumvirs Caesar and Pompey:

'Quis hoc potest videre, quis potest pati,
nisi impudicus et vorax et aleo,
Mamurram habere quod comata Gallia
habebat ante et ultima Britannia?'

'Who can see this, who can stand it, save the shameless, the glutton, and gambler, that Mamurra Mentula should possess what long-haired Gaul had and remotest Britain had before?'

Poem 29, 1–4

'Eone nomine, imperator unice,
Fuisti in ultima occidentis insula'

'Is it for this reason, unique commander, You were on that farthest island of the west?'

Poem 29, 11–12

Note that the 'unice' commander, described with not a little irony as 'beyond compare', is Julius Caesar and the farthest island of the west is Britannia.

The remoteness and mysterious 'edge of empire' quality of Britannia (*ultima*) is emphasized twice, while in all three instances the island is cited as an example of how the depredations of Mamurra, and of triumvirates Caesar and Pompey by extension, extend so far as to include Britannia despite it being so far from Rome. In the love poem 45 (22–23) of Septimius and Acme Britannia is used, with Syria, as a measure of Septimius's devotion.

Near contemporary Cicero's (106 BCE–43 BCE) *Epistulae ad Q. Fratrem* written between 60 or 59 to 54 BCE, finds the orator writing to Quintus Tullius, his brother, who is a *legatus* with Caesar's army on the second of Caesar's two British incursions. His words describe for us the dangers, mystery and intriguing qualities of the place, based, no doubt, on detailed descriptions penned in earlier correspondence to Cicero from Quintus.

In *De Natura Deorum* Cicero cites Britannia (with Scythia) as another example not just of distance and remoteness, but also of the prodigious extent of Roman rule.[7] These countries are uncivilized (*barbaria*), but the inhabitants there nevertheless recognise the workings of a rational human being when they see it. In the same treatise he marvels that the tides on the Spanish and British (*Britannicus aestus*) coasts ebb and flow without divine intervention:[8] naturally that is.

Despite the commercial attractions to British tin and other mineral deposits, we know little about anything that happened between Rome and Britannia until the mid-first century BCE when an inquisitive Rome arrived in 55 BCE with Julius Caesar. Continued expansion meant that the empire had extended its reach from the Alps and Cevennes to the Channel in the five years before the incursion, so Caesar's actions in trying to extend these boundaries would have been by no means unusual. Caesar, of course, was a shrewd man of the media, a persuasive reporter and a skillful politician, so it comes as no surprise that he states in his inevitably biased and one-sided Gallic War commentaries that his purported aim in invading Britain, his *casus belli*, was to stifle the military and economic support the Britons had been giving to the Gauls on the mainland. The corollary to this strategy was equally influential; luxury Roman goods available in the import-export markets were valuable bargaining chips in seducing tribes into the Roman political sphere: British chiefs might avail themselves of levels of opulence for home and table unknown or only dreamed about a few years earlier. Archaeological evidence comes in the form of wine jars deposited in the tombs of chiefs and noblemen, silver tableware and bronze plated furniture. Strabo describes ivory, high-end jewellery and glass. Other exports he mentions include short, coarse and dark wool from the diminutive and goat-like indigenous Celtic sheep, corn, cattle gold, silver, iron, hides, slaves and 'clever hunting dogs'. Numismatic evidence for this commerce comes from the widespread use of silver and gold coinage on the Gallic model throughout south east England at the time. Less tangible, less traceable entities such as Roman medicine, law and education would also have been attractive to the more enlightened or ambitious, Britons as witnessed on their increasingly frequent trips to the Romanized near continent, and even to the city of Rome itself.

The only risk for Caesar was that, in deploying legions over the unpredictable English Channel, he may leave the mainland territories in Gaul prone to attack and undo all the good work completed over the last few years. As it turned out this was a risk Caesar, the supreme opportunist, was willing to take, although the prosecution of the two forays turned out to be very unpredictable and uncertain at times. There was, though, another, far more rewarding pretext for the incursion over the Channel; this owes much more to the hoary civic institutions enshrined in the Roman Forum than to the misty battlefields and dense forests of Gaul. Caesar's invasions, or more accurately reconnaissance and intelligence-gathering expeditions, would make an impressive addendum to his already glowing *cursus honorum*. The celebrity to be gained by just attempting this foray into the unknown and dangerous world – never mind any success which accrued – would add priceless grist to his political machinations at this time. Caesar would also have been keen to postpone a recall to Rome, which would be required on the resignation of his province, where his many enemies could get at him.

According to Balsdon, the decision to send an expedition to Britain may have been taken a year before Caesar's armies set sail: 'The notion was in his mind, perhaps, in early 56, indeed when he was at Luca, and it may well have been for this project that those ships had been built on the Loire …' (Balsdon, *Julius Caesar*).[9] But there were clearly other motives beyond the militaristic.

In Michael Grant's *Julius Caesar*[10] we hear of a probable financial motive: 'Caesar himself like many others hoped for lavish loot of gold and silver and above all pearls'. And then there was the prestige and celebrity brought by conquering this exotic, mysterious land beyond the borders of the world. The British campaign became a kind of publicity stunt, a PR exercise to further his political aspirations. Campaigning against the barbaric Britons in an unknown, wild frontier was sure to impress and spotlight Caesar as the archetypal heroic Roman conqueror.

The Veneti tribe of Brittany may also have been a factor: they enjoyed a monopoly on British trade at the time, but Caesar's earlier attempts to disrupt this commerce and glean information through commercial espionage had failed, so stoking his curiosity and desire to investigate further:

'I could not find out anything about the size of the island, the names and populations of the tribes ... their methods of fighting or the customs they had, or which harbours there could accommodate a large number of big ships.'

De Bello Gallico 4, 20

More significantly, Caesar had reason to believe that the Britons had embarrassed and compromised his campaigns in Gaul. They had lent support to the efforts of the mainland Gauls against him and provided safe harbour for fugitives from the Gallic Belgae fleeing to Belgic settlements in Britain. Moreover, he believed that the Veneti of Armorica, who, as noted. controlled seaborne trade to the island, depended on military aid from their British allies in their conflict against him in 56 BCE (*De Bello Gallico* 3, 8–9). Strabo adds that the Venetic rebellion was fomented to prevent Caesar from travelling to Britain and disrupting their trade.[11]

So Britain, as noted, by the first half of the first century BCE was familiar to the educated and literate in and around Rome; it had a place in the vocabulary of philosophers, poets and their côteries, socialites, lawyers, politicians and rhetoricians. In short, it enjoyed a role in the public narrative; contemporary Romans would have expected Britannia to fall to Rome's relentless war machine, given that expansionism was a prominent facet of foreign policy at that time. From this perspective, the pressure was very much on Julius Caesar to go and investigate.

Caesar's efforts did little to dispel the island's reputation for mystery and danger and, for most Romans it remained a mysterious misty island located beyond the Ocean at the edge of the known world – *ultima Thule* – so great was the trepidation it evoked. If Caesar had intended the invasion as a full-scale campaign, invasion or occupation, then clearly it had failed. It also had not fully succeeded as a reconnaissance operation or a show of strength to deter further British aid to the Gauls. Nonetheless, going to Britain and taking Rome beyond the 'known world' carried such prestige for a Roman that the Senate decreed a *supplicatio* of twenty days on the basis of Caesar's report.[12] It may also be that this exercise established alliances and trade agreements with British kings in the area which smoothed and facilitated the later invasion of 43 CE.

As noted, Caesar's stated official motive for the incursion was to quell Gallic support from Britain: 'in almost all the wars with the Gauls military support had been offered to our enemy from that country'. However, the possibility of exploiting tin reserves and other mineral resources remains another motive. Cicero refers to the disappointing discovery (from his brother Quintus) that there was neither gold nor silver to be found in the island, although how this could have been established for certain in such a short and geographically limited visit – particularly as the Romans were hundreds of miles from the recognised source in Cornwall – remains problematic. As it happens silver was mined from soon after the Claudian invasion, although not in the areas penetrated by Caesar. Quintus is on safer ground with the chariots as British weapons of war:

> 'In Britain I am told there is no gold or silver. If that turns out to be the case, I advise you to capture a war-chariot and hasten back to us at the earliest opportunity.'
> Cicero, Ad Familiares, 7, 7 – to C. Trebatius Testa (who was serving in Caesar's army) on his way to Gaul, from Cumae, April 54 BCE.

The chariots were obviously a cause for concern back in Rome as this reference to Trebatius makes clear: 'look out, while in Britain, that you are not yourself taken in by the charioteers',[13] but it was not just the chariots:

> 'The result of the British war is a cause of anxiety for it seems that the approaches to the island are protected by astonishing masses of cliff. Moreover, it is now known that there isn't a pennyweight of silver in that island, nor any hope of booty except from slaves, among whom I don't suppose you can expect any instructed in literature or music.'
> Cicero Ad Atticus, 4, 17

Suetonius reports that Caesar was said to have gone to Britain in search of pearls.[14] Caesar did later dedicate a thorax decorated with British pearls to Venus Genetrix in the temple dedicated to her that he later built, and oysters were later exported from Britain to Rome.[15]

When Caesar landed in 55 BCE, Britain had an estimated population of between one and four million. The lowland southeast with its expansive tracts of fertile soil encouraged extensive arable farming, while communications developed along trackways – such as the Icknield Way, the Pilgrims' Way and the Jurassic Way – and along navigable rivers like the Thames. North of a line from Gloucester to Lincoln, workable arable land was less in evidence. Settlements were usually built on elevated ground and fortified, but in the southeast, *oppida* were established on lower ground, often at river crossings, suggesting that trade was increasing in importance. Trade between Britain and the continent had been growing since the Roman conquest of Transalpine Gaul in 124 BCE. Italian wine was being imported via the Armorican peninsula, mostly at Hengistbury Head in Dorset.

The following year, 54 BCE, Caesar went back. This time he was better prepared, he had learnt from his mistakes to some extent, and was working to a more adventurous strategy. For a start, he took with him a larger force: no fewer than 600 new, specially built transports and 28 ships of war constructed with the latest Venetic shipbuilding technology. The five legions and 2,000 cavalry were conveyed in ships better suited to amphibious beach landings, being broader and lower. Portus Itius (somewhere in the Nord-Pas-de-Calais) was the port of departure.

Caesar left Titus Labienus at Portus Itius to ensure the lines of supply. Interestingly and astutely, the naval ships were joined by a trade delegation in the shape of a flotilla of commercial vessels looking to secure business with the Britons. The fleet totalled 800 ships. If nothing else, this civilian contingent proved that, for them at least, Caesar's earlier foray had dispelled much of the anxiety and superstition relating to this strange place at the end of the world; money spoke and for the hopeful merchants Britannia was now a former *terra incognita*, stripped of its ancient terror.

Within twenty years the Roman Republic had dissolved, amid much bloodshed and corruption, and re-emerged as the Roman Empire after Octavian's decisive victory at Actium. The story of Britain's relationship with Rome during that period up to the Claudian invasion is one of procrastination, hesitation and false starts descending, under Caligula, into nothing short of farce. Nevertheless, much good diplomatic work was achieved, not least, as noted, the establishment of a number of client kingdoms and the beginnings of the process we call Romanization in the south east corner of Britain. Trade inevitably picked up under the new regime. When Claudius did invade his progress was rapid, because a number of the noblemen and decision makers already enjoyed a cordial relationship with Rome and were only too happy to facilitate Claudius' progress. Claudius was fortunate indeed to be able to benefit from and exploit Caesar's diplomatic and commercial legacy.

The emperor Augustus (r. 27 BCE–14 CE) toyed with the idea of invading in 34 BCE; 'he had set out to lead an expedition into Britain also, and had already advanced into Gaul ... when some of the newly-conquered people and Dalmatians along with them rose in revolt';[16] we hear that:

'These were the actions of Augustus at that time. He also set out to make an expedition into Britain, but on reaching the provinces of Gaul hesitated there. For the Britons seemed likely to make terms with him, and the affairs of the Gauls were still unsettled, as the civil wars had begun immediately after their subjugation. He took a census of the inhabitants and regulated their life and government. From Gaul he proceeded into Spain, and established order there too.'

Dio, 53, 22

Dio interestingly gives us another explanation for Octavian's first projected invasion, claiming that Octavian was anxious to emulate his adoptive father, Julius Caesar, particularly after the success in Illyricum seemed to give him an opportunity to add to his military triumphs. However, trouble in Pannonia, Dalmatia and northern Italy put a stop to that.

To this we can add Strabo's comments made about the same time. First he says that the Romans were loath to invade because they believed the Britons to be too weak a force to cross over and threaten Roman rule on the European mainland; and second, that the potential return on exacting tribute was already outweighed by the tax revenues payable from the island.[17] Strabo repeats this at 4, 5, 3, adding that British leaders had been in Rome making offerings to Augustus at the Capitol – in effect giving over the whole island to Rome. The significance of this being that these influential Britons represented a powerful pro-Roman faction in the island.

But there was another powerful influence urging for invasion, at least for the literate and chattering classes. We have seen how Lucretius and Catullus reference Britannia, and, in the case of Catullus, Julius Caesar himself, in the late republic. In the early empire two pro-Augustan poets, Virgil and Horace, mention the island in the context of imminent or accomplished invasion; it was everybody's expectation that Britannia was going to fall to the Romans. We have *ultima Thule* from Virgil in the *Georgics* as an example of Augustus' global suzerainty: 'the boundless ocean's God thou come, Sole dread of seamen, till far Thule bow Before thee', and 'Even now I long to escort the stately procession to the shrine and witness the slaughter of steers; and see how Britons raise the crimson curtain they are woven into' in the same poem (3, 25).[18] Horace gives us much the same propaganda: 'O shield our Caesar as he goes to furthest Britain, and his band, Rome's harvest! Send on Eastern foes Their fear, and on the Red Sea strand!'[19] – *in ultimos orbis Britannos*. Far off Britain was within the reach of Augustus and spoken of in the same way as other outposts of empire. Augustus, however, may not have thanked Horace for asserting that he would not become a god unless or until he conquered the Parthians, the Persians and the Britons.

Moreover, the debacles visited on the Romans by the *Clades Lolliana* (17 BCE) and at Teutoburger Wald (9 CE) were eloquent reminders of the huge risks involved in oversees aggression and most likely deterred Augustus from further risky expansionism in the north west.[20]

So all the plans of Augustus came to nothing and relations with Britannia and its tribes proceeded on the basis of diplomacy and trade agreements. Sporadic references to Britannia include British kings who sent embassies to Augustus in Rome, and kings received by Augustus as exiles – Dubnovellaunus and Tincomarus. Tacitus gives an example of cordial relations and at the same time rekindles the mystique of Britannia in his reports that some of Tiberius' (r. 14 CE to 37 CE) ships were blown off course to Britain during his German campaigns in 16 CE; they were promptly sent back whence they came by local rulers, the startled Romans telling tales of hurricanes, strange birds, monsters and figures half man-half animal, imagined or otherwise.[21]

The diplomacy and commerce continued until 40 CE when an exile from the Catuvellauni, Adminius, son of Cunobelinus, fled to the court of Caligula and led the ever-unpredictable emperor (r. 37 CE to 41 CE) to plan an invasion of Britain. The gossipy imperial biographer Suetonius tells us that, characteristically for Caligula, it was a complete shambles and that the 'invaders' never actually left Gaul; Caligula ranged his siege-engines on the Gallic coast facing Britannia, then, to everyone's astonishment (or maybe not), ordered his troops to gather sea shells from the beach – 'such was the booty due to Rome'.[22] This they did, a lighthouse was erected, a bounty of four gold pieces was announced and he bid the troops 'go rich and go happy!'

Verica was a British client king in the years before the Claudian invasion of 43 CE. Numismatic evidence suggests he was king of the Atrebates tribe and a son of Commius. He succeeded his elder brother Eppillus as king in about 15 CE, reigning from Calleva Atrebatum, Silchester. He was recognised as *rex*, king, by Rome and appears to have had long-standing and amicable trade and diplomatic links with the empire.

However, his territory was threatened from the east by the Catuvellauni, led by Epaticcus, brother of Cunobellinus, who conquered Calleva in about 25 CE. After Epaticcus's death ca. 35 CE, Verica regained some territory, but Cunobelinus's son Caratacus assumed power and conquered the entire kingdom some time after 40 CE.

Cassius Dio[23] says that Bericus (Verica) was exiled from Britain around this time and fled to Claudius. Suetonius refers to demands by the Britons that Rome return 'certain deserters'.[24] As *rex*, Verica was nominally an ally of Rome, so his exile gave Claudius a pretext, if he needed one, to invade Britannia and restore Verica to power.

The Roman client kingdoms in Britain were indigenous tribes who had elected to ally themselves with the Romans, seeing, no doubt, that discretion was the better part of any valour. It protected them from Roman aggression by assuming Roman protection, protection which at the same time deterred land grabbing expansionist interference from other hostile tribes. The Romans sometimes created or enlisted client kingdoms when they felt arm's length influence without direct rule was appropriate or desirable.

The system began when Julius Caesar restored Mandubracius as king of the Trinovantes, after he had been deposed by Cassivellaunus and then supported Caesar's second invasion of Britain in 54 BCE. The arrangement ran from 54 BCE–c. 39 CE. Caesar also established the Catuvellauni as a tributary state of Rome. Since 10 CE, both areas were ruled by Cunobelinus, who lost control to an anti-Roman faction led by his son Caratacus around 39 CE; this was to prompt that farcical 'invasion' by Caligula.

We have established that it seems likely that Augustus adopted a policy of establishing client kingdoms with regard to Britain as being sufficient to keep the island under control, in preference to a full scale invasion with its financial and manpower costs; at the same time, it chimed well with his general foreign policy of containment rather than expansion of the Roman empire. Financially the treasuries of Augustus and Tiberius after him would continue to benefit from the customs duty brought in by the flood of imports from the continent, as evidenced by excavations of pottery and grave goods: Colchester and other places including Silchester with the Atrebates; Bagendon (Cirencester), the Dobunni; Leicester, the Coritani; and North Ferriby, the Parisi.

Client kingdoms were particularly successful in the south east and included those ruled by Cogidubnus of the Regnenses (55 BCE-70s CE), Prasutagus of the Iceni (roughly Norfolk; c. 47–60 CE), Cartimandua of the Brigantes, and Boduocus of the Dobunni. The antecedents of the Regnenses, the Atrebates, had been client kingdoms of Rome since Caesar's first invasion in 55 BCE. Following the Roman conquest, Cogidubnus, who at some point received the Roman names Tiberius Claudius, ruled what had been the lands of the Atrebates. His people were now referred to as 'Regni' or 'Regnenses'. Cogidubnus was especially loyal to the Romans and after his death, probably in 73 CE, the kingdom was absorbed into the Roman province of Britannia.

The Claudian Invasion

But trouble was brewing: by the 40s CE, the Catuvellauni had replaced the Trinovantes as the most powerful kingdom in southeastern Britain, taking over the former Trinovantian capital of Camulodunum (Colchester), and were threatening their neighbours, the Atrebates. In 43 CE, after a century of Roman indecision and hesitation, Caligula's successor, Claudius, invaded, ostensibly to assist the client king Verica of the Atrebates who had been exiled after a revolt by the Catuvellauni. Aulus Plautius was appointed commander-in-chief and first governor of the province. The invasion force comprised four legions: the IX Hispana, the II Augusta, the XIV Gemina, and the XX Valeria Victrix, supported by 20,000 auxiliary troops from Thrace and Batavia in Germany. II Augusta was led by Vespasian who was to become emperor in 69 CE. This invasion was not without its problems, however: the troops who mustered on the coast of Gaul were apprehensive about what to them was just like sailing off the edge of the world; they mutinied. Nevertheless, once reassured by Claudius's influential freedman and secretary Narcissus that the world did not actually end where they stood – and encouraged to see a former slave in place of their general – they shouted out '*Io Saturnalia!*' (Saturnalia was the Roman festival in which social roles were reversed for the day).

The panic and mutiny evaporated, and the invasion force set sail in three waves, landing at Rutupiae (Richborough) and possibly also at Bosham harbour near Fishbourne; a legionary helmet of Claudian date has been found in Bosham harbour and is now in Lewes museum. From here the Romans set about subduing the Catuvellauni – first on the Medway and then on the Thames. The Medway battle was won by a flanking movement by the Batavians – special forces expert in swimming in full armour. Togodumnus, one of the Catuvellaunian leaders, was killed, but his brother Caratacus lived to fight another day out west. Claudius arrived with reinforcements, artillery and terrifying elephants for the attack on Camulodunum, the Iron-Age *oppidum* which was their key objective.

This was Claudius' big moment; this is exactly what he had planned the invasion for: personally taking the war to the enemy and capturing their royal capital, thus, theoretically at least, placing him amongst the great Roman commanders of the past, not least Julius Caesar whose efforts he now truly eclipsed. Claudius would now be a credible and memorable member of the Julio-Claudian *gens*: the people of Rome and of the Roman empire would see how he extended that empire by adding a new province and compensating for the theatrical shambles that Caligula had orchestrated, and, in so doing, restoring the glory of Rome in this very visible theatre of war, this new province.

Trade had been flourishing: excavations have revealed fine imported ware from Gaul and red Arretine from Italy as well as the glass Strabo mentions. Slaves too, captured from other tribes, were on the manifests: a six-man slave chain has been found at Lord's Bridge in Cambridgeshire.

Claudius led from the front and, according to Cassius Dio (c. 155 – c. 235 CE), the stronghold fell after sixteen days, allowing Claudius to enter the *oppidum* in triumph. Suetonius is less enthusiastic;[25] an impartial Josephus even less so, giving all the glory to Vespasian.[26] Roman armies at this time were in the habit of hailing their emperor as *imperator* when he had won a significant conflict; Dio tells us that, in the case of Claudius, this happened more than once, so we might assume that Colchester was not the only successful outcome in his three weeks in Britain. Cogidubnus was installed as a client king for the kingdom of Verica (Sussex); he received two tribes to control and was honoured with the title *rex et legatus Augustii in Britannia*, elevating him to native prince and Roman official. Eleven other tribes of south east Britain surrendered to Claudius with no loss and the Romans proceeded to infiltrate further west and north into the territory of the Durotriges and Belgae of Dorset and Wiltshire, retaining Camulodunum as a springboard for the incursions. The Romans duly established their new capital at Camulodunum and Claudius returned to Rome, his job done. The Arch of Claudius was built to honour Claudius's successful invasion of Britannia. Sadly, it has not survived, but happily, the inscription can still be seen at the Capitoline Museum. The arch was dedicated in 51 CE, although a preview of sorts could be seen on the reverse of coins issued in 46–47 CE and 49 CE depicting it surmounted by an equestrian statue between two trophies. The reconstructed inscription also can be found on the arches celebrating the same events at Boulogne-sur-Mer and at Cyzicus reads:

> 'The Roman Senate and People to Tiberius Claudius Caesar Augustus Germanicus, son of Drusus, Pontifex Maximus, Tribunician power eleven times, Consul five times, Imperator twenty-two times, Censor, Father of the Fatherland, because he received the surrender of eleven kings of the Britons defeated without any loss, and first brought barbarian peoples across the Ocean into the dominion of the Roman people.'
>
> ILS 216 (CIL 6, 920)

47 CE saw the measured governor and commander in chief Aulus Plautius giving way to Ostorius Scapula, a belligerent hawk if ever there was one; Ostorius Scapula exemplifies what happens when client kingdoms go wrong. Tacitus describes his uncompromising policy to 'tame everything this side of Trent and the Severn' as ill-advisedly 'reducing the nearest part of Britain into a province', which involved disarming those tribes which Plautius had trusted to retain their weapons.[27] Result: the first Iceni rebellion which Ostorius put down only after a close-fought battle. Prasutagus was installed as king after the revolt of the Iceni. The Iceni were allowed quasi-independence, with the expectation that the kingdom would revert to Roman control on Prasutagus' death. However, the king, invoking an agreement made with the Romans earlier, insisted on leaving control of his kingdom to his daughters. When he died in 60 CE, the Romans denied all knowledge, choosing to skate over any small print or codicil, and

seized control, thus inciting a second, more challenging, Iceni rebellion under Prasutagus' widow Boudica. After ruthlessly quashing Boudica's revolt, the Romans simply administered the territory as part of Britannia.

Soon after the 43 CE invasion Claudius was honoured with the agnomen 'Britannicus' as conqueror of the island. A frieze discovered at Aphrodisias in 1980 shows how seriously the Romans viewed this: 'Claudius subjugating Britannia' is a relief on the south portico of the Sebasteion, Aphrodisias on which Claudius is about to deliver a death blow to a cowering and beaten Britannia. He wears helmet, cloak, and sword-belt with scabbard. Britannia wears a tunic with one breast bare – like the Amazons on which she is presumably modelled.

To give some idea of the size of the Roman garrison in Britannia, at times the Romans maintained four legions in Britain, in total about 20,000 soldiers supported by a further 20,000 auxiliaries, so deploying a full legion would on average entail moving around 5,000 men, their carts, mules and horses, equipment and supplies, and the extensive baggage train. All of this needed to be protected.

Hadrian's Wall

Trajan had died in 117 CE; his reign can be characterised in Britannia as one of withdrawal from Caledonia and consolidation of all territories south of that. Hadrian, his successor, continued in similar vein, reinforcing frontiers and dealing efficiently with trouble-makers within those boundaries. He created *municipia* and established *coloniae* throughout his empire. In pursuit of this Hadrian spent much of his time actually visiting and inspecting his territories rather than just getting embroiled in politics in Rome as emperors before and after him so often did. For Hadrian it was the establishment of communities, the civil engineering infrastructures and military projects which appealed; trade would naturally flow from such relatively settled periods: inevitably, it was only a matter of time before Britannia figured on his never-ending itinerary, and for Britannia Hadrian had ambitious plans.

Hadrian, like Trajan, was a provincial from the same provincial city as Trajan, Italica in Hispania Baetica. This gave him a less Rome-centric view of his empire – Rome was mightily important but it was not the be-all and end-all of the Roman empire, which other emperors believed to be the case. Hadrian's view of his world was more universal, a bigger picture view which embraced the whole empire rather than just a few square miles in Italy. Indeed, Hadrian did more than anyone to demonstrate that Rome, even with its prodigious and cumbersome civil service, was a mobile, portable entity: where Hadrian was, Rome was. Traditionalists took a dim view of this: to them Hadrian was shirking his responsibilities and they carped, as they had done with an itinerant

Nero some sixty years earlier when he travelled to Greece. In the *Historia Augusta*, Hadrian is described as 'a little too much Greek', too cosmopolitan for a Roman emperor. It seems that the arch conservatism of the Catos some 200 years before was still alive and well, and xenophobia was still a factor in the Roman Weltanschauung.

Hadrian and Trajan were two very different men; Trajan's comfort zone was enshrined within the restrictions dictated and imposed by the *mos maiorum*: conservative and averse to too much change too quickly, continuing the age-old tradition of progress through empire building conquests. Not so Hadrian; Hadrian built in the grand style like Trajan, but his buildings were often characterised by a preference for aesthetics over utility; Hadrian's love was for Greek culture (and for the Greek youth Antinous). Hadrian's ambitious focus was on unification and for making the empire a one-nation empire in which defence was the order of the day all around the world; seventy-five years of relative peace says that Hadrian's policy was an unmitigated success. There were of course exceptions to this view: for example, the Jews would never have considered Hadrian a champion of their culture but, by and large, Hadrian was what was called 'a good emperor'.

Britannia provides another exception; despite its ambitious scale there is little aesthetic about the great wall that was erected after Hadrian's visit in 122 CE, but it is an unmissable and powerful symbol of defence and defiance, an emblem of Roman might and influence; it has been called the most military barrier in the Roman world by more than one historian.

A formidable defensive wall was seen as the way to put a stop to truculent natives once and for all. The *Scriptores Historia Augustae*[28] in the fourth century tells us that Hadrian wanted to build the wall to separate the barbarians from the Romans. The policy to curtail the extension of Empire in pursuit of a need to reduce defence costs – a wall was a much cheaper way of deterring attacks than financing a border army – was surely another reason; moreover, a wall was just as useful in controlling cross border trade and for collecting excise and supervising immigration.

The internal trade within the province – with goods traded for sale and consumption from other parts of Britannia – is beyond the scope of this book. However, the trade generated for onward transportation to the wall is important when it comes to defending the border from barbarian incursions which often emanated from beyond the empire.

The wall helped to provide a period of military stability in Britannia which, in turn, allowed Romanization to prosper and for trade to flourish. Wroxeter is a good example, where a forum was dedicated to Hadrian. Indeed, we can be sure that Hadrian's visit cultivated a surge in Romanization province-wide

Replica of the famous statue of Mercury by Flemish sculptor Giovanni da Bologna, completed in 1580 and in the Louvre. Located on the island of Källskär, Kökar, Åland archipelago, Finland. Mercury is one of the top gods in the Roman pantheon: his portfolio includes being the god of profit, commerce, merchants, messages, communication, travellers, boundaries (*limes*), trickery, and thieves (including shoplifters and pirates). (*ReinerausH via Wikimedia Commons/CC BY-SA 3.0*)

Amphorae were the basic containers for shipping oil and wine. Millions were carried over the seas and many have been found on the ocean bed in shipwrecks. This image shows amphorae designed for marine transport, recovered from shipwrecks of the Bronze Age, on display in the Museum of Underwater Archaeology at Bodrum Castle, Turkey. The museum archaeologists have devised a rack and roping device to illustrate how the cargo might have been kept from shifting. (*Ad Meskens via Wikimedia Commons/CC BY-SA 3.0*)

The title page of the *Description of Greece* by Pausanias housed in the Laurentian Library collection in Florence. Pausanius, along with Pliny the Elder, Strabo, the authors of the various *peripli* and Ptolemy, is one of our chief sources of information on Roman trade outside the empire. (*Public domain*)

The transportation of slaves was a significant part of Roman trade, shipping men, women and children to Rome. Here is a mosaic of an actor's mask of an old slave; Altes Museum, Berlin.

Fragment of a limestone mosaic depicting a Roman *venatio* fighting a tiger, c.300–400 CE. Originally from Torre Nuova. One of a set of five large mosaics of gladiators and venators and two smaller ones. The mosaics are now in the Salone of the Galleria Borghese in Rome. The importation of wild animals from Africa, Arabia and India was big business. (*Daderot/Wikipedia*).

Teuta was a truculent pirate queen from Illyria who caused Rome many problems, and a significant amount of revenue in lost trade. She reigned from 231 BCE to 228/227 BCE. Skanderbeg Museum in Kruja, Albania. (*Hyjnesha via Wikimedia Commons/CC BY-SA 4.0*)

Mail coach out on the *cursus publicus*. This is one of the most famous Roman tombstones in Austria and can be found in the wall of the Marienkirche, a church in Maria Saal.

Fresco depicting the Isis Geminiana, a *navis codicaria* (small river vessel) being loaded from the columbarium 31 of the necropolis at Via Laurentina, Ostia, 200–250 CE. (*Vatican Museums, inv. 79638/ Joel Bellviure*)

Floor mosaic in the Aula dei Mensores (hall of the grain weighers) in Ostia showing grain measurers (*mensores frumentarii*) at work. The second person from the left is carrying a sack of grain. Next comes a slave? His right hand is raised: with his hand and fingers he is indicating the number nine. In his left hand is an instrument: a rope with nine tickets, presumably of wood, used to count the number of sacks that had arrived from the harbour. The right half of the mosaic is taken up by three people around a grain measure. To the left is the actual measurer (*mensor*). In his right hand is a levelling stick (*rutellum*). In the centre is a porter who has just emptied a sack, or is about to take the contents of the measure to a warehouse. The person at the far right is indicating the number 5,000 with his right hand.

Roman mosaic from Veii (Isola Farnese, Italy), depicting an African elephant being loaded onto a ship, third–fourth century CE, Badisches Landesmuseum Karlsruhe, Germany. (*Carole Raddato via Wikimedia Commons/CC BY-SA 2.0*)

Sarcophagus found at Porta Latina in Rome showing a busy port scene. Now in the Vatican Museum (inv. 927).

The importation of bread into Rome – the *cura annonae* or corn dole – was done on a huge scale and was essential to the existence of Rome. This represents either a distribution of bread by a candidate for office (wearing the 'toga candida' or white toga of the electoral candidate); or, since he is seated upon a tribunal, and perhaps already an official, the white toga would, therefore, be a sign of a plebeian office, e.g., aedile of the plebs. Because there is no exchange of money or shopfront in this image, it cannot be a 'sale of bread', as often assumed. (*Public domain*)

Trajan's Market in Rome. Thought to be the world's oldest shopping mall, the arcades in Trajan's Market are now believed by many to be administrative offices for Emperor Trajan. The shops and apartments were built in a multi-level structure, and it is still possible to visit several of the levels. Highlights include delicate marble floors and the remains of a library. (*Adobe Stock*)

Ostia today: former harbour town of Rome. (*Adobe Stock*)

Mosaic showing the bow of a large cargo ship in the quay at Portus, in the Portus Collection Musei Capitolini, Rome (third century CE).

Portus: NASA Earth Observatory image by Jesse Allen, using Landsat data from the U.S. Geological Survey. On 27 July 2013, the Operational Land Imager (OLI) on Landsat 8 acquired this view of the ancient Roman port. The hexagonal Trajanic Basin now sits about 2km inland, and it is a reed-filled lake. Over the past 1,500 years the coastline has migrated westward as the outer Claudian Basin filled in naturally with silt and sediment.

Caspar was one of the Three Wise Men, along with Melchior and Balthazar, mentioned in the Gospel of Matthew, verses 2:1-9. This portrait is by Jan Hermansz van Bijlert and was painted around 1640. Caspar is important to us, not just because he brought incense along the Spice Road to the west, a commodity which was much in demand in Rome, but also, as a man of colour, he is representative of the many people of colour with whom the Romans came into contact. Our chapter on Roman xenophobia and *Romanitas* emphasises that the Romans for the most part were unconcerned about anything like our modern notions of race or ethnicity. People who looked different from the typical Mediterranean were not excluded from any profession or discriminated against and there are no records of stigmas or biases against 'mixed race' relationships. Attributes which are vital when building trade relationships overseas.

Bas-relief from Cabrières-d'Aigues showing the transport of barrels and amphorae, pulled by three *halciarii* (boatmen), of which only two have survived. (*Fabrice Philibert-Caillat via Wikmedia Commons/CC BY-SA 3.0*)

Floor mosaic with two different approaching ships in the harbour of Portus. On the left probably a Cladivata and on the right a Corbita.

Mosaic from the Syrian city of Basrah showing a bearded man, probably a caravan merchant, leading a camel train through the desert. (*Jadd Haidar via Wikimedia Commons/CC BY-SA 4.0*).

The Three Wise Men journeying to Bethlehem carrying their gold, frankincense and myrrh as gifts for the infant Jesus. (*Painting by James Tissot/Brooklyn Museum*).

The Three Magi, Byzantine mosaic c.565, Basilica of Sant'Apollinare Nuovo, Ravenna, Italy. As here, Byzantine art usually depicts the Magi in Persian clothing, which includes breeches, capes and Phrygian caps. (*Nina Aldin Thune via Wikimedia Commons/CC BY-SA 2.5*)

Trekking along the Amber Road.

Roman glassware found in the grave of a rich man in Himlingøje in present-day Denmark. Dated to second–third century CE.

A reconstruction of the interior of the Bronze Age Uluburun shipwreck, 1330–1300 BCE. The ship sank off the coast of Lycia and contained, amongst other cargo, ten tons of copper ingots, tin ingots and jars of resin and foodstuffs. (*Bodrum Museum of Underwater Archaeology, Turkey*)

A mural showing women dressed in traditional Hanfu silk robes, from the Dahuting Tomb of the Late-Eastern Han Dynasty (25–220 CE), located in Zhengzhou, Henan province, China. (*Public domain*)

In the first centuries BCE and CE, much Roman trade was taken up with the importation of fashionable goods like silks, precious stones, incense and ivory. This mosaic from a Roman villa at Sidi Ghrib (in present-day Tunisia) depicts two female slaves (*ancillae*) attending their mistress and assisting with her make-up. Note the mirror. (*Fabien Dany via Wikimedia Commons/CC BY-SA 2.5*)

Roman food was revolutionised by imports of spices and herbs from India, Arabia and Africa. This is a Roman mosaic from a house in Pompeii, second century BCE. (*Naples National Archaeological Museum*)

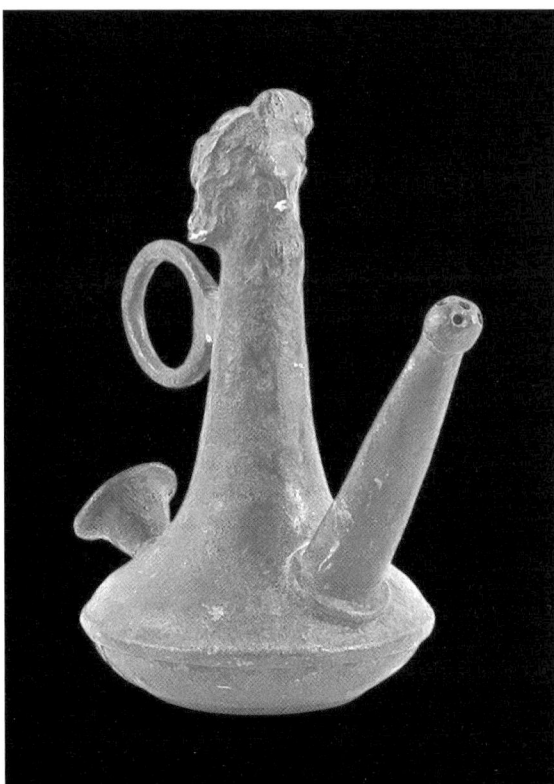

Incense, especially frankincense and myrrh, was another very popular commodity in Rome, imported from Arabia and east Africa. Incense burners of every shape and size were manufactured: this bronze creation features a face and a phallus.

Indian art in Pompeii: an ivory statuette of Lakshmi (first century CE), discovered in the ruins of Pompeii, 1930–1938. (*Sailko via Wikimedia Commons/CC BY-SA 3.0*)

Zhang Qian taking leave of Emperor Han Wudi for his expedition to Central Asia from 138 to 126 BCE, Mogao Caves mural, 618–712. (*Public domain*)

In 1996 some beautiful mosaics were uncovered by chance during road construction in the modern Israeli town of Lod, near Tel Aviv. Lod is ancient Lydda. It seems likely that the mosaics had been laid about 300 CE. The large rooms in which the mosaics were found probably belonged to an expensive private house and were reception or audience halls where visitors were greeted and entertained. Various birds, fish and animals are depicted. These surround a larger octagonal space populated by ferocious wild animals – a lion and lioness, an elephant, a giraffe, a rhinoceros, a tiger, and a wild bull – with a mountainous landscape flanking a *ketos*, or mythical sea creature. (*Public domain*)

A Maenad in a silk dress, a Roman fresco from the Casa del Naviglio in Pompeii, first century CE. A Maenad was a female follower of Bacchus, traditionally associated with divine possession and frenzy during the Bacchanalia. Silk, mainly from China, was hugely fashionable at the time. (*Naples National Museum*)

The cult of Bacchus was extremely popular. This shows the wedding of Dionysos and Ariadne. The Latin inscription identifies the girl for whom this sarcophagus was made as Maconiana Severiana, a member of a wealthy senatorial family. The front of the sarcophagus shows a Dionysiac revel, culminating in the discovery of the sleeping Ariadne. Ariadne's face was probably left unfinished to be completed as a portrait of Maconiana. Roman marble sarcophagus, 210–220 CE. (*Getty Museum, Pacific Pallisades CA*)

Bona Dea Marble Statue with epigraph; '*Ex visu iussu Bonae Deae sacr(um) Callistus Rufinae N(ostrae) Act(or)*' (Dedicated to Bona Dea by Callistus, slave of Rufina). *CIL*. XIV 2251. Antoninian, *Ager Albanus*, Italy.

just as much as it fostered military calm. London, Leicester and Caistor-by-Norwich also benefitted at the time with new civic buildings, while we know that York, Aldborough and Brough-on-Humber too would have seen a vigorous construction programme of public works and amenities along with the commerce which came with it. Local administration was increasingly the responsibility of local communities, leaving the army to respond flexibly to any local emergencies. This in turn led to an increasing influx of administrators and service industries to support the infrastructure projects, bringing in increasing numbers of Romans from all parts of the empire. The more they came the more Roman ways were inculcated over the length and breadth of the province. Local men and women would have profited, firing the businesses and trades in the towns. The countryside and rural economies would feel the benefits too, working the iron, tileries and ceramics workshops, for example, as well as the land.

A shrine was erected in York to Britannia as the divine personification of Britain; coins were struck, bearing her image, identified as BRITANNIA. By the end of 122, Hadrian had done his work and concluded his visit to Britannia. He never saw the famous wall that bears his name.

How were the legions and auxiliaries on and in the immediate proximity of the wall provisioned; how were the troops garrisoned up to the Antonine Wall, and the legions which made incursions into Celtic territory north of the wall? The answer lies in the construction of the fortress at Eboracum in 71 CE and its ceaseless development over the years until the withdrawal of the Romans. Eboracum was the storehouse for military provisions with lines of supply extending up to the forts just south of the wall.

Communications and connectivity were everything in the Roman world. As noted, much of Rome's enduring success as world leaders can be attributed to the Roman obsession with and expertise in road building, bridge building and its 'postal service'. The fact that the site of Eboracum was at the confluence of two navigable rivers (leading eventually to the Humber and to the North Sea only some fifty miles to the east) would have been influential factors in the decision the Romans made to site their northern stronghold and supply base where they did. As with any occupying army, the Romans had to move men and supplies and they had to trade. The rivers Foss and Ouse were connected to the Humber, Trent and Fosse Dyke, which gave access to the Witham at Lincoln and the Nene at Peterborough and so to the fertile farmlands of East Anglia; they also brought materiel, supplies, food, weapons, soldiers and horses to the fortress speedily and efficiently. They also fostered trade and provided a launching place for the deployment of soldiers in times of crisis or of routine defence, or to go north to build roads and forts. The Romans, then, put their rivers to good use: shiploads of goods would have come in on the Ouse via the Humber from the North Sea, and on the Foss; two possible wharves, excavated on the east bank of the River Foss, support this, as does large deposits of incinerated grain, found in a timber-structure on the north bank of the Ouse, which points to storehouses for the movement and storage of goods via the river.

One man who would have been familiar with this mercantile activity was Marcus Minucius Mudinus, *gubernator* (helmsman) of Legio V, who worked on the cargo boats plying up and down the Ouse. His altar (*RIB* 613), found in York's Micklegate, is dedicated to the 'Mother Goddess of Africa, Italy and Gaul' – adding a nice international flavour to the trade in and through York.

As well as the rivers, we have seen how an efficient road system and supply chain was required to support the needs of a garrison. The ordinary Roman soldier carried all of his kit and weapons with him. The Roman army had to be able to move from A to B in the most expeditious way possible.

In almost four centuries of occupation the Romans built about 2,000 miles of roads in Britain with the aim of connecting key locations by the most direct possible route. The roads were all paved and all-season and all-weather, to permit heavy freight-wagons to be used the year round, whatever the weather.

Before the Romans came Britain had few, if any, substantial bridges, so all rivers and streams would have been crossed by fords. Even well after the Romans had gone, many British towns remained at fording points, and the point nearest to the sea that a river could be forded was a major consideration in most journeys for trade and military supply and manoeuvres.

The Roman fortress would have exerted many varied influences on the local community and environment: at once a source of local labour and of women for conjugal relationships and prostitution, and at the same time a golden opportunity for trade and for the more venal elements in the local population to enrich themselves by running ancillary businesses in support of the garrison, or to enhance their standing in the community with a career in local government. The spiv has always been with us.

Canabae

A *canaba* was originally a hut or hovel, but from the time of Hadrian it denoted a town that emerged as a civilian settlement (*canaba legionis*) in the vicinity of a Roman legionary fortress (*castrum*). A settlement that grew up outside a smaller Roman fort was a 'vicus' (village). *Canabae* were also often divided into *vici*.

Permanent forts naturally were a magnet for anyone and everyone dependent on the military garrison and civilian traders and contractors who serviced the base; these all needed housing and feeding. They included traders, artisans, sellers of food and drink, prostitutes, and also unofficial wives of soldiers and their children; hence most forts had *vici* or *canabae*. Many of these communities became towns through synoecism with other communities; some are still towns today.

Chapter 10

Africa – Sub-Sahara and West Africa, Egypt, Nubia, Lake Chad

'There are four great kingdoms on earth: the first is the Kingdom of Babylon and Persia; the second is the Kingdom of Rome; the third is the Kingdom of the Aksumites: the fourth is the kingdom of the Chinese.'

The Persian prophet Mani, third century CE

Africa was explored at least as early as Queen Hatsheput's reign (1473–1458 BCE) when the Egyptians swerved round Nubia in order to trade direct with Somalia. Twelve hundred years later, in the third century BCE, the Ptolemies established Red Sea ports to facilitate their elephant hunting expeditions down Africa's east coast. Frankincense was the target for the Romans though and they soon realized that even modest boat loads brought a handsome profit – Pliny says (*NH* 13,4) 30 tons of it would bring in over one million sesterces back in Rome. Strabo gives us an idea of the extent of the trade when he reveals that 100 or more ships were conducting trade in Somalia and India via the Red Sea, bringing their trade to Egypt.

The ever- curious and restless Carthaginians were exploring the region from the fifth century, initially through Hanno.

Hanno the Navigator

Hanno was a Carthaginian explorer active from around the fifth century BCE, famous for his naval exploration of the west coast of Africa, the only source of which is a *periplus* translated into Greek. His precise route remains a matter of conjecture: some say he reached as far south as Gabon while others (Law 1978, p. 135) believe that he could not have got much further than the south of Morocco. Although referred to variously as *basileus*, *dux* and *imperator* he was most probably a high ranking official; Law (p. 121) says he was the son of Hamilcar. According to Warmington (*Carthage*, 1960, p. 62), the *periplus* has survived as 'the nearest we have to a specimen of Carthaginian "literature"' and one of the few extant accounts of ancient exploration penned by the explorer himself (Cary and Warmington 1929, *The Ancient Explorers*). Jona Lendering adds, 'This is the only known first-hand report on those regions before those of the Portuguese, which were written two thousand years later', adding 'we visit a mysterious island, have to fight hostile natives, survive an erupting volcano, and encounter gorillas'. (htttps://www.livius.org/articles/person/hanno-1-the-navigator/)

Lendering tells us that Hanno's orders were to:

'Found several colonies on the Moroccan coast; having done so, he established a trading post on a small island off the Mauritanian coast. After completing the original mission, he ventured further south, making a reconnaissance expedition along the African coast until he reached modern Gabon, where he was forced to return because he was running out of supplies. There is some reason to doubt the truth of the latter statement, because the Roman encyclopaedist Pliny the Elder says that Hanno circumnavigated Africa and reached the borders of Arabia.'

Necho II

Between 610 and 594 BCE, pharaoh Necho supposedly commissioned an expedition made up of Phoenicians, who, it is said, in three years sailed from the Red Sea around Africa back to the mouth of the Nile; and, in so doing achieved the first completion of the Cape Route. Herodotus' account may be credible because he stated with some disbelief that the Phoenicians, 'as they sailed on a westerly course round the southern end of Libya (Africa), they had the sun on their right' (4.42).

Besides Hanno and Necho II there were other explorers: one being a Persian prince, navigator and cavalry commander called Sataspes (ca 470 BCE).

Sataspes

Sataspes is, in Herodotus (4, 43), famous for *not* sailing around Libya, even though that was what he was ordered to do by his mother and Xerxes. We can let Herodotus relate the story:

'Sataspes was frightened by the length and loneliness of the voyage and so returned home without completing the task set by his mother. He had raped the virgin daughter of Zopyrus son of Megabyzus and was to be impaled by King Xerxes until Sataspes' mother, who was Darius' sister, interceded on his behalf, saying that she would impose a weightier punishment on him than Xerxes: namely, she would force him to sail around Libya, until he completed his voyage and came to the Arabian Gulf. Xerxes agreed, so Sataspes went to Egypt where he picked up a ship and a crew from the Egyptians, and sailed past the Pillars of Heracles ... he sailed south; but after many months at sea, always with more ahead of him than behind he turned and sailed back to Egypt. When he reached Xerxes he told him that when he was farthest away he sailed by a country of little men, who wore palm-leaf clothing; these, whenever he and his men put in to land with their ship, fled their towns into the hills; Sataspes and his men did no harm, and took nothing from the people except a few cattle. As to why he did not complete the voyage around Libya, he said his ship was becalmed [due to the horse latitudes]. But Xerxes did not believe him, and given that his task was incomplete, he impaled him, punishing him on the charge originally brought against him.'

Sataspes is credited with coining the term, 'the horse latitudes'. The horse latitudes lie about 30 degrees north and south of the Equator, characterised by sunny skies, calm winds, and not much rain – a high-pressure area where trade winds and the westerlies meet.

Polybius

In 146 BCE Polybius made the first Roman voyage along the north and west coasts of Libya west of Cape Bon, also known as Ras at-Taib, Sharīk Peninsula, or Watan el Kibli – a peninsula in far north-eastern Tunisia. Cape Bon is also the name of the northern most point on the peninsula, known in antiquity as the Cape of Mercury. We are reminded by Marijean Eichel (1976) that Pliny (*HN* 5, 9) tells us that under Scipio Aemilianus' command in Africa, 'Polybius the historian went round in a flotilla provided by the general in order to explore that continent'. Polybius confirms this in his *Histories* (34, 15, 7) when he tells us that his motive for the voyage was 'to increase the readers' knowledge of hitherto little known regions'.

Eudoxus of Cyzicus

The Greek explorer Eudoxus (fl. 130 BCE) was commissioned by Ptolemy VIII of Egypt to explore the Arabian Sea. Poseidonius and Strabo (*Geography* 2, 3) both report that he was the first Greek to sail the monsoon wind system of the Indian Ocean in 118 and 116 BCE. Arab sailors had been doing just that for some time already.

Poseidonius gives us more detail and reveals that a shipwrecked Indian sailor had been rescued from the Red Sea and taken to Ptolemy VIII in Alexandria, presumably to discuss trading opportunities. The Indian offered to guide Greek ships to India, so Ptolemy appointed Eudoxus of Cyzicus to lead this explorative operation with two voyages from Egypt to India, the first in 118 BCE. This was deemed a commercial success when Eudoxus came back laden with a cargo of incense and precious stones – so much so that a second voyage left Egypt in 116 BCE.

Strabo, whose *Geography* is the only extant source, was sceptical but it is now generally agreed that it has some credence. During the second century BCE Greek and Indian ships were meeting to trade at Arabian ports like Aden (Eudaemon), although attempts to sail beyond Aden were discouraged and involved 'a long and laborious coast-hugging journey'. The Greeks needed the expertise of Indian pilots in order to avoid the Arabian ports and establish direct commercial links with India. Result: Greek ships were soon using the monsoon winds on their voyages to India so that by 50 BCE there was a notable increase in the number of Greek and Roman ships sailing the Red Sea via the Indian Ocean.

George Hourani (1995, pp. 24–26) tells us more about the establishment of direct sailing routes from Egypt to India, ancient knowledge of the monsoon winds, and details about Eudoxus and Hippalus, another Greek navigator.

Hippalus

The author of the *Periplus of the Erythraean Sea* believed that it was Hippalus who discovered the direct route from the Red Sea to Tamilakam over the Indian Ocean, which he achieved by plotting the sea and the exact location of the trade ports along the Indian coast. Pliny the Elder claimed that Hippalus discovered not the route, but the monsoon wind also called *Hippalus* (the south-west monsoon wind). André Tchernia clarifies that Pliny's connecting of the wind with the navigator was based on a common pronunciation: in the Hellenistic period the name of the wind was *Hypalus* and only in Roman times did the spelling *Hippalus* come into use. Mariners were familiar with the wind in Hellenistic times and it had previously been used by the Himyarites (an ancient Semite people of the south-western part of the Arabian peninsula, who ruled much of southern Arabia before the sixth century CE) and Indian sailors to cross the Indian Ocean.

We should not underestimate the importance of Hippalus' discovery to trade in the region: before him Greek geographers believed that India's west coast extended from west to east. Hippalus was probably the first westerner to realize its north–south direction. Only with this insight would anyone crossing the Arabian Sea appreciate that it was a quicker route to southern India than hugging the coastline.

The use of Hippalus' direct route was a major factor in generating the prosperity of trade contacts between the Roman province of Aegyptus and India from the first century BCE onwards. From Red Sea ports like Berenike capacious ships crossed the Arabian Sea to the Malabar coast and the port of Muziris, the Tamil kingdoms of the Pandyas, Cholas and Cheras in present-day Kerala and Tamil Nadu. Hippalus is thought by some to have been the captain of Eudoxus' ships.

The Domestication of the Dromedary Camel

A camel, of course, is just as important in commercial transportation by land as ships are in sea transport. Like horses, the camel started life in North America and eventually arrived in Arabia and Asia via Beringia (the land and maritime area between the Lena River in Russia and the Mackenzie River in Canada). They were first domesticated around the third millennium BCE. Think of camels and you think of them as cavalry mounts or transports in the military, as tourist attractions or, most importantly for us, pack animals on long- and short-distance trade routes, plodding sedately laden with spices, precious minerals, silks, grain, incense and other such goods, usually westwards toward the receptive markets of the Mediterranean.

A camel train will rarely progress faster than human walking speed. For centuries camels' ability to withstand harsh conditions made them perfect for communications and particularly trade and transportation in the desert regions of North Africa and the Arabian Peninsula. Camel trains have also long been deployed in trans-Asian trade, including along parts of the Silk Road.

The abstract to Sophie Habinger's *Mobility and Origin of Camels in the Roman Empire* (2020) [https://www.sciencedirect.com/science/article/abs/pii/S1040618220302627#:~:text=In%20general%2C%20camels%20are%20multifunctional,military%20and%20civil%20trade%20context] confirms that:

> 'Although camels are not indigenous to Europe, they have been found at several sites from several Roman provinces dating from the beginning of the 1st century AD onwards. It must have been beneficial to bring them there. Based on finds of remains from juvenile individuals (e.g. from Tanais), it has been suggested that the Romans might have systematically bred camels within Europe ... In general, camels are multifunctional animals that can be used in many different ways. In the Roman Empire they were used as beasts of burden, both in a military and civil trade context. The camel

rider units of the Roman army, the so-called *dromedarii*, were mostly used for the logistics that accompanied warfare. Probably the first function one might think of is them being part of caravans, transporting trade goods. This was of greatest importance in North Africa, the Near East associated with the incense trade in Arabia, and along the trade routes to Central Asia and China, for example along the so-called Silk Road. The Bactrian camels found in the Greek cities on the northern shore of the Black Sea served this purpose. In addition to their adaption to arid environments, they were also superior to other means of transport available at that time for other reasons. Unlike carts, camels do not rely on roads and require a smaller work force. In addition, they are also a faster option when compared to oxcarts in arid conditions.'

Sarah Bond, in Caitlin Green's article in *Forbes Magazine*, 'Were There Camels in Roman Britain? New Evidence Suggests Camels Were Common Across The Empire', reminds us that camels were of particular importance in the trade for incense and that Pliny the Elder (*NH* 12.32) observed that frankincense passed through Sabota – Shabwa, capital city of the South Arabian kingdom of Ḥaḍhramaut – on camels through a single gate. Bactrians could carry 220–270 kg up to 25 miles a day, while Diodorus Siculus (2.54.6) goes as heavy as 400 kg. The camel guides sold camel hair and milk to traders as well as their caravan services. Hadhramaut is a region in South Arabia, comprising what is now eastern Yemen, parts of western Oman and southern Saudi Arabia.

Strabo remarked that it was king Ptolemy Philadelphus who had opened up a route to Berenike for traders and camels as an alternative to the Red Sea route due to its often dangerous and unpredictable weather and navigation. Berenike and Myos Hormos were the most important of the Red Sea ports, and merchants often used camels to travel to and from Coptos – making them a crucial transport link between the Nile region and the Red Sea.

Green adds that 'Camel teeth found at Greenwich Park, near … Londinium likely come from a temple complex that sat along a busy Roman road' and concludes:

'All told, the finds from Greenwich thus seem to fit into the general pattern of Roman-era finds of camel remains across Europe, and there consequently seems little reason not to interpret them in a similar manner, that is to say as evidence of the presence and use of Roman camels, probably primarily as pack animals/beasts of burden. Certainly, if the Romans were willing to transport elephants across the Channel, as they may well have done, then there seems little reason to think that they wouldn't have done the same with camels, particularly given that camels were apparently being fairly widely employed elsewhere in north-western Europe then.'

Camels only really came into their own in Egypt around 500 BCE, in lands further west it took until the Roman period. In 46 BCE Julius Caesar captured twenty-two camels from Juba, king of Numidia. Pliny tells how back in 70 BCE the Romans built a new road through the territory of the troublesome Garamantes, the *Iter Praeter Saxa*, possibly usable by camels and not horses Sitwell, p. 67 suggests, leading to Roman supremacy for a short while. Two Roman expeditions followed, with Garamantian assistance: Septimius travelled south for three months and Julius Maternus for four. He turned up in the land of Agisymba 'where the rhinoceri roam'.

West Africa

'The roads to the land of the Sudan and to all the countries of east and west were brought into use for trade and all kinds of goods ...'
Ibn al-Saghir, ca. 902–3 CE

Sonja Magnavita opens her article, '*Initial Encounters: Seeking Traces of Ancient Trade Connections between West Africa and the Wider World*' with an interesting suggestion and gives us an early example of industrial espionage and attempts to mitigate it:

> 'Phoenicians, Carthaginians and Romans are said to have had knowledge of diverse luxury articles of the inner African continent and purchased them over concealed trade routes. That these trade routes were kept strictly confidential is one of the explanations given by some authors as to why the written sources of Antiquity do not tell us of the luxuries obtained or the routes leading to them. Herodotus is the only historian who acknowledges trade enterprises undertaken by the seafaring Carthaginians, namely a 'silent trade' in gold at a still unknown place somewhere on the west or rather northwest coast of Africa.'

Add to this the inherent difficulty in precisely locating places mentioned by classical authors and we have a complex and seemingly intractable problem when it comes to trade to and from west Africa. Magnavita goes on to say that 'Before the first Arab textual sources appeared towards the end of the first millennium AD, virtually nothing tangible was reported on the regions beyond the southern fringes of the Sahara', and asks the question as to 'whether trans-

Saharan trade contacts prior to the Arab conquest of North Africa, yet not unambiguously traceable by written sources, are detectable archaeologically'. Magnavita continues:

> 'Excavations at these sites [Kissi in Burkina Faso] revealed that a number of valuable goods from various parts of Africa and the wider world were finding their way into the West African Sahel earlier and, more importantly, on a larger scale than previously thought. All in all, thousands of beads made of different materials, more than a thousand of them being of glass, as well as brass jewellery and cowries were found among other goods brought to the Sahel from far distant regions. While the cowries were identified as *Cypraea moneta* [the money cowrie], deriving most likely from the Indian Ocean, the origin of the glass used to manufacture most of the glass beads was chemically traced to the Middle East and some of the tested copper alloys to regions along the Mediterranean Sea, possibly including Carthage. Other objects of likely northern origin found at Kissi include the first known West African swords as well as curved daggers and wool textiles, most of these dated to pre-8th century AD contexts.'

Magnavita concludes from this that these findings indicate that initial encounters involving the exchange of valuable items between the West African Sahel and the wider world were not initiated by merchants who came into North Africa along with the Arab armies, as previously thought. On the contrary, they prove that a flow of luxury objects reached the Sahel from beyond the Sahara throughout the first millennium CE, thus encompassing not only the early Islamic period but also Late Roman and Byzantine times.

There are intriguing glimpses of possible Roman trade in the region. The Janus bronze statuette found at Zangon Dan Makéri in southern Niger south of the Sahara 'potentially may have derived from pre-Arab cross-desert contacts. Stylistically dated to second century AD Roman North Africa the circumstances of its discovery remain obscure'. But 'without any knowledge of the archaeological context it derives from, it is not possible to conclude on whether it was really brought to the Sahel in Roman times'. Indeed, Magnavita asserts 'the same is true for the sporadic Roman coin finds made here and there in the Sahara and in sub-Saharan Africa ... To date, no Roman coin has ever been excavated at a West African sub-Saharan archaeological site'.

We are on safer ground with trade from Roman North Africa into the lands of the Garamantes, a tribe famous in classical times for their tattoos and ritual self-scarring. Tacitus, hinting at their piratical nature, informs us that they assisted the rebel Tacfarinas and raided Roman coastal settlements. According to Pliny the Elder, in response to continuous Garamantian raids, Lucius Cornelius Balbus and other Romans captured fifteen of their settlements in 19 BCE.

Tacfarinas

Tacfarinas (d. 24 CE) was a Numidian Berber from Thagaste in the province of Proconsular Africa (modern Souk Ahras, in Algeria); he had deserted from Rome's auxiliary Numidian cavalry and led his own Musulamii tribe along with an ever-changing coalition of other Berber tribes in a war against the Romans in North Africa during Tiberius' reign (14–37 CE).

> 'Tacfarinas assembled a band of robbers, ready for plunder and rape. Later, however, he knocked them into shape like soldiers in regular battalions with standards. He was, therefore, no longer the chief of some undisciplined rabble, but was commander of the tribe of the Musulamii.'
>
> Tacitus, Annals 2, 52, 1

The Roman land-grabbing that took place under Augustus of the traditional grazing grounds of the Musulamii, who had reverted to a pastoral lifestyle in the high plateaus of the Aures Mountains, lay behind the hostilities. In fact, Polybius wrote that he had never seen more sheep, goats, cows, and horses than in Africa. Tacfarinas' persistent guerrilla raids caused severe disruption of the province's grain production and exports to Rome – never a good thing for the aggressor when it threatened civil disorder in the capital itself. Tacfarinas knew full well that much of the Numidian grain was consumed by Legio III Augusta. Stationed at Ammaedara (Haidra), the legion needed nearly 2,000 tons every year and yet more was shipped to Rome. The Roman presence had been felt in northwest Africa for generations of Tacfarinas' family: the Romans had reinforced their permanent foothold in 146 BCE, when they levelled Carthage and extended Roman hegemony over the Berber kingdom of Numidia next door. Roman Africa joined Sicily as one of the empire's premier wheat baskets.

It took the Romans some considerable time to wipe out Tacfarinas due to the Numidians' agility and mobility, and the support they gained from the many desert tribes including the Moorish leader Mazippa; from the south of Numidia, nearest to the desert, came the Gaetulians, old allies of the Musulamii, and from the coast, near Gigthis, the Cinithii. However, the Roman governor of the neighbouring province of Africa, the proconsul Marcus Furius Camillus, and Legio III Augusta defeated the rebels in 17 CE. Next year, however, Tacfarinas hit back and annihilated a detachment of III Augusta under a new governor, Lucius Apronius, who blamed his legionaries for the humiliation and restored discipline with recourse to the outdated tradition of decimation, flogging every tenth man to death. Having done this, he went on to defeat his quarry near a town named Thala but was unable to bring an end to the war. The rebel army was now striking out and threatening the Roman towns along the coast. Tacfarinas was finally captured and killed in 24 CE.

One consequence of the war was that the entire Tunisian plateau became subject to Roman land taxation and a wholesale conversion to grain cultivation. The registration was conducted by Publius Cornelius Dolabella soon after Tacfarinas' death and completed in 30 CE; we know this from the stone markers laid down by the Roman surveyors, some of which can still be seen today. They extend as far as the Chott el Jerid on the province's southern border. The Musulamii and other tribes were probably permanently excluded from their former grazing areas.

We have seen how the Romans were contemptuous of so-called 'barbarians' – that is, anyone not Roman; nomadic people, whom they termed *incondite* (vulgar) or *vagi* (wanderers) were considered the 'lowest of the low' at *Annals* 3, 21. Hence, Tacitus' description of the Fenni (nomadic hunter-gatherers of north-east Europe) as 'incredibly primitive and shockingly destitute' and of the Sarmatians, steppe horsemen of south-east Europe, as 'looking repulsive' in *Germania* 46.

We cover Roman trade with the African territories on the west bank of the Red Sea in our discussion of the *Periplus of the Erythraean Sea* below. However, there is much more to African-Roman commerce than that: Roman trade extended south beyond Egypt into Nubia and lower Africa, with economic and political interaction between Romans and Africans in the southern regions.

We will see how important the Red Sea ports were to Roman trade with India and beyond: however, Egyptians and Romans also used the Red Sea as a trade route to access sub-Saharan Africa, benefitting from cheaper sea transport and enjoying friendly relations with trading stations like Ptolemais Theron in the Kingdom of Aksum, governed by King Zoskales (*Periplus* 5). The main port was Adulis, which Strabo records was 340 miles and five-days sailing south of Theron, which itself was 450 miles down the Barbaroi coast (*Periplus* 4). Rome's trading tendrils were extending further and further from the borders of her empire. Pliny calls the region Anzania, where, he reports, shiploads of turtles were fished by the *Ichthyophagoi* (fish eaters) and their shells freighted back to the Roman empire where most often they were cut into panels and polished up to adorn expensive furniture in expensive villas (*NH* 6,34). Pliny adds that native Africans brought 'much ivory, rhino horn, tortoiseshell and apes to Aulis'. Arab ships also called in there from Yemen. The Aksumites were in control of the lucrative trade in ivory, sending it to a port in Ethiopia called Koloe

Ptolemais Theron, or 'Ptolemais of the Hunts', was an ancient harbour built during the Ptolemaic period (305–30 BCE) as one of the main hunting stations for much sought after elephants. Ptolemais Theron was only one of a series of such elephant-hunting stations along the Red Sea coast of Africa, Adulis being perhaps another. Pliny the Elder and Diodorus Siculus also mention the hunting of elephants.[1]

The early Ptolemies had observed the value of war elephants in the military strength of the Seleucids. Unable to acquire Indian elephants, they tried to capture them from the neighbouring regions of Africa. Although these animals helped in the Battle of Raphia, they proved unstable in battle situations; the fact that the African species were intimidated by the Asian species did not help and led to the Egyptians eventually abandoning the use of the animals in war.

Pliny reveals that Ptolemais Theron is a place where shadows vanished under the noontime sun (meaning that the sun reached its zenith) forty-five days before and forty-five days after midsummer. Pliny claims that this gave Eratosthenes a clue as to how to calculate the circumference of the Earth.[2]

The Aksum Empire

> *'The Aksum Empire was the result of two world hubs sharing their collective learning about agriculture, and rose to become a great power in the ancient world because it formed a crucial link between East and West on the supercontinent of Afro-Eurasia.'*
>
> *David Baker*, Khan Academy[3]

David Baker tells us how in around 1000 BCE a major agrarian civilization arose in the Northern Horn of Africa, popularly known as D'mt. This mysterious kingdom flourished from the tenth- to the fifth-centuries BCE, formalizing and intensifying their trade relations with Egypt. They began organising the mass exportation of agricultural goods, along with intricate stone jewellery. When the kingdom of D'mt fell, smaller kingdoms populated the area which adopted iron and began exporting their metalwork. Arabia and Egypt began to influence Aksum's architecture, increasing the literacy of its people, and introducing the pre-Islamic polytheistic Arab religion.

For many years, Aksum was simply a small settlement in the Northern Horn, acquiring over time more land and wealth from trade. Then in 30 BCE everything changed with the Roman annexation of Egypt bringing Aksum into the Roman world's orbit. Trade routes shifted west from the Persian Gulf and overland Asian routes moved nearer the Red Sea with the result that Aksum soon became a hub of overseas trade between the Roman Empire and India with their own navy patrolling the Red Sea to protect their increasingly valuable trade.

So Aksum was now a mercantile power, operating trade between India and the Mediterranean in ivory, gold, emeralds, silk, spices, agricultural products, salt, exotic animals, manufactured goods, and a lot more.

Looking back at its height in the third century CE, some ancient writers considered Aksum to be one of the four great powers of the world, rubbing shoulders with Rome, Persia, and China.[4] It rose to become one of the most sophisticated agrarian civilizations of the ancient African world.

As we saw at the head of this chapter, the third-century CE Persian prophet, Mani, puts into context for us the commercial might of Aksum:[5]

'There are four great kingdoms on earth: the first is the Kingdom of Babylon and Persia; the second is the Kingdom of Rome; the third is the Kingdom of the Aksumites: the fourth is the kingdom of the Chinese.'

We have already noted that in the case of Rome, trade was just as important as the serial warfare they conducted; indeed, they were interdependent. The same can be said of Aksum. Ibrahim Anoba in his *Commerce and Trade in Ancient Africa* (2019) asserts that:

'It was their facility at trade and commerce that set them apart in ancient history. Those that were not farmers, laborers, or soldiers were merchants. Evidence from Tigray strongly supports the theory that the Aksumite civilization was defined by its complex market economy; commodities like labor, slaves, ivory, and incense, among many other goods, were either bartered or exchanged using legal tender. Commercial activities in Aksum have been linked to kingdoms and empires as far away as China, Persia, and Rome (and, later, Byzantium).'

Anoba reminds us that British archaeologist Sheila Boardman noted, in her chapter in '*The Exploitation of Plant Resources in Ancient Africa*', that the commercial activities in Aksum might have been responsible for the increase in crop variety and the growth of the market economy across the entire East Africa region. She argued that before the Mid- to Late-Aksumite period, the range of crops planted was limited to flax, barley, and teff. But under Aksumite rule, the production extended to some twelve other species, most of which were cash crops like oil and fibre plants, all of which points to a robust interest in both agriculture and market exchange.[6]

Aksum City expanded rapidly in a rather haphazard way due to the rapidity of its growth, building many grandiose monuments; the wealthiest citizens were buried in increasingly elaborate tombs marked by huge *stelae*, adorned with intricate carvings. Aksum had its bureaucrats, priests, soldiers, merchants, and artisans; it minted its own coinage with successive dynasties inscribed onto gold coins which have been unearthed by archaeologists from Rome to Persia to India – testament to the reach of Aksum's trade in the region.

Naval power brought the obvious advantage of protecting trade: it facilitated the transportation of troops, enabling Aksum to expand its borders, which is exactly what happened in the third century CE when the Aksum Empire controlled North Ethiopia, parts of Sudan and the southern Arabian Peninsula, most notably what is today Yemen. The empire's wealth enabled it to acquire weapons and ships-a-plenty and with no comparable power in East Africa to oppose them, the Aksum Empire's growth and expansion were largely unrestrained and so it became one of the foremost powers of the ancient world, and one of the first complex agrarian civilizations in Africa.

Aksum set up a state-controlled elephant ivory trade with the Roman Empire, exchanging valuable goods such as gold, silver, textiles and iron, while King Zoskales (ca. 100 CE) was a respected negotiator and was conversant in Greek. His realm included the ancient city of Adulis, the main emporium of Axum, in modern-day Eritrea. In exchange for gold and silver tableware from the Empire and Egyptian or Syrian fabric, Roman merchants purchased precious goods from the hinterland of ancient Africa: ivory, rhinoceros horn, hippopotamus hides, tortoise shell, emeralds or slaves. All of these were much in demand, probably more as a signal of wealth (and extravagance) as much as anything else (Apuleius, *Metamorphoses* 2, 76, 8).

Ivory, Ebony and Rhinoceros Horn

But it was ivory which enjoyed the biggest cachet in Rome. Furniture was inlaid with it at great expense (Juvenal 11, 120–124), while Clement of Alexandria deplored 'tripods fashioned of ivory, couches inlaid with ivory on silver feet' and questions that 'surely a simple loaf can be served on something other than an ivory footed table ... a simple box bed can deliver the same rest as an ivory couch' (*The Instructor* 2, 3). The *stylus*, combs, brooches, and hairpins all got the ebony and ivory treatment, while Martial (14, 83) adds back-scratchers to a list which also included abaci, dice, writing tablets, cash boxes and medicine chests. He tops it all when he introduces us to a woman who had her dentures made from white ivory (1, 72). Pliny reports that so frantic did the trade get that artisans resorted to splitting elephant bones and whitening them to masquerade as elephant tusk ivory (*NH* 8,4). We even hear of legionaries paying blacksmiths to fashion sword hilts and silver chains – an unintended consequence of which was surely making the show-off soldiers a more attractive target on the battlefield than they were already (*NH* 33,54). Josiah Osgood in his chapter (3, 78–79) in *The Oxford Handbook of Social Relations in the Roman World* tells us that girls from well-off families could play with ivory dolls – tragically they have been found as grave goods in burials of deceased children.

The Romans sold iron to the Aksumites, which exceeded local supplies both in quantity and quality. For instance, Roman iron was used for spears crafted for elephant hunts and, presumably, weaponry. In addition, the coastal area around Adulis was a source of rare and precious volcanic glass, known as obsidian, a material which fascinated the Romans who believed it to possess magical properties. Textiles too were on offer with Egyptian linen, coloured cloaks and scarves; Roman empire pots and pans made from brass and copper were popular as well.

A Roman labourer would have to put in two weeks of work before he could afford one pound of Somali myrrh. African cassia was by no means cheap either. Sailing east brought the Roman trader into frankincense country, mostly around Cape Elephas in Somalia which the Romans called the Spice Promontory – the outer tip of the Horn of Africa which was forty-days' sail from Egypt and nearly 1,500 miles from the southernmost point of the Roman empire.

In addition, Roman traders exchanged goods such as ivory and myrrh with local African traders in the face of competition from Arabic traders, and traded valuable items like cassia, silverware, precious stones, and slaves in ports such as Mosyllon, Opone, and Rhapta. As a measure of the economic importance of Aksum to Rome, a permanent Roman merchant colony was established on Diodorus Island, accessible to the mainland by a causeway, but because of the frequency of pirate raids the Romans relocated their operations to the nearby, easily defensible island of Oreine. The Roman settlement was defended all year-round and remained in operation for many centuries.

Beyond Adulis, Roman ships progressed further down the eastern coast of Africa beyond Bab-el-Mandeb, at which point the ships bound for India left the Red Sea and entered the Indian Ocean. The merchant vessels engaged in African trade continued their voyages down the coast, making use of local ports for shelter and business where, given the increasingly uncivilized settlements, Roman merchants were obliged to deal with natives organized in small, self-governing tribal communities.

Despite the occasional opposition from some locals, the Romans calculated that the risks were worth it given the abundant resources in the markets of what is today Somalia of myrrh and frankincense, always much in demand in Rome.

Indeed, the Romans referred to the Horn of Africa as the 'Spice Promontory' or 'Aromatic Lands'. So receptive were the markets to these special commodities that the Romans began organizing long-distance trading expeditions, conducted in larger and better-suited ships. However, all was not exactly plain sailing: the Romans were not the only interested party, since Arab traders also sailed to the Horn of Africa, competing with the Roman merchants for business.

Proceeding down the coast, the Romans first arrived at the small port town of Avalithes, which, importantly, controlled access to the Red Sea, but was ruled by one of the more fractious tribes. Here, the Romans swapped their tat – low-value goods such as shiny glass baubles, Egyptian olives, grain, and tin – for high end myrrh, ivory, and tortoise shells. Even more commercially important was Mosylon, located at the tip of the Horn of Africa. Mosylon handled most of the cinnamon coming from India and was the source of *cassia*, a special type of cinnamon.[7] Due to its high quality and scarcity at the time in Rome, the imported cinnamon was typically deposited in the Romans' Royal Treasury. This cinnamon hub of Africa also exported incense, used in religious rituals, gums, ivory, and tortoise shells.

Red Sea Ports

Augustus (r. 27 BCE–14 CE) was responsible for significantly growing the amount of Roman trade passing through Red Sea ports; it was increased dramatically when he brought Egypt under Roman control in 30 BCE. Strabo tells us that; 'in his day 120 vessels sailed regularly from Egypt to India, whereas previously very few made the journey'.[8]

There were now two major trade routes emerging under the Roman Empire spanning 3,000 miles or so. The southern route that went down the Red Sea and then along the eastern coast of Africa to Rhapta, close to present-day Dar es Salaam; the second also progressed down the Red Sea but then turned east across the Indian Ocean to ports in India. The journey down the coast of Africa from Egypt took about two years to complete, while the return trip to India was closer to one year.

Ships carrying goods bound for both Africa and India left the Red Sea ports between July and September. Vessels bound for African ports then headed to Cape Guardafui on the Horn of Africa and then south to Rhapta. They then proceeded to India, sailed to Aden and Qana' on the southern coast of Arabia, to take advantage of the monsoon winds to cross the open waters of the Indian Ocean to destination southwest India.

The *Periplus of the Erythraean Sea*[9]

The *Periplus of the Erythraean Sea* (Περίπλους τῆς Ἐρυθρᾶς Θαλάσσης) was written by an unknown Greek-speaking Egyptian; it is also known by its Latin name, *Periplus Maris Erythraei*; it is a Greco-Roman *periplus* written in a blend of classical and common (*koine*) Greek that describes shoreline navigation and trading opportunities from Roman-Egyptian ports such as Berenice Troglodytica on the Red Sea coast and others along the Horn of Africa, the Persian Gulf, Arabian Sea and the Indian Ocean, including the modern-day Sindh region of Pakistan and south-western regions of India. Generally speaking we can describe the genre as literally 'a sailing-around' ... a logbook recording sailing itineraries and commercial, political, and ethnological details about the ports visited. In the pre-map era it functioned as an atlas-cum-traveller's handbook. Among much else it gives us our earliest information about the inhabitants of the coast of East Africa, pre-dating by more than half a millennium any other comparable written references.

The *Periplus of the Erythraean Sea* has been called 'a social and geographical landmark of the first order ... one of the most fascinating books that have come down to us from antiquity'.[10] Today, it is generally agreed that it dates from between 40 and 50 CE, so significantly predating Pliny's *Natural History*, published between 73 and 77 CE.[11] Schoff says of it:

> 'The Periplus of the Erythraean Sea is one of those human documents, like the journals of Marco Polo and Columbus and Vespucci, which express not only individual enterprise, but the awakening of a whole race toward new fields of geographical discovery and commercial achievement. It is the first record of organized trading with the nations of the East, in vessels built and commanded by subjects of the Western World. It marks the turning of a tide of commerce which had set in one direction, without interruption, from the dawn of history.'

Schoff gives us a detailed description of the Arabian coast section of the voyage:

> 'Directly below this place is the adjoining country of Arabia, in its length bordering a great distance on the Erythraean Sea. Different tribes inhabit the country, differing in their speech, some partially, and some altogether. The land next the sea is similarly dotted here and there with caves of the Fish-Eaters, but the country inland is peopled by rascally men speaking two languages, who live in villages and nomadic camps, by whom those sailing off the middle course are plundered, and those surviving shipwrecks

are taken for slaves ... Navigation is dangerous along this whole coast of Arabia, which is without harbors, with bad anchorages, foul, inaccessible because of breakers and rocks, and terrible in every way. Therefore, we hold our course down the middle of the gulf and pass on as fast as possible by the country of Arabia until we come to the Burnt Island; directly below which there are regions of peaceful people, nomadic, pasturers of cattle, sheep and camels.'

Periplus of the Erythraean Sea, 20

The first port they called at in India was Barbaricum. The *Periplus* describes it:

'The ships lie at anchor at Barbaricum, but all their cargoes are carried up to the metropolis by the river, to the King. There are imported into this market a great deal of thin clothing, figured linens, topaz, coral, storax, frankincense, vessels of glass, silver and gold plate, and a little wine. On the other hand, there are exported costus, bdellium [resin of myrrh], lyceum [a Solanaceous herb], nard, turquoise, lapis lazuli, Seric skins, cotton cloth, silk yarn, and indigo. And sailors set out thither with the Indian Etesian winds, about the month of July, that is Epiphi: it is more dangerous then, but through these winds the voyage is more direct, and sooner completed.'

Periplus of the Erythraean Sea, 39

James Hancock tells how, once in India, the Romans would visit ports along the coast from Barbaricum, on the Indus River, Muziris (Cranganur) on the south-western Malabar Coast, and then Sri Lanka. The important trading partners were the Tamil dynasties of the Pandyas, Cholas, and Cheras in southern India. The first major spice trade centre in the world was Muziris, in Kerala on the south-western coast of India. He adds that it was probably established by 3,000 BCE, and remained one of India's most important trading ports through the Roman period.

Hancock continues:

'In the *Akananuru*, a collection of ancient Tamil poetry, it was described as 'the city where the beautiful vessels, the masterpieces of the Yavanas [westerners], stir white foam on the Periyar, river of Kerala, arriving with gold and departing with pepper'. Black pepper was the major export of this great emporium, constituting three-quarters of the bulk of the west-born cargo, but other Indian trade items included locally gathered ivory and pearls, and semi-precious stones and silks from the Gangetic Valley and East Himalayan regions.'[12]

Africa – Sub-Sahara and West Africa, Egypt, Nubia, Lake Chad

The *Periplus* comprises 66 sections, each of which is the length of a short paragraph. The shortest is:

> 'From Malao (Berbera) it is two courses to the mart of Moundou, where ships anchor more safely by an island lying very close to the land. The imports to this are as aforesaid [Chapter 8 mentions iron, gold, silver, drinking cups, etc.], and from it likewise are exported the same goods [Chapter 8 mentions myrrh, douaka, makeir, and slaves], and fragrant gum called *mokrotou* (cf. Sanskrit *makaranda*). The inhabitants who trade here are more stubborn.'[13]

Numerous trade goods are mentioned in the *Periplus*, but some are unique in the ancient literature, leading to some creative guesswork as to what they might be.

Obviously, each stop on the journey presented a trading opportunity with different local commodities offered for trade – sometimes for gold coins and other times for barter, including goods like cloth, silver and gold statues, cereals, wine, and olive oil. Hancock tells us that frankincense and myrrh from South Arabia were extremely popular in India, along with gold and silver, for which the Indians traded their locally produced pepper, cotton, and pearls, along with silks they had obtained from Chinese traders:

> 'On the trip down the African coast, Egyptian linen, glass, wine, and metal products would be traded for African ivory, tortoiseshell, myrrh, and frankincense, along with cinnamon, Indian cloth, sashes, and fine muslins obtained from their trade with Indian merchants.'

The journey home was potentially just as lucrative, their ships replete with all manner of goods. They would head back to the Egyptian entrepôts of Myos Hormos and Berenike from where their goods were sent overland on camel caravans, and then shipped to Alexandria, the commercial hub of Egypt, where the magnificent range of goods, much of them much coveted luxury items, were sold: Arabian frankincense, Sri Lankan and Chinese cinnamon, Indian pepper, pearls and precious stones, Chinese silks and porcelain, African myrrh, ivory, rhinoceros horn, and tortoiseshell.

Here are some of the entries, translations by Schoff unless otherwise indicated:

- *Muza looks promising:*
  'The market-town of Muza is without a harbor, but has a good roadstead and anchorage because of the sandy bottom thereabouts, where the anchors hold safely. The merchandise imported there consists of purple

cloths, both fine and coarse; clothing in the Arabian style, with sleeves; plain, ordinary, embroidered, or interwoven with gold; saffron, sweet rush, muslins, cloaks, blankets (not many), some plain and others made in the local fashion; sashes of different colors, fragrant ointments in moderate quantity, wine and wheat, not much. For the country produces grain in moderate amount, and a great deal of wine. And to the King and the Chief are given horses and sumpter-mules, vessels of gold and polished silver, finely woven clothing and copper vessels. There are exported from the same place the things produced in the country: selected myrrh, and the Gebanite-Minaean *stacte*, alabaster and all the things already mentioned from Avalites and the far-side coast. The voyage to this place is made best about the month of September, that is Thoth; but there is nothing to prevent it even earlier.'

Trans. Lance Jenott'

- *The Frankincense kingdom*

'After Eudaemon Arabia there is a continuous length of coast, and a bay extending two thousand stadia or more, along which there are Nomads and Fish-Eaters living in villages; just beyond the cape projecting from this bay there is another market-town by the shore, Cana, of the Kingdom of Eleazus, the Frankincense Country; and facing it there are two desert islands, one called Island of Birds, the other Dome Island, one hundred and twenty stadia from Cana. Inland from this place lies the metropolis Sabbatha, in which the King lives. All the frankincense produced in the country is brought by camels to that place to be stored, and to Cana on rafts held up by inflated skins after the manner of the country, and in boats. And this place has a trade also with the far-side ports, with Barygaza and Scythia and Ommana and the neighbouring coast of Persia.'

Periplus of the Erythraean Sea, §27

- *Somalia*

[Ras Hafun in northern Somalia is believed to be the location of the ancient trade centre of Opone. Ancient Egyptian, Roman and Persian Gulf pottery has been recovered from the site by an archaeological team from the University of Michigan.]

'There is another market-town called Opone ... and in it the greatest quantity of cinnamon is produced, (the arebo and moto), and slaves of the better sort, which are brought to Egypt in increasing numbers; and a great quantity of tortoiseshell, better than that found elsewhere.'

Periplus of the Erythraean Sea, §13

In ancient times, Opone operated as a port of call for merchants from Phoenicia, Egypt, Greece, Persia, Yemen, Nabataea, Azania, the Roman Empire and elsewhere, as it enjoyed a strategic location along the coastal route from Azania to the Red Sea. Merchants from as far afield as Indonesia and Malaysia called on Opone, trading spices, silks and other goods, before heading south for Azania or north to Yemen or Egypt on the trade routes that spanned the length of the Indian Ocean's rim. As early as 50 CE Opone was famous as a centre for the cinnamon trade, along with the trading of cloves and other spices, ivory, exotic animal skins and incense.

The ancient port city of Malao, situated in present-day Berbera in north central Somaliland, is also mentioned in the *Periplus*:

'There is another market-town, better than this, called Malao ... There are imported into this place ... many tunics, cloaks from Arsinoe, dressed and dyed; drinking-cups, sheets of soft copper in small quantity, iron, and gold and silver coin, not much. There are exported from these places myrrh, a little frankincense, (that known as far-side), the harder cinnamon, duaca, Indian copal and macir, which are imported into Arabia; and slaves, but rarely.'

Periplus of the Erythraean Sea, §8

Under the Western Satraps, Barigaza was one of the principal centres of Roman trade in the Indian subcontinent. The *Periplus* describes the many goods bought and sold:

'There are imported into this market-town (Barigaza), wine, Italian preferred, also Laodicean and Arabian; copper, tin, and lead; coral and topaz; thin clothing and inferior sorts of all kinds; bright-colored girdles a cubit wide; storax, sweet clover, flint glass, realgar, antimony, gold and silver coin, on which there is a profit when exchanged for the money of the country; and ointment, but not very costly and not much. And for the King there are brought into those places very costly vessels of silver, singing boys, beautiful maidens for the harem, fine wines, thin clothing of the finest weaves, and the choicest ointments. There are exported from these places spikenard, costus [Saussurea costus], bdellium, ivory, agate and carnelian, lycium, cotton cloth of all kinds, silk cloth, mallow cloth, yarn, long pepper and such other things as are brought here from the various market-towns.'

Periplus of the Erythraean Sea, §49

Damirica or Limyrike is Tamilagam (Tamil தமிழகம்) – the 'Tamil country' which served as a hub for trade in the Gangetic plain:

> 'Besides this there are exported great quantities of fine pearls, ivory, silk cloth, spikenard from the Ganges, malabathrum from the places in the interior, transparent stones of all kinds, diamonds and sapphires, and tortoise-shell; that from Chryse Island, and that taken among the islands along the coast of Damirica.'
>
> *The Periplus of the Erythraean Sea, §56*

As noted above, other gazetteers of places, place names and Roman roads can be found in the *Ravenna Cosmography*, the *Peutinger Table* and the *Antonine Itinerary*.[14]

Other trade-related *peripli* in and around Africa and the Atlantic Europe seaboards include:

- *The Periplus of Himilco the Navigator*, parts of which can be found in Pliny the Elder and Avienius.
- *The Periplus of Hanno the Navigator*, a Carthaginian explorer who explored the coast of Africa from present-day Morocco southward at least as far as Senegal in the sixth or fifth century BCE.[15]
- The *Periplus* of the Greek Scylax of Caryanda, in Caria, who allegedly sailed down the Indus River and then to Suez on the initiative of Darius I. This voyage is mentioned by Herodotus, and his *periplus* is quoted by Hecataeus of Miletus, Aristotle, Strabo and Avienius.
- The *Massaliote Periplus*, a description of trade routes along the coasts of Atlantic Europe, by anonymous Greek navigators of Massalia (now Marseille, France), which possibly dates to the sixth century BCE, also preserved in Avienius.
- Pytheas of Massalia (fourth century BCE), *On the Ocean* (Περί του Ωκεανού), has not survived; only excerpts remain, quoted or paraphrased by later authors, including Strabo, Diodorus Siculus, Pliny the Elder and in Avienius' *Ora maritima*.
- *The Periplus of Nearchus* surveyed the area between the Indus and the Persian Gulf under orders from Alexander the Great. He was a source for Strabo and Arrian, among others.
- *On the Red Sea* by Agatharchides. Fragments preserved in Diodorus Siculus and Photius.
- *The Periplus of Scymnus of Chios* dated to around 110 BCE.

* * *

Africa – Sub-Sahara and West Africa, Egypt, Nubia, Lake Chad 133

Goods from the Far East generally arrived in Rome through two principal trade routes: the Red Sea and the Persian Gulf. This binary traffic brought a constant stream of exotic goods flowing into the Roman Empire.

The Red Sea Route

The Red Sea corridor option was by no means simple: it required a sea voyage of 2,800 miles from India to the Red Sea port cities, followed by an arduous caravan trek of 236 miles across the Egyptian Desert, and then another 472 miles by ship to Coptos on the Nile and Alexandria, thence to the Mediterranean and the Italian ports of Ostia and Puteoli, giving a total distance of 3,500 miles. On the other hand, the Persian Gulf corridor meant a trip by ship of 1,460 miles from India to the confluence of the Tigris and Euphrates and then by caravan across the Syrian desert for 870 miles, resulting in a total of 2,330 miles. To get to India, Chinese silk had already spent another 3,100 miles on the road across the steppes, the craggy mountainous and desert terrain of central China to the Indian ports.

All this allowed comfortable …

> 'Romans to adorn themselves with cosmetics and perfumes made with cinnamon from Sri Lanka, myrrh from Somalia, and frankincense from Yemen, and to wear clothing of translucent silk from China. The streets were filled with fragrant smoke from frankincense and myrrh wafting from burners at the base of statues of the Roman emperor, and the Roman cuisine was spiced with pepper and ginger from India.'
>
> Hancock, J. (2 June 2021) https://member.worldhistory.org/article/1761/the-eastern-trade-network-of-ancient-rome/

We get a vivid picture of the potential sensuousness of the foods and scents on offer at a banquet described in the second-century CE Roman novel *The Metamorphoses* by Apuleius:

> 'And now, with responsive desire melding with mine into mutual passion, the odour of cinnamon came exhaling from her open mouth, she tongued me ravishingly with her honeyed tongue.'

During another seduction, a temptress admits, 'The lovely face of your brother, my husband, still lingers in my eyes, the cinnamon odour of his ambrosial body still haunts my nostrils.'[16]

Eastern fragrances also had a public health role when huge braziers of incense were burned at the Colosseum to eliminate the stench of the blood and gore left frying in the unrelenting sun. Funerals too were sweet smelling with the deceased honoured with the burning of copious quantities of incense. Pliny the Elder reported that at the funeral of Nero's (r. 54–68 CE) consort Poppaea, a full year's supply of Rome's incense was consumed; so much so that apparently the economy of the Roman Empire was compromised.

Pepper and Ginger

To give some idea of the popularity of pepper we need only observe that Apicius, the famous gastronome, includes pepper in 349 of his 469 recipes. This is how Pliny the Elder described the allure and value of pepper:

> 'Why do we like it so much? Some foods attract by sweetness, some because they look good, but neither the pepper pod nor its berry has anything going for it. We only want it for its sharpness – and we will go all the way to India to get it. Who was the first to try it with food? Who was so anxious to develop an appetite that hunger would not do the trick? Pepper and ginger both grow wild in their native countries, and yet we value them as we do gold and silver.'[17]
>
> 'Ginger, in fact, grows in Arabia and in Troglodytica, in various cultivated spots, being a small plant with a white root ... the price at which it sells is six denarii per pound. Long pepper is very easily adulterated with Alexandrian mustard; its price is fifteen denarii per pound, while that of white pepper is seven, and of black, four.'[18]

Silk

Silk was so popular that it attracted sumptuary legislation in Rome, usually ineffective, to restrict or prohibit the wearing of silk on both economic and moral grounds. Men, not surprisingly, were amongst the loudest critics although they were no strangers to dressing in silk themselves: Juvenal, writing around 110 CE, was appalled 'by luxury loving women who find the thinnest of thin robes too hot for them; whose delicate flesh is irritated by the finest silk tissue'. Seneca the Younger (3 BCE–65 CE) moaned:

> 'I can see clothes of silk, if materials that do not hide the body, nor even one's decency, can be called clothes ... Wretched flocks of servants work hard so that the adulteress can be seen through her translucent dress, so

that her husband has no better an idea than any stranger or foreigner about his wife's body.'[19]

Coptos

What would we find in the markets at Coptos? Sacks of gold and silver coins, fabricated tin, copper, iron, locally produced barley, wheat and sesame oil, Alexandrian glass vessels, grape juice, and wine from Italy and Syria, and purple cloth from Phoenicia. Coptos buzzed with trading and transport, attracting merchants and financiers from Rome, Egypt, Arabia, and India.

Hancock gives us some detail:

'The merchandise arriving at Coptos was carried overland by camel caravans to the Red Sea ports of Berenike and Myos Hormos. It took about seven days for the caravans to make their way to Myos Hormos (110 miles) and twelve days to more southerly Berenike (230 miles). Myos Hormos was closer to Coptos than Berenike, but the strong northerly winds of the upper Red Sea made voyages to southern African ports slower and more difficult from there. Berenike was sheltered from the high northern winds by the Ras Banas peninsula and ultimately became the premier trade emporium on the Red Sea. It remained a major trade center for almost 800 years, linking the Mediterranean basin, Near East, and Egypt with the African coast, India, China, and Southeast Asia.'

https://www.worldhistory.org/article/1761/the-eastern-trade-network-of-ancient-rome/

As noted, Muziris in Kerala was the first significant spice trade centre in the world. It is thought to have been established by 3000 BCE, and remained one of India's most important trading ports through the Roman period. Black pepper was the major export but there was more: for example local ivory and pearls, and semi-precious stones and silks from the Gangetic Valley and East Himalayas. The *Periplus* tells of Tamil merchants exporting from Muziris 'all kinds of transparent gems, diamonds [from the Ganges] and sapphires from Sri Lanka' – again paid for with silver and gold bullion. The high local prices can be accounted for partly by the fact that the Tamils believed that different jewels came with different levels of good fortune and good health for the wearer, no doubt inculcating a policy of aiming high to achieve the best outcomes in life'.

The traders would ply back to the Egyptian ports of Myos Hormos and Berenike. There, as noted, consignments were despatched overland on camel caravans to the commercial hub of Roman Egypt, that was Alexandria.

William Dalrymple argues in his *The Golden Road* that the Red Sea Route was 'much bigger and historically more significant than the overland route from China'.[20] Indeed, Pliny the Elder complains about 'the significant outflow of gold from the Roman world to India due to extensive Indian exports. Roman demand for Indian goods such as silk, gemstones, spices, and ivory led to a trade balance heavily favouring India. This is evident from the discovery of more Roman coins in India than in any country except Italy.'

Dalrymple continues:

'Sir Mortimer Wheeler was digging south of modern Pondicherry at Arikamedu in the 1930s and 40s, and established the existence of Indo-Roman trade in the 1st century CE. However, he incorrectly interpreted his finds solely in terms of Roman merchants trading to India: he failed to give Indian merchants and shipowners any agency in this trade, which they undoubtedly had.'

The sheer scale of the trade has until now been grossly underestimated. According to latest research, custom taxes on the Red Sea trade with India, Persia, and Ethiopia may have generated as much as one-third of the income of the Roman exchequer. This is evidenced by the Muziris Papyrus as noted above – a shipping invoice taken out by an Alexandria-based Egypto-Roman financier for the purchase of goods from an Indian merchant based in far-away Muziris on the coast of Kerala. The Muziris Papyrus, purchased in 1980 for the Austrian National Library, and first published in 1985, is a remarkable historical document, including details of container contents, insurance, and legal provisions.[21] Dalrymple continues 'The Papyrus gives precise details of one particular cargo sent to the Egyptian port of Berenike from Muziris aboard the ship *Hermapollon*. The total value of the goods – calculated as worth 131 talents, 'enough to purchase 2,400 acres of the best farmland in Egypt or a premium estate in central Italy – is jaw-dropping'. Further archaeological evidence comes in the shape of Arikamedu outside Pondicherry and Berenike in Egypt, which have provided compelling evidence of ancient trade connections between India and the Mediterranean.

The Persian Gulf Corridor

Exotic luxuries from Southeast Asia also arrived at Rome through the Persian Gulf, with silk and pepper shipped first by Indian and then by Persian crews to the central Persian Gulf ports, where they were then on-shipped by caravans north towards Syrian Antioch. Some silk and other goods reached central Syria via the Silk Road, but by the first century CE, Chinese silk was being moved to ports of the Indian subcontinent for the last leg of transportation to the Mediterranean via sea routes.

The city of Palmyra controlled most of the caravan trade through Syria to Rome. Popularly known as the 'Bride of the Desert', it was in an oasis halfway between the Mediterranean Sea and the Euphrates River. We learn from inscriptional and archaeological evidence from the early-second century CE of some of the goods passing through here: salt, dried foods, purple cloth, perfumes, prostitutes, silk, jade, muslin, spices, ebony, incense, ivory, precious stones, and glass.

Palmyra's commercial success owes much to the delicate diplomatic line it trod between those with vested trade interests in the region: bellicose Rome and the belligerent Persian Empire, Parthia, the Kingdom of Kush, and the nomadic desert tribes of the desert. The Palmyrene traders were thus able to tap into the caravan trade routes linking the eastern Mediterranean cities with the ports of the Persian Gulf and western coast of India.

Hancock explains how the Palmyrenes shrewdly eschewed the use of middlemen, electing instead to establish colonies at critical points along their extensive trade routes. There were enclaves of Palmyrene traders scattered across the far-flung corners of the ancient world from Babylon in Mesopotamia, Coptos in Egypt, and Merv on the Parthian border. Palmyrenes even sailed with their merchandise on the Red Sea.

Palmyra became part of the Roman province of Syria under Tiberius (r. 14–37 CE) in about 14 CE, while Hadrian (r. 117–138 CE) declared it a free city in 129 CE. During the reign of Septimius Severus (r. 193–211 CE) the city was elevated to a Roman *colonia*, the highest civic status that could be accorded a city of the empire, so its inhabitants now enjoyed full Roman citizenship.

The Red Sea route from Southeast Asia was clearly much longer than the Persian Gulf corridor, but it became the route of choice for the Romans. Why? The Red Sea – Nile route was about a third longer than the Persian Gulf – Syrian Desert alternative, but it involved a much shorter overland caravan journey and therefore was cheaper and less susceptible to attack and plunder. Second, the Romans had almost full control of the Red Sea corridor to India in the second and third centuries CE, while they controlled the head of the Persian Gulf only intermittently. This meant that the goods shipped by the Romans through the Persian Gulf corridor were subject to the tariffs charged by Palmyran and Parthian middlemen.

But the Romans kept trading through both routes to safeguard themselves against shortages caused by unpredictable weather and equally unpredictable political vagaries. Hancock explains how:

'The Romans essentially had two seasons of delivery, a spring one in Antioch and a late-summer one in Alexandria. Goods headed to the Red Sea corridor would have left India between December and January, arrived at the Red Sea in February, and got to Alexandria in August. Goods travelling through the Persian Gulf corridor would have left India for the Gulf in November, arrived there between January and February, and made their way to Antioch between April and May.'

The operation of a trade network using more than one route ensured that the Roman markets would receive Indian Ocean imports at different times of the year and from multiple sources, and all the commercial benefits that brought.

The Canal of the Pharaohs

The modern 120 mile Suez Canal (officially opened on 17 November 1869) is not the first time the Mediterranean Sea was linked to the Red Sea for reasons of trade and travel. A smaller canal was constructed under pharaoh Senusret II (r. 1897 to 1878 BCE) or, much later, Ramesses II (r. 1279–1213 BCE). Another canal, probably building on the first, was constructed in the reign of Necho II (610–595 BCE), but according to Darius the Great's *Suez Inscriptions* and Herodotus (2, 158), the only fully functional canal was engineered and completed by Darius I (522–486 BCE):

'Psammetichus left a son called Necos, who succeeded him upon the throne. This prince was the first to attempt the construction of the canal to the Red Sea – a work completed afterwards by Darius the Persian – the length of which is four days' journey, and the width is such as to admit of two triremes being rowed along it abreast. The water is derived from the Nile, which the canal leaves a little above the city of Bubastis, near Patumus, the Arabian town, being continued thence until it joins the Red Sea.'

Darius I of Persia ruled over Egypt after it had been conquered by his predecessor Cambyses II.

Aristotle (384–322 BCE) tells us in his *Meteorology* (I 14 P 352b), that:

'One of their kings [Egypt's pharaohs] tried to make a canal to it (for it would have been of no little advantage to them for the whole region to have become navigable; Sesostris is said to have been the first of the ancient kings to try), but he found that the sea was higher than the land. So he first, and Darius afterwards, stopped making the canal, lest the [salty] sea should mix with the river water and foul it.'

Strabo (17, 1, 25) mentions Sesostris' attempt to build a canal, and Pliny the Elder (24–79 CE) wrote that it was Ptolemy II Philadelphus who finally succeeded when he solved the problem of different water heights by using a system of locks which his engineers invented in 274 BCE:

> 'Next comes the Tyro tribe and the harbour of the Daneoi, from which Sesostris, king of Egypt, intended to carry a ship-canal to where the Nile flows into what is known as the Delta; this is a distance of over 60 miles. Later the Persian king Darius had the same idea, and yet again Ptolemy II, who made a trench 100 feet (30 m) wide, 30 feet (9 m) deep and about 35 miles long, as far as the Bitter Lakes.'

William Petrie explains how Darius the Great's *Suez Inscriptions* comprise five Egyptian monuments, including the Chalouf Stele,[22] that commemorate the construction and completion of the canal linking the Nile River with the Red Sea by Darius I:

> 'King Darius says: I am a Persian; setting out from Persia I conquered Egypt. I ordered to dig this canal from the river that is called Nile and flows in Egypt, to the sea that begins in Persia. Therefore, when this canal had been dug as I had ordered, ships went from Egypt through this canal to Persia, as I had intended.'
>
> *Darius Inscription*

The monuments were located along the Darius Canal through the valley of Wadi Tumilat and, as Carol Redmount says, probably recorded sections of the canal as well.[23] The canal left the Nile at Bubastis. The inscription on a pillar at Pithom records that in 270 BCE the canal was again reopened by Ptolemy II Philadelphus. In Arsinoe, Ptolemy constructed a navigable lock, with sluices, at the Heroopolite Gulf of the Red Sea, which allowed the passage of vessels but prevented salt water from the Red Sea from mingling with the fresh water in the canal.

Morris Silver tells us that remains of an ancient west–east canal through the ancient Egyptian cities of Bubastis, Pi-Ramesses, and Pithom were discovered by Napoleon Bonaparte and his engineers and cartographers in 1799.[24] Their findings, recorded in the *Description de l'Égypte*, include detailed maps that depict the discovery of an ancient canal extending northward from the Red Sea and then westward toward the Nile.²⁵ In 1855 French cartographers discovered the remnants of the north–south section of Darius' Canal past the east side of Lake Timsah and ending near the north end of the Great Bitter Lake.²⁶

Redmount says Islamic texts tell us the canal had been silted up by the seventh century, but was reopened in 641 CE by 'Amr ibn al-'As, the Muslim conqueror of Egypt. The canal functioned until closed in 767 in order to stop provisions and trade reaching Mecca and Medina, which were in rebellion.²⁷

Egypt

Egypt changed everything when it was annexed by Rome in 30 BCE after Octavian's success at the Battle of Actium. First, it eliminated a powerful enemy in Antony and Cleopatra VII, and second, it opened up the vital Red Sea shipping lane which itself gave access to the Indian Ocean and to India itself. It was less than ten years before over 100 Roman ships were plying back and forth from India, and this goes a long way to explain how our curious Roman jostling in the markets of Rome saw before his eyes such a plethora of strange, exotic and exciting goods, such a diversity of commodities: silks, incense, spices, slaves, sapphires and other precious jewels. Wild animals never encountered before by a Roman could be marvelled at the games, tearing each other apart and mauling to death gladiators, prisoners of war and Christians.

Cosmas Indicopleustes, a merchant of Alexandria and cosmologist, certainly brings the unicorn to exciting life. He lived in the sixth century and travelled to India, and gave us a description of a unicorn based on four brass figures he saw in the palace of the king of Ethiopia:

> 'It is impossible to take this ferocious beast alive; and ... all its strength lies in its horn. When it finds itself pursued and in danger of capture, it throws itself from a precipice, and turns so adeptly in falling, that it takes all the shock on the horn, and so escapes safe and sound.' (*Cosmas Indicopleustes*, 11.7)

Climate and physical geography obviously played a part in drumming up eastern trade: countries with climates similar to Italy and the wider Mediterranean could usually be relied on to produce similar goods, thus restricting demand and the opportunities for imported trade; Pliny cites olive oil, roses, myrtle and wine as examples (*NH* 13,2). The further east the Romans traded the more unusual, exotic goods they discovered and coveted for the home market. Pliny again gives us a special, if bewildering, example in a popular, modish perfume:

'We will now move on to what is the very height of refinement in these articles of luxury, indeed, I may say, the pinnacle of them all ... the 'regal' unguent ... it consists of myrobalanus, costus, amomum, cinnamon, comacum, cardamum, spikenard, marum, myrrh, cassia, storax, ladanum opobalsamum, Syrian calamus and Syrian sweet-rush, oenanthe, malobathrum, serichatum, cyprus, aspralathus, panax, saffron, cypirus, sweet marjoram, lotus, honey, and wine. Not one of the ingredients in this compound is produced either in Italy, that conqueror of the world, or, indeed, in all Europe, with the exception of the iris, which grows in Illyricum, and the nard, which is to be found in Gaul.'

Economically, it was a dream come true for Augustus (as Octavian later became known) – tax revenues of unimaginable and ever growing size garnered by the quarter rate tax on this trade – the *tetarte* – began to roll in. The *tetarte* was the 25 per cent tax levied on Indian Ocean imports before the Severan period. By 100 CE, according to Raoul McLaughlin (2010), the taxes were bringing in sufficient revenue to finance one third of the cost of running the entire empire, arguing that some one billion sestertii worth of goods at retail were imported each year, generating 250 million sestertii in tax revenues.[28] The GDP of the Roman Empire has been estimated at between 9–20 billion sestertii per annum, giving between 11 per cent and 5 per cent of GDP derived from the Indian Ocean. Cobb shows how this worked:

'Strabo specifically mentions that double duties (τέλη διπλάσια) were charged on imports, which F. De Romanis has suggested refers to an initial *tetarte* on Indian Ocean goods when they entered Egypt (via the Red Sea ports), and then a subsequent *tetarte* for those goods shipped from Alexandria to [Rome and] other provinces of the Empire.'[29]

We are familiar with the inextricable link between trade and military expansionism: the *tertarte* allowed Augustus to effect a wholesale change to his military by introducing a full time career-based professional army to replace the seasonal levies, and in so doing helped secure his borders, control subject nations and enforce the Pax Romana. And thereby stimulating domestic and overseas trade especially with India and China.[30] This army, regular and auxiliary, would eventually number around 300,000 professional soldiers and it owed its existence and conditions of service largely to the *tetarte*.[31]

The disposable income of many Romans increased too. When Augustus plundered the treasures to be found in Alexandria (themselves purloined by an avaricious Cleopatra from Egyptian sacred shrines), and then exacted two-thirds of the wealth of the richest Egyptians, all this bloated the coffers of Imperial Rome.[32] Augustus put it to good use when he distributed the bullion to Roman citizens; apart from increasing markedly disposable wealth, it also bought Augustus popularity (and therefore less troublesome disaffection) and boosted international trade. The hand-out gave every Roman citizen 400 sesterces (more than three months' pay for a labourer) and similarly rewarded the soldiery.[33] The average Roman's spending power increased dramatically and generated a consumer boom – spent not on essentials but rather on all those luxuries which were flooding into Roman markets from the east. Paulus Orosius remarked on a rise in property prices and a doubling of the price of some goods (6,19); he chose not to mention any inflationary consequences of all this money flowing into the economy. Suetonius echoes the impact on property prices and adds the depressing impact on the interest rates for loans, thus fuelling inflation yet further? The usual 12 per cent had fallen to 4 per cent.[34] Lower interest rates had the additional effect of attracting more and more merchants anxious to procure loans to finance more trips east to acquire more luxurious, in vogue goods. Add to this the Romans' control of the Red Sea ports with its direct route to India and we have an extraordinary trade boom: Strabo went to see for himself and reported an increase in India-bound vessels from less than 20 to 120.[35]

The Book of Revelation has something interesting to say about Roman trade. It was probably written in the reign of Domitian (81–96 CE) by a certain John of Patmos. He was astute enough to understand that the destruction of Babylon (Rome) he prophesied was due, in part at least, to the merchants of Rome and their transactions; the warnings regarding the frailty and fickleness of extravagance and wealth, the boom and the corresponding bust, were there for anyone who cared to look:

> 'The merchants of the earth will weep and mourn over her because no one buys their cargoes any more ... cargoes of gold, silver, precious stones and pearls; fine linen, purple, silk and scarlet cloth; every sort of citron wood, and articles of every kind made of ivory, costly wood, bronze, iron and marble; cargoes of cinnamon and spice, of incense, myrrh and frankincense, of wine and olive oil, of fine flour and wheat; cattle and sheep; horses and carriages; and bodies and souls of men. They will say, "The fruit you longed for is gone from you. All your riches and splendor have vanished, never to be recovered". The merchants who sold these things and gained their wealth from her will stand far off, terrified at her torment. They will weep and mourn and cry out: "Woe! Woe, O great city, dressed in fine linen, purple and scarlet, and glittering with gold, precious stones and pearls! In one hour such great wealth has been brought to ruin!" Every sea captain, and all who travel by ship, the sailors, and all who earn their living from

the sea, will stand far off. When they see the smoke of her burning, they will exclaim, "Was there ever a city like this great city?" They will throw dust on their heads, and with weeping and mourning cry out: "Woe! Woe, O great city, where all who had ships on the sea became rich through her wealth! In one hour she has been brought to ruin!"

Revelations 11–19 trans. New International Version[36]

McLaughlin points out that the majority of goods cited in this passage emanate from Rome's eastern markets, far beyond the boundaries of the empire.[37] When markets start to dry up, when demand diminishes, when the gold and silver bullion exports to Arabia, India and China are no longer sustainable, then trouble surely looms.

Nubia

South of Egypt lay Nubia. The Egyptians called the Nubians the Kush. From about the third century BCE to the third century CE, northern Nubia was invaded and annexed to Egypt, ruled by the Greeks and Romans; it was known in the Graeco-Roman world as Dodekaschoinos. After the Romans took control of Egypt Derek Welsby records how they and the Nubians fixed the southern border of Egypt at Aswan,[38] with Kush becoming a client kingdom. But the Kushites aspired to better than this and, oppressed by heavy taxation, revolted against the Romans.

Strabo describes how the Kushites 'sacked Aswan with an army of 30,000 men and destroyed imperial statues ... at Philae'. After the initial victories of Kandake ('Candace') Amanirenas the Kushites were defeated and Napata was sacked. Unperturbed Candace resumed the fight and, according to Robert Jackson, in 22 BCE led a large Kushite force north to attack Primis (Qasr Ibrim).[39] Welsby adds (64–65) that after a Kushite assault on Primis the Kushites despatched ambassadors to negotiate a peace settlement with Petronius the Roman commander which ended with favourable terms. Trade between the two nations increased and, according to Jackson and Welsby (pp. 64–65), the Roman Egyptian border was extended to 'Hiera Sykaminos' (Maharraqa). This arrangement, Welsby concludes, 'guaranteed peace for most of the next 300 years' and there is 'no definite evidence of further clashes'.

Lake Chad

The thirst for gold and spices led the Romans to launch a number of expeditions into the west of Africa, east of Nubia, between the first century BCE and the fourth century CE. There were five routes used:

- *The Cornelius Balbus expedition*: which, according to Pliny, was the first Roman expedition through the Sahara and was led by Cornelius Balbus, who in 19 BCE probably reached the Niger River near Timbuktu. He set off from Sabratha in Libya with 10,000 legionaries and took the Garamantes' capital at Fezzan. He then sent a squadron of his legionaries further south across the Ahaggar Mountains to explore the 'land of the lions'. There they found the Niger River, which they believed flowed into the Nile. In 1955, Roman coins and ceramics were unearthed around Mali.
- *The Suetonius Paulinus expedition*: the second was in 41 CE, led by Suetonius Paulinus, who was the first to lead an army across the Atlas mountains. After ten days' march he reached the snow-capped summits and later arrived at the Gerj river, and then marched into the semi-desert country south of Morocco. There is evidence, in the shape of coins and fibulae, of Roman business in Akjoujt and Tamkartkart near Tichit in Mauritania.
- *The Flaccus expedition*: took place in the first century CE, destination Lake Chad, with two Roman expeditions aiming to reach it: Septimius Flaccus and Julius Maternus reached the 'Lake of Hippopotamus' (as it was called by Ptolemy) having moved from Tripolitania on the coast and travelling through the Garamantes' territories, leaving a small garrison on the 'lake of hippopotamus and rhinoceros'. Ptolemy reports that in 50 CE Septimius Flaccus finally reached the Bahr Erguig, Chari, and Logone Rivers near Lake Chad, described as the 'land of Ethiopes' (or 'black men') and called *Agisymba*.
- *Matiernus expedition*: Ptolemy tells us that in 90 CE Julius Matiernus left on a trade expedition from the Sirte Gulf, reaching the oases of Cufra and Archei, and then marched on with the king of the Garamantes to the Bahr Salamat and Bahr Aouk Rivers, near modern-day Central African Republic. He returned to Rome with a rhinoceros with two horns, that was exhibited in the Colosseum.
- *Valerius Festus expedition*: Pliny wrote that in 70 CE this was a rerun of the Balbus expedition heading toward the Niger River.[40] Festus penetrated the Air Mountains as far as the Gadoufaoua plain. We learn from the *Cambridge History of Africa* (p. 284) that Gadoufaoua (Touareg for 'the place where camels fear to tread') is a site in the Tenere desert of Niger, famous for its huge fossil graveyard, where remains of *Sarcosuchus imperator*, popularly known as Super Croc, have been found. Festus finally arrived near Timbuktu.
- Other routes included: travelling up the Nile Valley through Egypt towards the Great Rift Valley; along the western coast of Africa toward

the Sénégal River; and along the coast of the Red Sea toward the Horn of Africa, and modern Zanzibar.

Evidence of a Roman presence is provided by the Heinemann-University of California, p. 514:

'Roman objects are, indeed, found in the Sahara, and, significantly, along the western caravan route. Numerous Roman artefacts have been found at the Garamantes' capital of Germa in the Fezzan. Most striking is the large Roman-style mausoleum found there, evidence either of Roman presence or of Romanization of the elite. Between Germa and Ghat in the Hoggar have been found Roman ceramics, glass, jewellery and coins dating from the 1st to the 4th centuries. Farther down the route, at the oasis of Abelessa, is the site known locally as the Palace of Tin Hinan ... it seems to have been a fortress, in one room of which was found the skeletal remains of a woman, along with a number of Late Roman objects, including a lamp, a golden bracelet and a 4th-century coin. Finally, there was a cache of Roman coins found at Timissao only 600 kilometres from the Niger.'

Chapter 11

Arabia

Moving east into the Arabian Peninsula we find Roman merchants trading who are additional to those active in the Red Sea ports in east Africa and western Arabia, as described in the *Periplus of the Erythraean Sea*. These bring us into contact with the silk routes which snaked their circuitous way from the far flung borders with China.

Herodotus got it largely correct when he recorded:

'It would seem to be a fact that the remotest parts of the world are the richest in minerals and produce the finest specimens of both animal and vegetable life… and Arabia is the only place that produces frankincense, myrrh, cassia, cinnamon, and the gum called ledanon. All these, except the myrrh, cause the Arabians a lot of trouble to harvest… I have said enough about the perfumes of Arabia. Let me only add that the whole country exhales a more than earthly fragrance.'

Herodotus 3, 106–107, 113

Observing the fruits of the traders' ongoing efforts on display and for sale in Rome's bustling markets and shops in the clogged streets, Pliny complained; 'At the smallest reckoning 100 million sesterces [of gold = ca 16,660 English pounds] is the sum which every year India, the silk-growing country of northern China, and the Arabian Peninsula take from our Empire. Such is the cost to us of our luxuries and our women'. He was clearly not convinced that time, and particularly money, was well spent satisfying the demand for fine and exotic goods, or on indulging the cravings of well-off women.[1] He was right to be concerned about the amount of gold and silver bullion that was expended on paying for these fripperies and the impact that was having on Rome's balance of payments.

We have noted Juvenal's disgust at the fashion for translucent silk; the expensive tastes of comfortably off Roman women had long been a cause for anxiety and insecurity – mixed with not a little misogyny – amongst their menfolk well before Juvenal's day. As early as 195 BCE Livy points out, in the debate relating to the repeal of the Oppian Law, that women are only fit to go shopping; 'Women cannot hold magistracies, priesthoods, celebrate triumphs, wear badges of office, enjoy gifts, or booty; elegance, finery, and beautiful clothes are women's emblems, this is what they love and are proud of, this is what our ancestors called women's decoration'.[2]

Soon after, women were financially targeted by the *lex Voconia* of 169 BCE where we find binding references to women frittering away their inheritances on frivolities – the changes here to their ability to inherit involved overturning their supposedly inviolable right to do so under the revered Twelve Tables.[3]

Rome's eastern activities in Arabia coincided roughly with the Han Empire's expansion west into Central Asia, bringing prodigious quantities of Chinese silk westwards.

Daniel C. Waugh tells us that there were several routes to and from the East: in the north, trade passed through the Caucasus, crossed the Caspian Sea and then went up the Amu Darya (Oxus) river. More important was the route from the Mediterranean through Damascus and Palmyra to Mesopotamia. From there, merchants either could sail down to the Persian Gulf or head northeast through Parthia to Central Asia.[4]

Maës Titianus

Maës Titianus has a significant place in the history of Rome's connections with the east. He was most likely a Roman merchant: Ptolemy tells us that he was a Macedonian and a Greek speaker whose parents were merchants of Syrian and Roman extraction.[5] He moved to Hierapolis in Roman Syria around 100 CE. Apparently, Maës despatched an expedition the purpose of which was economic: to 'streamline the trade in Chinese silk'. The expedition has gone down in history as having travelled farthest east along the Silk Road from the Mediterranean, although this is disputed: other Greeks may well have ventured further east before the Silk Road: it seems that the Greco-Bactrians may have initiated expeditions from Alexandria Eschate – a city founded by Alexander the Great at the south-western end of the Fergana Valley (modern Tajikistan) in 329 BCE. They reached as far east as Kashgar and Ürümqi in Xinjiang, so becoming the first known contacts between China and the West around 220 BCE. Strabo relates that the Greco-Bactrians; 'extended their empire even as far as the Seres (Chinese) and the Phryni'.[6] Also in India, the Indo-Greeks under Menander I led conquests as far as Pataliputra, probably the farthest known eastern foray by the Greeks.

In the early-second century CE Maës' expedition passed through central Asia and reached the Stone Tower,[7] in or around the Pamir Mountains close to the border with China; here business would be conducted with Chinese merchants.

The final destination of the agents was the city of Sera Metropolis, which is probably the ancient city of Wu Wei.[8] Nothing much is known of him, apart from a brief mention in Ptolemy's *Geography* whose knowledge of Maës was gained through a secondary source, Marinus of Tyre:

> 'Marinus tells us that a certain Macedonian named Maes, who was also called Titian, son of a merchant father, and a merchant himself, noted the length of this journey [to the Stone Tower], although he did not come to Sera in person but sent others there.'
>
> *Ptolemy, 1, 11, 7*

The Stone Tower, the exact location of which is unknown, marked the midway point on the Silk Road and was the most important landmark – a place where caravans paused to allow travellers and pack animals to take on provisions, rest, and for the merchants to trade goods. Ben Chao (32–102 CE), the Chinese diplomat, explorer, and general of the Eastern Han Dynasty, with an eye on trade opportunities as well as things military, intercepted the group and made sure they were taken eastward to the Chinese capital Luoyang, where they were granted an audience before the Han Emperor He. Since the travellers spoke Greek and were with Parthian merchants they did not identify themselves as Roman. Thus, the Chinese had no idea they were dealing with subjects of Da Qin (the Roman Empire). Chinese records written in the Hou Hanshu state that the encounter took place in 100 CE. In line with protocol the Maës merchants offered tribute to Emperor He by gifting rewoven Syrian silks and imperial gold coins that bore the image of Emperor Trajan. 'They in turn were given Han silks as diplomatic gifts and then sent on their long way back to Syria. It would take them twelve months to return home, some two years for the round-trip. When they returned, knowledge of their experience spread around the Roman world and for the first time Romans in Egypt and Syria knew of a superpower in the Far East that produced large quantities of silk and steel'.[9]

When the significant advantages of the India Ocean monsoons were discovered in the first century BCE it allowed direct passage across the ocean and back, avoiding the hazardous coastal route with its twin dangers posed by dangerous reefs and even more dangerous pirates.

Of course, much depended on the ever-changing volatile political situation in the region. The Roman–Parthian Wars (54 BCE–217 CE) were a series of conflicts between the Parthian Empire and the Romans, the first in what would be 682 years of Roman–Persian mutual belligerence. Waugh tells how:

'The Parthians even managed to take Jerusalem before being driven back by the Romans, who then aggressively extended their control of the western end of the trade routes in the first and second centuries CE. In particular, the Romans established suzerainty over the Nabataeans, the rulers of Petra, and then in 115 CE under Emperor Trajan were able briefly to hold Ctesiphon, in the Parthian heartland. Trajan built a major road connecting Damascus with the Gulf of Aqaba and the Red Sea.'

Despite it all there was still significant commerce going on in the background. Waugh describes how a Chinese ambassador reached Parthia in 97 CE and reported on Parthian efforts to confine the trade to the overland route in order to avoid paying the customs duties required in taking the circuitous sea route around Arabia. In 166 CE another Chinese source reported that Roman merchants, who apparently claimed they were ambassadors from the Emperor, reached one of the Chinese ports. Waugh adds that the trade along the silk roads was amplified by the emergence of the Kushan Empire as the most powerful state sitting astride the routes reaching up into Central Asia and crossing Afghanistan and northwest India.

Incense and the Incense Route

It was the fragrances frankincense and myrrh which most excited Roman traders; we have seen that for climatological and botanical reasons these could only be obtained from southern Arabia, Ethiopia, and Somalia. Pliny informs us that 'frankincense trees covered an area close on 1.3 million hectares up in the Dhofar highlands producing more than 1,000 tons of frankincense for the Sabaean kingdom' *(NH* 12, 32). Arab merchants fetched these exotic, luxury, high-priced and highly prized commodities from along the Incense Route, which at first began at Shabwah in Hadhramaut, the easternmost kingdom of South Arabia, and ended at Gaza, then a port north of the Sinai Peninsula on the Mediterranean Sea. All were part of Arabia Felix – the name says it all and gives us an idea of how the region was regarded by the Romans – literally a place of good fortune. However, things being what they were, the Romans simply did not have enough goods for sale or exchange in their holds or on their camels' backs for simple bartering in the incense trade, so they were forced to pay for frankincense and myrrh with Roman gold and silver. Pliny the Elder tells us that top line frankincense commanded a price of 10 silver denarii per pound weight; quality myrrh (*stacte*), however, went for up to 50 denarii (200 sesterces) – the salary a skilled labourer could earn for fifty-days' work in the first century CE.[10] Gold and silver are of course, subject to finite resources being available, so this valuable commerce was in itself always economically unsustainable and potentially limited. The business was not helped by the fact that it was, according to Strabo, (16, 4, 22), usually a one-way trade, with the Arabians declining any goods the Romans had to offer in exchange while the Romans filled their holds with incense, sardonyx, red quartz, haematitis (red jasper), coloured crystals, diamonds – and onyx at Petra, the centre for the purple amethyst trade – expending more bullion in the process.

Incense was important in satisfying a huge demand from elite Roman women; it was a highly desirable accoutrement and a fashion statement of considerable significance. But it was not just the latest thing for those women who could afford it; incense played a major role in Roman religion, as it had in Greek religion in earlier days. Incense smouldered slowly and smokily in temple niches, on altars, on incense dishes and in incense lanterns in every kind of religious ceremony, including sacrifice (to conceal the rank smells) and at domestic religious rites – giving off its heady, near intoxicating fragrances. Prodigious quantities of incense were burnt away in all manner of excess: at public ceremonies, at the games (to hide the stench from animal carcasses and human corpses rotting way under a relentless sun) and in ceremonial processions, whence it graduated to official ceremonies, especially those which required divine approval, and then to private houses to demonstrate not just wealth but also that one's host was right on trend. Indeed, it was an essential part of ceremonies celebrating births, coming of age and marriages, and at funerals for the comfortably off.[11] Pliny was less than happy with the general extravagance of it all, wondering how much actually found its way to the gods on Olympus and how much ended up 'expended on spirits of the underworld' (*NH* 12, 41). Tacitus chimes in by reminding us that Poppaea, Nero's late wife, was not cremated in the usual Roman way, but her body was stuffed with incense 'following the custom of foreign princes' (*Annals* 16,6). We have mentioned that Pliny, though, tops this prodigious extravagance when he records that Nero used up more incense at Poppaea's funeral than was produced in the whole of Arabia in a single year (*NH* 7, 53).

Incense was there too as a votive at the beginning and end of long journeys, especially sea journeys, many of which were no doubt trade voyages.[12] It could also be found smoking away over the legions waiting for divine approval before joining battle. Indeed, archaeological finds at Dura-Europus reveal fifty days in the military calendar when the whiff of incense was required.[13] Not a day went by, it seems, in the Roman religious calendar, as listed by Ovid in his *Fasti*, that was not accompanied by incense smouldering noiselessly in the background.[14]

The Farasan Command and Muza

As a visible indicator of the importance with which the Romans considered their Arabian trade we need look no further than the Farasan Command where, in the second century CE, the Romans established a naval base on the Farasan Islands some 25 miles off what is now the Saudi Arabian coast, 600 miles from the Roman empire's southern borders and 2,500 miles from the city of Rome; these coral islands were of considerable strategic importance, commanding as they did the gulf sea lanes and the exit and entrance to the Red Sea.

The port of Muza, on the mainland opposite the Farasans, was the first reached by the Romans sailing to Arabia Felix; the *Periplus* (7, 8, 16, 21) informs that 'the entire place teems with Arab shipowners, charterers and sailors'. Here the Romans could pick up top-drawer myrrh (*Periplus* 24), *stacte* (liquid myrrh sap – Pliny *NH* 12, 35).

But it was not just the incense that the Romans craved and sent on its way towards a receptive Rome: indeed, spices, gold, ivory, pearls, precious stones, and textiles were all strapped to the camels and loaded onto wagons as they wended their plodding way along the desert tracks.

Southern Arabia is rich in bright white marble which the Romans used as ballast; but when the merchant ships reached Ostia or Portus this was offloaded and sold to Roman stoneworkers who fashioned it into perfume phials and incense jars. When ground down to an abrasive residue it was used to whiten stained teeth and remove tartar (Pliny *NH* 36,41; 37, 54).

Medicines

Public medicine as practiced in Rome, particularly from the latter years of the Republic, was actually Greek medicine conducted usually by Greek physicians; before that it was very much a domestic affair – family medicine administered by *pater-* and *materfamilias* largely based on traditional folk remedies. Medicine was an essential element in the unquenchable popular taste for the mystical, macabre and chthonic and a preoccupation with the dark arts within the shadier corners of Roman society.

The practice of dark arts and the accompanying medicine was often barely distinguishable from what might be called conventional medicine. They had their roots in folk religions and ancient folk medicine, insinuating themselves in cultures and civilizations in Egypt, Mycaenae, the Middle and Near East and Etruria, as old Italic traditions and practice, before flooding into Rome on the tide of Greek culture and Hellenization. Medicine and witchcraft have in common the use of medicinal herbs on an industrial scale. For example,

Thessaly was home to the world's most repellent witches and their *herbae nocentes*, pernicious herbs; when the witches here cast their spells even the gods above stop to listen, and are sometimes persuaded to do the witches' will. Lucan describes their *noxia pocula*, noxious potions, in his *Pharsalia* (6, 633ff). Both Pliny (*NH* 12, 35) and Arrian (*Animals* 4, 36) attest to the rich store of medicinal herbs available in Arabia and India.

Flavourings

Back in Rome, by the first century CE it had become *de riguer* among the wealthier and ostentatious to entertain on a grand scale, and one of the ways to impress was to serve up exotic dishes with novel flavourings – flavourings which originated in the east and included ginger, cinnamon, nard, cumin, vanilla and incense. Nard, or spikenard, is an aromatic amber-coloured essential oil derived from *Nardostachys jatamansi*, a flowering plant.

What did the Romans have to offer in exchange or to reduce the huge expenditure in bullion? Not that much: bales of cloth and expensive purple-dyed fabric made up in the Arabian fashion, some decorated with gold thread and Roman blankets. Saffron dyes were traded too, as was Cyperus which had medical properties and which the Arabians could not grow enough of to satisfy demand.

* * *

Myrrh and frankincense owe much of their enduring fame to the three Biblical Magi who visited the infant Jesus in his Bethlehem manger, where they paid due homage and showered him with gifts of gold, frankincense and myrrh from their treasure chests. By then the wise men had had warning that Herod had Jesus in his sights so they went straight back home by a different route.

Trogodytic Myrrh trees (the best) grew in most of south west Arabia and in the horn of Africa opposite, while frankincense bushes had a similar distribution but the best came from Dofar and belonged to the Sultanate of Oman.

Strabo compared the huge volume of this westbound traffic to an army on the march. The Incense Route ran along the western edge of Arabia's central desert about 100 miles inland from the Red Sea coast; Pliny the Elder tells us that the journey comprised sixty-five stages punctuated by stopping stations for the camels and traders. Both the Nabataeans and the South Arabians grew fabulously wealthy through the transport of goods destined for lands beyond the Arabian Peninsula going west. Pliny may be simplifying the economics when he tells us that these are the world's richest nations since such prodigious wealth flows into them from the Roman and Parthian empires, for they sell the produce of the seas or of their forests, while they buy absolutely nothing in return.

The Metropolitan Museum of Art in New York has it that previous nomads in northern Arabia, the Nabataeans, had settled in southern Jordan by 312 BCE; Petra (ancient Raqmu) was the capital of the Nabataean kingdom, strategically situated at the crossroads of several caravan routes that linked the lands of China, India, and South Arabia with the Mediterranean world. A pivotal position which allowed them to rise from a poor nomadic desert kingdom to one of the main beneficiaries of this east-west trade as intermediaries. The reputation of the Nabataean kingdom spread as far as Han-dynasty China, where Petra was known as Li-kan.[15] James Elroy Fleckerer (1884–1915) sums up the attitude of the Nabataeans to commerce in his poem, *The Gates of Damascus:*

'Four great gates has the city of Damascus,
And four Grand Wardens, on their spears reclining,
All day long stand like tall stone men
And sleep on the towers when the moon is shining ...

'Some men of noble stock were made: some glory in the murder-blade:
Some praise a Science or an Art, but I like honorable Trade!
Sell them the rotten, buy the ripe! Their heads are weak; their pockets burn.
'Aleppo men are mighty fools. Salaam Aleikum! Safe return!'
ll. 1–4, 57–60

The emperor Trajan obviously saw the potential here in 106 CE when he annexed the Nabatean kingdom and absorbed it into the province of Arabia. Desert Petra lost out too when the much more accessible northern city of Bostra (Busra) was given the privilege of being the capital. Antioch, Palmyra and Alexandria gained at Petra's expense.

It was not just the Romans who went to great civil engineering lengths to preserve their natural resources and trade. The Arabs from the south built many irrigation works to maximise their limited rainfall, not least the dam at Marib which is mentioned in the Koran. It was a huge 1,800 feet long and over 50 feet high. Like the Romans, they were great builders of roads, thinking nothing of hacking their way through mountains and other rocky terrains. Roads meant tolls and tolls meant taxing the endless streams of caravans carrying incense and herbs to the west.

Other beneficiaries included the Minaeans, Gerrhaeans and the Sabaeans.

The island of Tylos – which we call Bahrain – was in Dilmun, established by 2000 BCE and influential as a middleman in trade between the civilizations of

Mesopotamia and the Indus Valley. By Roman and Parthian times there was a large port on the mainland opposite called Gerra which was the endpoint for caravans from south Arabia and the source of revenues from the trans-shipments which took place here with goods bound for Parthia by sea. The contemporary botanist Theophrastus tells us that the island of Bahrain was a rich source of cotton and timber, some of which presumably found its way to Rome. Bahraini pearls were regarded as the second best in the ancient world, bettered only by those from Ceylon (Sri Lanka).

The Expedition of Gallus

Gaius Aelius Gallus was the second *praefectus Aegypti* (governor of Roman Egypt) serving from 26 to 24 BCE. We learn of his expedition to Arabia Felix from Strabo, Cassius Dio and Pliny the Elder. Strabo's account is the most detailed, getting most of his information from Aelius Gallus himself, who was a personal friend of Strabo.[16]

Augustus' orders to Gallus were to undertake a military expedition to Arabia Felix in 26 BCE, where he was to either strike treaties making the Arabian people *foederati* (client states), or to conquer them if they resisted. Gallus, according to Mommsen, had over 200 ships built (including 130 transports) and sailed with 10,000 legionaries.

In 25 BCE Gallus left Cleopatris (today's Suez) on the Red Sea, leading his expedition to subjugate the Kingdom of Sheba and capture its capital Ma'rib on the south-western tip of the Arabian Peninsula in today's Yemen. He landed at Leuce Kome, a Nabataean trading port on the north-western Arabian coast, which was under the rule of King Obodas III, Rome's ally. We learn from *Romans on the Arabian Peninsula* (2021) how the Nabataeans were to provide guides for the Romans and provide supplies early in the expedition.[17] Nabataea occupied territories corresponding with modern Israel, Jordan and Saudi Arabia. The Roman commander received support from Petra, with 10,000 soldiers under the command of Syllaeus, and from the king of Judea – Herod the Great, with 500 men. The expedition took fourteen days and as a result of storms, a large number of Roman vessels were sunk. Strabo blames Syllaeus for this, who, in his opinion, intentionally concealed another, safer route – by land.

Gallus besieged Ma'rib unsuccessfully for seven days, after which he was forced to withdraw due to the ravishes of plague, over-extended supply lines, and an unforgiving desert environment.

Gallus arrived back in Alexandria in sixty days. The supporting Roman fleet occupied and destroyed the port of Eudaemon (modern Aden), securing the all-important Roman merchant route to India.

Sabaea

The Sabaeans were ancient South Arabians occupying Saba in today's Yemen; its capital was Ma'rib. We learn about some of their strict religious practices from Muslim writer Muhammad Shukri al-Alusi in his *Bulugh al-'Arab fi Ahwal al-'Arab*:

> 'The Arabs during the pre-Islamic period used to practise certain things that were included in the Islamic Sharia. They, for example, did not marry both a mother and her daughter. They considered marrying two sisters simultaneously to be the most heinous crime. They also censured anyone who married his stepmother, and called him dhaizan. They made the major hajj and the minor umra pilgrimage to the Ka'ba, performed the circumambulation around the Ka'ba tawaf, ran seven times between Mounts Safa and Marwa sa'y, threw rocks and washed themselves after sexual intercourse. They also gargled, sniffed water up into their noses, clipped their fingernails, removed all pubic hair and performed ritual circumcision. Likewise, they cut off the right hand of a thief and stoned Adulterers.'

The Sabaeans were the strongest of the many tribes occupying the Arabian Peninsula and in the first century BCE, Mar'ib was a vital trading centre through which all trade between the Mediterranean countries, especially Egypt, and India passed. Sabaea was never conquered by either the Persians or the Romans. Photius, in his ninth-century CE *Bibliotheca*, tells us about 'the Sabaeans, the largest of those in Arabia, possessing all kinds of wealth', while Pliny nearly a century before had described them as 'the most wealthy, owing to the fertility of their forests in producing scents, their gold mines, their irrigated agricultural land and their production of honey and wax'.[18]

Chapter 12

Parthia and the Sasanian Empire

So the end of the first century BCE saw an explosion of international trade forming a commercial melting pot which included five mighty powers: the Roman Empire, the Parthian Empire, the Kushan Empire, the nomadic confederation of the Xiongnu, and the Han Empire.

The Parthian Empire (also known as the Arsacid Empire) emerged from the mid-third century BCE, and lasted until 224 CE. Situated as it was on the routes passing between the Roman Empire and the Chinese Han Empire, Parthia was obviously strategically important for all lucrative east–west trade. Parthia also produced commodities itself to be traded, especially carpets and traditional woven fabrics. Many Parthian merchants became very wealthy as resellers of Central Asian and Chinese wares, particularly silk. But political instability and a seemingly constant state of war with the Roman Empire was a drag on cultural and economic development, as well as deterring traders from passing through the region.

With characteristic high-handed Roman xenophobia, the Romans initially dismissed the Parthians as a rabble of 'wild men from the east'. A description, as Sitwell points out, Crassus would have taken issue with had he survived the Battle of Carrhae and its aftermath. Steve Hill in his dissertation, *Defining the Alter Orbis: The Roman View of Parthia in the Early Principate* (2003) examines in some detail the Roman attitude to the Parthians: his abstract tells us:

'During the reign of Augustus the idea of Parthian Empire as an alter orbis was developed. For the Romans of the early Principate, the kingdom of the Arsacids represented the antithesis of their own values, embodying the vices of despotism and licentiousness. In the absence of a decisive military victory, the Roman people used this image of the Parthians to assert their own sense of superiority, while also acknowledging the formidable military strength of their eastern neighbour. This depiction of the Parthians (and later the Persians) was to persist throughout the centuries, despite increased contact through diplomacy and trade. As a result, the rivalry between the two powers never diminished, despite long periods of relative peace.'

Isaac (2004, p. 371) adds that the Parthian kingdom was of sufficient importance 'to guarantee it a special place in the Roman perception of foreigners'.

We can see from this University of Washington article that:

'They established their first treaty in 92 BCE with their future rivals, the Romans, in an effort to defeat their common enemy, the Seleucids. As the Seleucids weakened, the Parthians absorbed much of their territory. By the middle of the first century BCE, the Parthian Empire was at its zenith, both stable and strong.'[1]

At its zenith, the Parthian Empire stretched from the northern reaches of the Euphrates, in what is now central-eastern Turkey, to present-day Afghanistan and western Pakistan.

Following the diplomatic efforts of Zhang Qian into Central Asia in the reign of Emperor Wu of Han (r. 141–87 BCE), the Han Empire of China sent a delegation to Mithridates II's court in 121 BCE. Zhang Qian was a Chinese diplomat, explorer, and politician who served as an imperial envoy to the world outside of China in the late-second century BCE. He was one of the first official diplomats to bring back valuable intelligence about Central Asia, including the Greco-Bactrian remains of the Macedonian Empire and the Parthian Empire. He was a key pioneer for the future Chinese conquest of lands west of Xinjiang, including much of Central Asia and lands south of the Hindu Kush. This trip was of such importance since it led to the creation of the Silk Road that marked the beginning of globalization and substantial trade between the countries of the east and west.

From the first century BCE, the Romans and Parthians were embroiled in a series of indecisive, costly wars which went on and on for almost three centuries. The cause was often disputes over Syria, Mesopotamia and Armenia, with these lands passing to and fro first to Roman hands, and then back to the Parthians in successive battles. The only real outcome was to deplete resources on both sides: the resultant stalemate gave way to almost a century of peace.

In 114 CE, Roman forces once again penetrated Parthia and Rome was able to permanently retake many of the disputed territories.

Patrick Scott Smith tells us how:

'Mithridates II (r. 124–88 BCE) would take over [from Artabanus I (r. c. 127–124 BCE)] and become Parthia's greatest ruler. Mithridates would not only strengthen Parthia's hand in Elam, Characene, Mesopotamia, and Bactria but he also added Albania and Armenia and captured the Syrian city of Dura-Europos in the west. With frontiers now stretching between the

Mediterranean Sea and China, Parthia became a geographical juggernaut and true superpower.'

https://www.worldhistory.org/Parthia_(Empire)/

Soon afterwards Parthia and Rome were in conflict again: Phraates III (r. 70–57 BCE) lost Armenia, Albania, and Gordyene in northern Mesopotamia to the Romans, with the consequence that his sons, Orodes II and Mithridates IV, assassinated him. The resulting civil war saw Orodes II (r. 57–37 BCE) kill his brother and reconquer the capital city of Seleucia. In 53 BCE, Marcus Licinius Crassus, one of the three First Triumvirates and a very rich man, invaded Parthia near Carrhae with catastrophic results. Crassus was hoping to emulate the military successes of his fellow triumvirs Pompey and Caesar, and, as governor of Syria, launched a calamitous invasion of Parthia. Hill (pp. 5–6) adds that this invasion, which Plutarch tells us was a private enterprise rather than a policy of the Roman state, cost Crassus not only his own life, but also that of his son and most of his army. Orodes had despatched his general, Surena, to deal with the matter: with Parthian archers on horseback deployed with deadly effect, Crassus and his army were annihilated, and the Roman *aquilae* (standards) were seized; a huge psychological and foreign policy blow for Rome, up there with Teutoburger Wald, Trasimene and Cannae.[2] Later, forging alliances with a number of neighbouring kingdoms, including Armenia, Mark Antony instigated a campaign against Parthia with a huge force in 36 BCE. Then, to make things doubly worse for Rome, the Parthians proceeded to retake Armenia with the defeat of Mark Antony in 32 BCE.

These two defeats brought Rome to the negotiating table and persuaded them that the Parthians, barbarians though they were, were a force to be reckoned with – a league above the traditional Roman perception of eastern peoples as soft and effeminate. Both sides now saw sense and so to avoid a stalemate in a conflict which would serve simply to weaken each side in mutual attrition a treaty was agreed. In the words of Raoul McLaughlin:

'In 20 BCE Augustus secured a long-term peace agreement with the Parthian King Phraates IV. This agreement allowed both rulers to concentrate their military activities on other frontiers and thereby enlarge their respective empires.'[3]

Hill (p.6) adds the testimony of Cassius Dio (*Augustus* 54,8):

'It was in this year that the Parthian king Phraates IV returned to Augustus the standards which had been lost at Carrhae, along with the surviving prisoners from Crassus' army. Yet this diplomatic success was presented by the Augustan government as a triumph of Roman might, and was celebrated with all the trappings of a great military victory, such as a Parthian arch, a temple to Mars Ultor which housed the recovered standards, and a series of commemorative games.'

Hill asks the important question, 'How did Augustus manage to reverse what has been described as the 'loss of face and appearance of weakness', suffered by the Romans after the defeat at Carrhae, without scoring a decisive victory over the Parthians on the battlefield?' Answering:

'Nevertheless, they could not view the Parthians in the same dismissive manner as they did other eastern races, as they had always to acknowledge the formidable military strength of the Arsacids. Therefore, it was necessary for the Romans to create an image of this rival empire which acknowledged their martial prowess, whilst at the same time asserting the ultimate superiority of their own society. Once established, this depiction of the Parthians (and later the Sassanid Persians) was to persist throughout the centuries, despite increased contact through diplomacy and trade. As a result, tensions between the two powers never diminished.'

Contact with China

The Han embassy opened official trade relations with Parthia via the Silk Road yet did not achieve the military alliance they wanted against the confederation of the Xiongnu.[4] As noted, the Parthian Empire became extremely wealthy from the taxes imposed on the Eurasian caravan trade in silk, the most highly-prized and priced luxury good imported by the Romans.[5] Pearls were also in demand and a valued import from China, while the Chinese in return purchased Parthian spices, perfumes, and fruits.[6] Exotic animals were also given as gifts from the Arsacid to Han courts; in 87 CE Pacorus II of Parthia sent lions and Persian gazelles to Emperor Zhang of Han (r. 75–88 CE).[7] Besides silk, Parthian goods bought or bartered by Roman merchants on the trade routes and in the markets included iron from India, spices, and fine leather.[8] Caravans travelling through the Parthian Empire brought west Asian and sometimes Roman luxury glassware to China.[9] The merchants of Sogdia served as the primary middlemen of this vital silk trade between Parthia and Han China.[10]

97 CE saw the Chinese general Ban Chao, the Protector-General of the Western Regions, send his envoy Gan Ying on a diplomatic mission to the Roman Empire. Gan visited the court of Pacorus II, Parthian King of Kings,

at Hecatompylos before heading for Rome.[11] Gregoretti tells how Pacorus was intent on establishing a far-reaching and viable trade-route through East Asia and India to the Mediterranean Sea with obvious economic benefits for Parthia. This planned long trade-route would greatly benefit the economy of the Parthian Empire.[12] In order to achieve this, Pacorus bolstered relations with those other powers with whom he was able to establish long distance trade, most notably Han China.

Gan got as far west as the Persian Gulf, where the Parthians hoodwinked him into believing that an arduous and dangerous sea voyage around the Arabian Peninsula was the only way to reach Rome.[13] Gan Ying swallowed this; he reported back to the Han court and delivered a detailed report on the Roman Empire based on the spurious accounts of his Parthian hosts. William Watson speculates that the Parthians would have been relieved at the failed efforts by the Han Empire to open diplomatic relations with Rome, especially after Ban Chao's military victories against the Xiongnu in eastern Central Asia. However, we know from Chinese records that a Roman embassy, possibly a group of Roman merchants, arrived at the Han capital Luoyang via Jiaozhi (northern Vietnam) in 166 CE, during the reigns of Marcus Aurelius (r. 161–180 CE) and Emperor Huan of Han (r. 146–168 CE).[14] It may be coincidental, but Antonine Roman golden medallions dated to the reigns of Marcus Aurelius and his predecessor Antoninus Pius have been discovered at Oc Eo, Vietnam (among other Roman artefacts in the Mekong Delta).

Travel in Parthia was extremely tough and knowledge of geography haphazard to say the least. War was never far away and the Antonine Plague killed millions, but despite it all business contacts were made and with them the spreading of ideas and initiatives, beliefs were compared, and traditions exchanged amongst these different peoples; all the while valuable goods were shipped over long distances, bought and sold, forwarded into newer markets through trade, barter, gift giving, and the payment of tribute.[15] Transport over land used river craft and pack animals, king amongst which was the strong Bactrian camel. Travel by sea depended on the prevailing monsoon winds across the Indian Ocean, which blow from the southwest during the summer months and from the northeast in the autumn.

To facilitate all of this, an extensive network of strategically-placed trading posts (*emporia*) was set up to enable the exchange, distribution, and warehousing of goods.

Isodorus of Charax, a Parthian Greek writing around 1 CE, described some of these posts and routes in his *Parthian Stations*, essentially an itinerary from the Graeco-Roman metropolis of Antioch to India following the caravan stations maintained by the Arsacid Empire, the Parthian ruling house. Isidore must have penned it sometime after 26 BCE, as it refers to the revolt of Tiridates II against Phraates IV, which occurred in that year. We learn from *Trade between the Romans and the Empires of Asia*[16] that:

> 'Routes crossed the Syrian Desert via Palmyra to Ctesiphon, the Parthian capital, and Seleucia on the Tigris River. From there the road led east across the Zagros Mountains to the cities of Ecbatana and Merv, where one branch turned north via Bukhara and Ferghana into Mongolia and the other led into Bactria. The port of Spasinu Charax on the Persian Gulf was a great center of seaborne trade. Goods unloaded there were sent along a network of routes throughout the Parthian empire – up the Tigris to Ctesiphon; up the Euphrates to Dura-Europos; and on through the caravan cities of the Arabian and Syrian Desert. Many of these overland routes ended at ports on the eastern Mediterranean, from which merchandise was distributed to cities throughout the Roman empire.'

The Sasanian Empire

The Sasanian Empire succeeded the Parthian Empire and prevailed in the region for more than four centuries, from 224 to 651 CE; it re-established the Persians as a major power to compete with the Roman Empire. Sasanian rule brought with it a high point in Persian civilization, 'characterized by a complex and centralized government bureaucracy, and revitalized Zoroastrianism as a legitimizing and unifying force of their rule'.[17] They also founded imposing new cities – Ardashir Khwarra, Bishapur and Veh-Antiok-Shapur; constructed grandiose monuments and public works; and financed cultural and educational institutions. The empire's cultural influence extended way beyond its borders – including Europe, Africa, China, and India. Sitwell adds, 'Commerce flourished ... and sophisticated new banking systems grew up to deal with it – our word 'cheque' is of Persian origin.[18]

As with many other things Persian, trade and industry under the Sasanians flourished transitioning from the domestic to the urban.

The Sasanians made use of two trade routes: the Silk Route in the north, and another skirting the southern Sasanian coast. The factories of Susa, Gundeshapur, and Shushtar were renowned for their production of silk, rivalling the Chinese factories. Guilds were established, viable roads and bridges were built and defended and facilitated state post, communications and merchant caravans to link Ctesiphon with the other provinces; harbours were built in the Persian Gulf to expedite trade with India. Sasanian merchants travelled extensively far and wide and slowly but surely ousted Romans from the lucrative Indian Ocean trade routes.¹⁹ Fascinatingly, we have recent archaeological evidence from the northern gate of the Takht-e Suleiman historical site which shows that the Sasanians made use of special commercial labels affixed on goods as a way of promoting their brands and distinguishing between different levels of quality.²⁰ The Iranian Cultural Heritage News Agency tells us how:

> 'The labels are in the form of two seals engraved on earthenware vessels and are discovered on the top layer of soil near the northern gate. Archaeologists hope to unravel bureaucratic relations of the era.
>
> 'Located in a mountainous area of north-western Iran and 42 kilometres north of Takab, Takht-e Suleiman (the 'Throne of Solomon') is one of the most interesting and enigmatic sacred sites in Iran.'²¹

Frye tells us that Khosrau I further extended the already vast commercial network,²² and that the Sasanian state now inclined towards a monopolistic control of trade, with luxury goods assuming a far greater role in the trade than ever before, and the great activity in building of ports, caravanserais, bridges and the like, was linked to trade and urbanization. How far the Romans were involved in this it is difficult to tell. Frye continues:

> 'The Persians dominated international trade, both in the Indian Ocean, Central Asia and South Russia, in the time of Khosrau, although competition with the Byzantines was at times intense. Sasanian settlements in Oman and Yemen testify to the importance of trade with India, but the silk trade with China was mainly in the hands of Sasanian vassals and the Iranian people, the Sogdians.'

What were the principal exports from the Sasanian Empire? Silk, woollen and gilded textiles, carpets and rugs, hides, and leather and pearls from the Persian Gulf. There were also goods inbound from China including paper and silk and spices from India. All of these would have had Sasanian customs taxes imposed on them, and many would have been re-exported to Europe, including the Roman Empire.²³

Metals were important to the Kingdom, which witnessed a surge in increased metallurgical production, thus earning Iran a reputation as the 'armoury of Asia'. Most of the Sasanian mining centres were at the fringes of the Empire – in Armenia, the Caucasus and above all, Transoxania. The extraordinary mineral wealth of the Pamir Mountains led to a legend among the Tajiks: when God was creating the world, he tripped over the Pamirs, dropping his jar of minerals, which spread across the region.²⁴

The Kushan Empire

The Kushan Empire was formed by the Yuezhi in the Bactrian territories in the early-first century CE. It spread to encompass much of what is now Uzbekistan, Afghanistan, Pakistan, and Northern India. We hear of Vida Kadphises, king of Bactria (r. 102–127 CE) sending envoys to Rome,[25] while various Roman sources describe the visit of ambassadors from the Kings of Bactria and India during the second century. The *Historia Augusta*, on Hadrian (117–138), reports that 'The kings of the Bactrians sent supplicant ambassadors to him, to seek his friendship'.

Also in 138 CE, according to Aurelius Victor and Appian, Antoninus Pius received Indian, Bactrian, and Hyrcanian ambassadors.[26] Hill tells us that:

> 'The summer capital of the Kushan Empire in Begram has yielded a considerable amount of goods imported from the Roman Empire – in particular, various types of glassware. The Chinese described the presence of Roman goods in the Kushan realm: 'Precious things from *Da Qin* [the Roman Empire] can be found there [in Tianzhu or North-western India], as well as fine cotton cloths, fine wool carpets, perfumes of all sorts, sugar candy, pepper, ginger, and black salt.'
>
> *Hou Hanshu*[27]

We learn from McLaughlin that excavated storerooms have yielded up more than 100 years' of treasure, including from the Roman Empire: bronze figurines decorated with classical deities, steel weights, glass bowls, painted vases and cut glass goblets depicting the Pharos Lighthouse at Alexandria, gladiator fights and a duel between Hector and Achilles.[28] Strabo says that 120 Roman ships were engaged in this trade in the Augustan age amounting, according to McLaughlin, to tens of thousands of tons if the ships only carried 300 ton payloads.[29]

Chapter 13

India

We have covered the Indian sub-continent's contacts with the Roman empire as indicated in the *Periplus of the Erythraean Sea* in the chapter on Africa above. This trade was of two distinct types; commodities which originated in the India sub-continent and trade in goods which arrived in India from central Asia and China. The first is terminal trade, the latter is transit trade.

History of Trade and Commerce in India

The fact that India is surrounded by sea on two of its triangular sides was and is an enormous advantage in spreading Indian business around the world and receiving trade from all around the world.

During the Hellenistic and Roman periods, India was the premier exporter of silk, cotton, sugar and precious stones. Of course, India was also a major exporter of spices to the west; this was conducted by sea and through the Spice Route.

Most commodities sold to Rome were exported in exchange for gold and silver. India was by now one of the leading business centres of the world with, commercial towns like Harappa and Mohenjo-daro having emerged around 2600 BCE. India had built strong business relations with other countries like Mesopotamia and trade took place between the two nations involving gold, silver, terracotta pots, precious stones, pearls and the like.

What made India an attractive proposition when it came to trade? Rao reminds us that the Hindu mercantile community soon acquired a reputation for entrepreneurship, its enterprising nature, resilience and trustworthiness. Goods manufactured in India were known for their high quality, while many goods produced in India were unique and were not available from anywhere else. Finally, the Hindus were skilled shipbuilders; they were excellent mariners with a prodigious knowledge of and expertise in sea routes, winds and other aspects of meteorology and navigation. This enabled them to travel to distant and foreign lands efficiently and relatively safely in order to conduct international trade.[1]

One of the first steps taken in forging commercial relations with the Indians came in 20 BCE when Augustus wintered on Samos and received a number of trade delegations. Dio takes up the story:

'Augustus, for his part, returned to Samos [in 20 BCE] and once more passed the winter there. In recognition of his stay he gave the islanders their freedom, and he also attended to many matters of business. For a great many embassies came to him, and the people of India, who had already made overtures, now made a treaty of friendship, sending among other gifts tigers, which were then for the first time seen by the Romans, as also, I think by the Greeks. They also gave him a boy who had no shoulders or arms, like our statues of Hermes. And yet, defective as he was, he could use his feet for everything, as if they were hands: with them he would stretch a bow, shoot missiles, and put a trumpet to his lips. How he did this I do not know; I merely state what is recorded. One of the Indians, Zarmarus, for some reason wished to die – either because, being of the caste of sages, he was on this account moved by ambition, or, in accordance with the traditional custom of the Indians, because of old age, or because he wished to make a display for the benefit of Augustus and the Athenians (for Augustus had reached Athens). He was therefore initiated into the [Eleusinian] mysteries of the two goddesses, which were held out of season on account, they say, of Augustus, who also was an initiate, and he then threw himself alive into the fire.'

Dio, 54, 9, 8–9 trans, E. Cary https://lexundria.com/dio/54.9/cy

The Indus River Valley Civilization

The Indus River Valley Civilization, also known as the Harappan civilization, was a Bronze Age civilization in the north-western regions of South Asia, lasting from 3300 BCE to 1300 BCE. It developed the first accurate system of standardized weights and measures, some as accurate as to 1.6 mm, as marked on an ivory scale found in Lothal.

In architecture and infrastructure construction, Harappans demonstrated considerable skills with dockyards, granaries, warehouses, brick platforms, and protective walls. The ancient Indus sewerage and drainage systems developed and deployed in cities throughout the region were far more advanced than any found in contemporary urban sites in the Middle East, and even more efficient than those in many areas of Pakistan and India today. Harappans created sculpture, seals, pottery, and jewellery from materials, such as terracotta, metal, and stone. They were excellent metallurgists.

Evidence shows Harappans participated in a vast maritime trade network extending from Central Asia to modern-day Iraq, Iran, Kuwait, and Syria. The civilization's economy depended on it; it was facilitated by major advances in transport technology. The Harappan Civilization may have been the first to use wheeled transport in the form of bullock carts. It also appears likely that they built boats and other watercraft – a claim supported by archaeological discoveries of a huge, dredged canal used as a docking facility at Lothal.

Until relatively recently it was generally believed that the Indus civilization, being land-locked, could only depend on a limited trade route leading to Mesopotamia and Elam through Baluchistan and south-western Iran. Indeed, it was the belief that there was hardly any sizeable international trade which could have powered the cultural activity of the Indus people. Recent explorations have, however, uncovered several Harappan ports 'giving a coastal aspect to the Indus civilization and suggesting a brisk sea-borne trade between the Indus people and the Sumerians in the late-third and early-second millenniums BC'. Thus, the entire 875-mile coastline of Kutch, Kathiawar, and South Gujarat was studded with Harappan ports in the second millennium BCE with some already established as early as the third millennium.

The earliest, and the most important, sheltered harbour was Lothal, which the Harappans developed into a large emporium and servicing station. 'Situated as it is at the head of the Gulf of Cambay it served as the warehouse of its rich rice, cotton, and wheat-growing hinterland. The inhabitants exported agricultural and marine products and imported the raw materials such as gemstones and metals needed for domestic consumption and for supplying the processing industries in order to sustain a large population'.

Rao continues:

'The principal exports of Lothal were ivory, shell inlays and ornaments, beads of gemstones and steatite, and, perhaps, cotton and cotton goods …The Kathiawar coast abounds in conch shell. The raw material and rejected pieces of shell found in the factories outnumber the finished products, suggesting that shell was worked for export. Lothal was also an important center for ivory-working. That elephants were reared here is indicated by the occurrence of elephants' tusks and femurs. The minute details of its anatomy depicted on the sealings are further evidence of intimate knowledge of the animal. From a merchant's house in the bazaar street, shell bangles, two Indus seals, eight gold pendants similar to those found in the Royal Cemetery at Ur, and sherds of Reserved Slip Ware were recovered. Obviously he was engaged in trade with foreign countries.'

The author of the *Periplus* knew well that there was much more to the world than the Red-Sea-centric coastal lands he describes. To the east of the Ganges he notes Chryseë – the Golden: the very last land heading east. To the north lay This, a land difficult to get to, with is magnificent inland city Thinae; silk came from here to markets in Bactria and Barygaza and to the Ganges and southern India. One hundred years later Ptolemy (c.100 – c.170 CE) was able to help us out with an extensive gazetteer of coasts, islands and hinterlands in this *Ultima Thule* of the east, but that was all. Names and nothing else. In fact, he got his geography wrong when he described the Indian Ocean as a larger version of the Mediterranean, with south eastern Asia skewed south and west to append to Africa near Zanzibar. His 'Golden Chersonese' may roughly be Malaysia and Myanmar (Burma) with its two emporia (markets), Takola and Sabana – Takola being near where Yangon (Rangoon) is today.

Barbarikon

An important port engaged in the Indian Ocean trade between India, the Middle East and the Mediterranean. It was near the modern city of Karachi. Tightly controlled procedures and bureaucracies, apparently to ensure commercial transparency, were conducted here and were probably repeated in other west-facing ports, not least at Minnagar where toll booths were manned by four or five officials who interrogated all traders. According to McLaughlin:[2]

> 'Roman cargo offloaded at Barbaricon was assessed by a customs official known as the *Antapal* (Officer in charge of Boundaries) who examined the quality of the incoming cargo and stamped delivery batches with his distinctive seal. He also collected road and ferry tolls ... [he] kept customs and a 'network of spies in the guise of traders' who he could send to the 'king with information about the quantity and quality of incoming merchandise. The king would forward this information to the Superintendent of Toos so that agents in the main city knew exactly what foreign merchants were bringing into the city'.

The aim was that the agents understood 'that nothing can be kept secret and all information is known through the omniscient power of the king'. Customs taxes were usually one-fifth value although a wide range of goods were at one-tenth; these included silk, mail armour, arsenic sulphide (to produce vivid paints), red arsenic, wine, ivory, skins, insect products, raw wool, and antimony sulphate (realgar) for alloys and eye shadow. Realgar had medical applications too: for wounds bleeding out to staunch bleeding, and in asthma cases and other chest diseases involving too much mucus.[3] Diamonds, precious stones, coral and pearl attracted the highest tax.[4] Merchants who failed to comply and had not collected a seal were punished with yet higher taxes.

Once through these barriers the trader had to cry out the quantity and price of his goods three times.

The Saka (Indo-Scythian) Kingdom

India's Saka era stretched from about the middle of the second century BCE to the middle of the first century CE. The Saka dynasty was founded by a chieftain named Maues (r. c. 130–120 BCE) who invaded Bactria (in modern Afghanistan) and India about 130 BCE and held sway over the modern-day regions of Afghanistan, Pakistan and northern India. The Saka were responsible for the spread of Buddhism in Central Asia and India. They also introduced coinage and urban planning to the region. They eventually fell to the Sasanians. Scythia in the area that is now Pakistan with its capital at Minnagara (modern-day Karachi) features a lot in Western maps and travelogues: the Ptolemy world map and *Periplus of the Erythraean Sea* mention Scythia in the Indus Valley, as does the Roman *Tabula Peutingeriana*.

The city-port of Barygaza was a destination for Roman traders, several hundreds of miles south of the Indus region. Mines were state run and the jewels traded at the port here by Romans were bought through government agents who imposed a purchase tax, the profits from which went straight into the treasuries. Suetonius reveals how the Saka, a nation previously unknown to the Romans, sent envoys under Azes to Augustus in 26 BCE seeking an alliance since they were under immediate threat from the Parthians.[5] Four years later a second embassy followed, the envoys travelling overland to Roman Antioch and then on to Samos; Strabo reports that only three of the emissaries survived the journey.[6]

The Saka came bearing gifts for Augustus, described thus by Strabo: 'Presented by eight naked servants besprinkled with sweet-smelling odours and clad only in loin cloths'.[7]

The Sakas' other commercial wealth lay in its agricultural economy established inland from the coast. From here the Romans imported a new type of millet unknown elsewhere in the empire: this proved very fertile when sown in Italy, outyielding traditional Italian crops.

But it was the gemstones mined in northern India which really caught the eye of the Roman merchant. As noted, there was a seemingly inexhaustible market in Italy for gemstones of all kinds and colours with which to bedeck fashion-conscious elite Roman women. To Pliny this was the main market – so important did he think gems were to Roman trade and culture that he devoted a whole chapter to them in his *Natural History*.[8]

Rome-bound cargoes, then, included grain and gemstones but also agate, onyx, cotton and spices – including costus, bdellium, lyceum and Himalayan nard; and then there was the Chinese silky yarn, quartz and ivory, rice, ghee and female slaves. Italian wine was mainly what the Saka could barter with in exchange, although Arabian and Spartan wines also feature, as did lead, tin, glass and copper.

The Satavahana Dynasty

This dynasty was located largely in the Deccan Plateau of India from the late-second century BCE to the third century CE. Carla Sinopoli tells us how 'the Satavahanas participated in (and benefited from) economic expansion through intensification of agriculture, increased production of other commodities, and trade within and beyond the Indian subcontinent'.[9] The Satavahanas controlled the Indian sea coast, and so also dominated much of the trade. Charles Higham gives us information on two important Satavahana trade centres: Pratishthana and Tagara. Others included Kondapur, Banavasi and Madhavpur. Nanaghat was the site of an important pass that linked the Satavahana capital Pratishthana to the sea.[10]

The ten ports on the Konkan coast were mainly engaged in local trade.[11] Kalliena was the only city-port dealing with foreign merchants as a state-controlled emporium. A horde of low value classical bronzes manufactured in Campania has been unearthed near Kolhapur which Tomber describes as 'antique junk'.[12]

AD 50 saw the Sakan king Nahaphana seize Satavahana possessions down the coast, but their return later was perfectly timed as this coincided with Vespasian (r. 69–79 CE) completing the construction of his majestic Flavian Amphitheatre (the Colosseum). Vespasian needed scores of exotic animals for his grand opening ceremony and Satavahana was a major exporter of all manner of astonishing and savage beasts which would tear each other to shreds and do likewise with unfortunate *in vivo* slaves, criminals and prisoners. Rhinos, leopards, tigers, huge snakes, monkeys and hyenas all passed through Kalliena on the first stage of their journeys.[13]

Eventually Semylla replaced Kalliena as the port of choice; being further south it was less vulnerable to hostile raids from the Saka; here Roman traders loaded up with cotton fabrics, spices and onyx.

The Tamil Kingdoms in the South of India

As noted already, the apex of India was torn between the three ruling houses of Tamil India (Tamilakam) – the Pandyas, Cheras, and Cholas – who fought each other for hegemony over what is now southern India and Sri Lanka. The Chera chiefs ruled over the south-western coast of Tamilakam, with the first rulers referenced in Sangam literature in the first century CE. Karur was their capital – an important port for trade in the jewel and spice trades. Modern Kerala gets its name from the Chera Dynasty.

The chief economic activities in Tamil country were agriculture, weaving, pearl fishing, manufacturing and construction. Paddy-field crops like rice were the most important staple cereal, which was also a medium of exchange for internal trade. Other common crops included pepper, millets, grains and sugarcane. The textile industry thrived in Madurai and Urayur, while Korkai was the centre of the pearl trade. Written testaments from Greek and Egyptian voyagers tell us that the fishermen who dived into the sea avoided attacks from sharks by bringing up the right-whorled conch and blowing on the shell.[14] Unsurprisingly convicts were deployed as pearl divers. *The Periplus* mentions that 'Pearls inferior to the Indian sort are exported in great quantity from the markets of Apologas and Omana'. Prior to export pearls were woven together with muslin cloth and were obviously the most expensive product imported by Rome from India.[15]

The Tamil economy was dependent on foreign trade. Literary, archaeological and numismatic sources all attest to the commercial relationship between Tamilakam and Rome. With Augustus in 27 BCE came a great boost in their trade, reaching its peak during Nero's reign, after which it slowly declined until the death of Caracalla (217 CE), when cotton and industrial products were still imported by Rome, and then it more or less ground to a halt. It was revived again under the Byzantine emperors. In the first century, under the early Roman emperors, there was, as we have seen, a huge demand for luxury items, especially beryl. Most of the articles of luxury mentioned by the Roman writers came from Tamilakam. In the declining period, cotton and industrial products were still imported by Rome. The exports from the Tamil country included pepper, pearls, ivory, textiles and gold ornaments, while the imports were luxury goods such as glass, coral, wine and topaz.[16] To the exports we can add other lucrative commodities: fine muslins and jewels, especially beryls; drugs, spices and condiments as well as crepe ginger, and other cosmetics all commanded a good price; plus pepper which, according to Pliny, sold at fifteen silver denarii a pound. Sapphire and a variety of ruby were also exported, as were ivory, spikenard betel, diamonds, amethysts and tortoiseshell. The government reaction to all this bounty was to finance infrastructure such as good harbours, lighthouses, and warehouses to stimulate overseas trade yet further.

The ships left Tamilakam carrying their valuable cargoes which were, on landfall, then transported in camel trains from the Red Sea to the Nile, then up to Alexandria, finally reaching Rome.[17] Evidence of a Tamil trading presence in Egypt can be found in Tamil inscriptions on pottery in Red Sea ports.

Domestic trading was *laissez faire*, mainly through barter in busy market places, conducted by merchant associations and commercial lending institutions. Merchants formed guilds which functioned independently, without state interference.

The Tamil country engaged in lively overseas trade with Rome. Pepper, pearls, timber, ivory, textiles and gold ornaments were exported from Tamilakam, in exchange for luxury goods such as glass, coral, wine and topaz but foreign trade generally (and particularly pepper) brought in much internationally-convertible Roman currency – gold and silver bullion again. Archaeology in the form of hoards attest to this, with finds containing hundreds, even thousands of Imperial Roman coins, mainly silver denarii and gold aurei.

Paint pigments
In Rome the colour of a host's dining room wall was a matter of some importance to both host and guest. Radiant colours were all the rage, leading to the importation of indigo in large quantities for use by interior decorators as an outline or to depict light and shade. Undiluted it was black, but watering down produced a gorgeous purple blue which could not fail to attract admiration. Pliny, however, was not impressed:[18]

> 'Nowadays, when purple is used even for colouring walls, and when India sends to us the sludge of her rivers, and the toxic blood of her snakes and her elephants, you never get a high quality artwork. Everything, in fact, was much better when the resources of art were so much fewer than they are today. Yes, so it is; and why is that? Because it is the paint, and not the hard work that goes into genius, that we are obsessed with.'

Black pigment reputedly came from burnt ivory.

But it was not just the colour of the walls that exercised Pliny. He was wise enough to know that the cost of all these spices, all this incense, pepper and silk – renewable resources all – was draining the Roman economy of an unsustainable and finite resource; the bullion payments could not, would not continue forever. He computes the cost to Rome of the plethora of eastern trade from Egypt to India based on, to him, newly divulged information: how much? A massive 50 million sesterces every year. He also assessed the total bullion expended on underwriting the Far East business, including China. The figure increases by 100 per cent, to 100 million, lamenting that this is the price we pay to satisfy vain women and amass exorbitant luxuries.[19]

Chera

Chera did particularly well out of trade with the Romans and with north India. Gurukkal asserts that:[20]

> 'The geographical advantages, like the favourable Monsoon winds which carried ships directly from Arabia to south India as well as the abundance of exotic spices in the interior Ghat mountains (and the presence of a large number of rivers connecting the Ghats with the Arabian Sea) combined to make the Cheras a major power in ancient southern India.'

Spice and black pepper were the money spinners;[21] the *Periplus Maris Erythraei* gives us the detail and adds that Muziris was the prime centre in the Malabar Coast, which according to the *Periplus*, 'abounded with large ships of Romans, Arabs and Greeks'. But it was by no means always plain sailing: in the second century CE, according to McLaughlin,[22] 'a Cheran king named Netunceral attacked and seized Roman ships'. The *Pattirruppatta* describes how the king; 'captured the uncivilized *Yavanas* [Romans] of harsh speech, poured oil on their heads and tied their hands to their backs and took their precious and beautiful vessels and diamonds'. They were either enslaved or a ransom was required for their release. How interesting to see the Romans for a change being criticised for their diction, by these 'bar-bar' speaking 'barbarians'.

Steel was also much prized by the Romans. According to Sasisekharan:[23]

> 'There are several ancient Tamil, Greek, Chinese and Roman literary references to high-carbon Indian steel. The crucible steel production process started in the sixth century BCE at Kodumanal in Tamil Nadu, Golconda in Telangana, Karnataka and Sri Lanka. This steel was termed "the finest steel in the world" by the Romans who referred to it by the term "Seric". It was exported to Rome, Egypt, China and the Middle East by 500 BCE. The steel was exported as [ingots] of steely iron that came to be known as "Wootz".'

The Pandyas

The Pandyas are mentioned by the Greek Megasthenes (fourth century BCE) who writes about a south Indian kingdom being ruled by women. He described the Pandya queen at the time, *Pandaia* as the daughter of Herakles.

Pliny refers to the Pandya ruler of Madurai as does the author of the *Periplus of the Erythraean Sea*, who describes the riches of a 'Pandian kingdom'; Ptolemy describes the country of the Pandyas as *Pandya Mediterranea* and *Modura Regia Pandionis*. Strabo relates that an Indian king called Pandion in 20 BCE sent

Augustus 'presents and gifts of honour'.²⁴ These amounted to pearls, precious stones and ... a giant elephant. We can speculate that the 50-million-sesterces-worth of pearls Augustus donated to the prestigious Temple of Jupiter Optimus on the Capitoline came from the Pandyans.²⁵ The first-century Greek historian Nicolaus of Damascus met, at Antioch, the ambassador sent by a king from India 'named Pandion or, according to others, Porus' to Augustus in c.13 CE.²⁶ While there is no direct evidence of trade between Rome and the Pandyans it seems likely that there was, given the contacts made by the Pandyans.

The Roman emperor Julian received an embassy from Pandya about 361 CE.

The Ganges

When the author of the *Periplus* describes the northeast coast of India he tells us that 'this region extends far inland and produces a great many cotton garments'.²⁷ He also reveals the existence of a port on the Ganges which 'shipped out cinnamon, Gangetic nard, pearls and the very finest quality cotton garments – known as Gangetic cottons'. Roman traders learnt that there were gold mines in the area and there were Indians that minted gold coins and sold precious stones. Ptolemy tells that 'near the Ganges River are the Sabarae in whose region diamonds are found'. He also notes how large quantities of high-quality nard were produced in the eastern Himalayas and the region exported exotic birds including roosters with colourful plumes, white crows, and talking parrots.²⁸

We know that Seneca the Younger wrote a book about India, but sadly it has not survived.²⁹

Chapter 14

Sri Lanka and Myanmar (Burma)

The somewhat perilous Palk Strait separating India from Sri Lanka was used by Indian merchants to access the eastern seaboard of India loaded with goods from Rome from the Malabar Coast.[1] These merchants also stopped at Sri Lanka (Taprobane), ruled then by the Anuradhapura Kingdom. Roman traders received goods in this way, including ivory, turtle-shell, pearls, gemstones and cotton clothing. Strabo saw that Sri Lanka 'sends great amounts of ivory, tortoise-shell and other merchandise to the markets of India'. Pliny also tells us that to 'procure pearls Indians go to the islands, the most productive of which is Taprobane'.[2]

As it is, we have on record only two visits to Sri Lanka by Romans; first that by a freedman of Annius Plocamus in the first century CE, which led to the despatch of a delegation from Sri Lanka to Rome during the reign of the emperor Claudius (41–54 CE);[3] and then that of Sopatros, probably in the fifth century CE.[4] Given that products from Taprobane were readily available in Indian markets there was no real need to travel to Sri Lanka to obtain them.[5] Moreover, it has been argued that anyone 'sailing between Egypt and the west coast of India during the southwest monsoon would have arrived in India in September or October. In order to take advantage of the northeast monsoon for their return journey, they would have had to depart India shortly thereafter, some time in November, so little time would have been available for even a brief trip to Sri Lanka.[6] Indeed, as McLaughlin suggests, these Indian merchants, for obvious reasons, would have discouraged Roman intervention in the Sri Lankan market.[7]

But a Roman tax collector changed all that for good when that freedman of Annius Proclamus found himself lost at sea in 52 CE. A storm blew him off his course bound for southern Arabia and he found himself beaching at Sri Lanka 14 days later.

Mc Laughlin takes up the story:[8]

'The Roman crew were brought to the court of the Anuradhapura King Bhatikabhaya (35–63 CE) where they learned the Sinhalese language. Amongst the ship's cargo was a trade consignment of Roman coin including denarii that impressed the king with its high-quality silver content. The silver content of Indian coins fluctuated according to the fortunes of the issuing kingdom and consequently their coins were rarely minted as pure bullion. By contrast all Roman denarii issued in this era were pure silver and this indicated to the Sinhalese that Rome was a stable and highly prosperous regime.'

As noted, the upshot was a Sinhalese delegation to Claudius in Rome to initiate trading relations led by Rachias (Raki).

After the success of this diplomacy, Roman ships began to cross directly to Sri Lanka and in so doing gave them more time to explore the markets there and in eastern India before the monsoon returned. They visited twelve cities and five harbours on the Sri Lankan coast as depicted on Ptolemy's map. Roman merchants also visited two trade centres (emporia) on the Sinhalese coast called Modurgi and Talacori. Here they were able to load up with rice, honey, ginger, beryls and purple amethyst gemstones.

Myanmar (Burma)

The author of the *Periplus* has it that the Himalayan region in the far north yielded the 'best cinnamon', known as malabathrum. He assumed that this area was on the border with Thinae (China) and describes for us how the cinnamon trade was 'conducted by an inland tribal people called the Sesatai or Besadae'. Ptolemy, with characteristic Greco-Roman stereotyping of foreigners, claims them to be 'short, stooping, ignorant, uncultivated, with broad foreheads and pale skin'.[9] He adds that Burma produces 'very much gold' and possessed 'well-guarded metal'. Martial describes how Domitian had Bengal tigers prowling around the Roman arenas.[10]

By the mid-second century CE Roman vessels were sailing around the Malay Peninsula, giving them access to markets in Thailand. Gold aurei minted by Antoninus Pius (r. 138–161 CE) and Marcus Aurelius (161–180 CE) have been unearthed at Oc-eo in southern Vietnam.[11] Around the same time Roman traders were getting reports that 'direct contact could be made with China by sailing north from Zabia into a sea called the Great Gulf (the South China Sea).[12] McLoughlin adds:

'These accounts proved to be correct as the Chinese army had an important military base in the region called Rinan ('South of the Sun'). Rinan was on the northeast coast of Vietnam where the Red River flowed into the Gulf of Tonkin. From this place Roman subjects would have been able to meet state-agents of the Chinese Empire and in AD 166 direct contact was made.'[13]

Chapter 15

China and the Silk Road

Roman Trade beyond the Empire before Commerce with China

Here is a summary of the state of Roman trade before commerce with China took off:

- By the end of the first century CE the total cost of running the Roman Empire was about 1,000 million sesterces per annum; 70 per cent went on maintaining the Empire, with over 700 million sesterces spent on the military, its navy and 30 legions stationed around the empire
- one of the largest costs was the grain-dole offered to 200,000 citizens in Rome which accounted for 48 million sesterces worth of grain imported into Rome on state-contracted private vessels. One third of this originated in Egypt, filling a fleet made up of over 100 ships
- Prodigious as it was, it was surpassed by the huge levels of commerce that spiralled between the Roman Empire and the lands of the east. By the first century CE, the value of Indian goods entering Roman Egypt exceeded 1 billion sesterces per annum
- We know that taxes levied on trade within the Empire yielded little revenue for the Roman State. However, revenues exacted from quarter-rate border taxes were massively lucrative and required minimal state infrastructure to manage and collect
- The Roman mines too were a high-value, low maintenance income stream generating, at high levels of production, over 120 million sesterces of gold and silver per year during periods of high-level production. This suggests that by the second century AD, the Roman Empire was operating on total revenues of about 1,100 million (1.1 billion) sesterces per year
- On the debit side Pliny computed that over 100 million sesterces of Roman bullion was exported out of the Empire every year by businessmen conducting eastern trade. Or, the equivalent to 10 per cent of the imperial budget and probably more silver bullion than the Empire was capable of mining annually. Result: 'a steady drain of precious metal wealth from the Roman economy that over time began to destabilise imperial currency.

As mine production declined, the Roman regime had to find new ways to pay for the Empire, or lose its dominance over the western world.'

By the time Augustus took over the reins of power in 27 BCE Rome was clearly the largest consumer economy in the world. Our extensive journey so far to the borders of the Roman Empire and beyond has taken in the lands of the Celts and the Nordic countries, Africa, Arabia and India. Our final out-of-empire destination is China and the Silk Roads which led over the Asiatic deserts and steppes to bustling markets in India and the Levant, and thence to Rome and the wider Mediterranean.

We have noted that the Romans were aware of India, but territories further east remained virtually unknown until the first century BCE, when silks started turning up in the markets, to the delight, no doubt, of vain fashionistas eager to out-silk their friends and dinner guests. For the most part these were women, but men too enjoyed the kudos that wearing silk garments brought to the party.

This chapter describes how the Romans overcame the vast distance, the inhospitable geography and climate, and the equally hostile Parthians who were jealously protecting the silk and incense routes between China and India. We have met Maës Titianus, who despatched an expedition to the Chinese border to 'streamline the trade in Chinese silk' around 100 BCE. We know of the journeys made by the Graeco-Bactrians who reached as far east as Kashgar and Ürümqi in Xinjiang, so becoming the first known contacts between China and the West around 220 BCE. We know about the 97 CE diplomatic mission led by Gan Ying, and Zhang Qian – Chinese diplomat, explorer, and politician – who served as an imperial envoy to the world outside of China in the late-second century BCE. In 165 CE Marcus Aurelius made use of merchant ships when he sent envoys, the Antun delegates, east to make contact with the Chinese; the crew wintered in India before sailing to Burma and around the Malay Peninsula 1,000 miles away, eventually reaching Thailand and then the southern tip of Vietnam – a further 500 miles away – in the summer of 166 CE. The envoys reached the Chinese outpost of Rinan, from where they were taken under guard to Luoyang, the Han capital about 1,000 miles away with samples from their cargo. Even with the benefits of what can only be described as highly-efficient Chinese 'motorways', this would have taken several weeks of flat-out riding. In the event, an international incident was fortunately avoided at the Han capital: as we have seen more than once, it was customary and expected for envoys:

> 'To offer costly diplomatic gifts to foreign rulers as tokens of respect and measures of prestige. However, the Antun delegates had no high-value offerings for the Han court and no costly Roman merchandise to present

as gifts. In place of imperial gifts they offered the Han Emperor some of the cargo samples that had been removed from their ship at Rinan to be conveyed to the palace at Luoyang. These items were a collection of relatively ordinary eastern goods and Han officials were disappointed because they had expected to receive Roman jewellery, objects fashioned from delicate red coral and exquisite western fabrics dyed with vibrant colours. *The Hou Hanshu records*: 'They offered elephant tusks, rhinoceros horn, and turtle-shell. This was the very first time there was communication [between our countries]'.

McLaughlin (2014) p. 209

Because of the sheer ordinariness of the gifts (which they probably could have obtained from the Indian markets anyway) the *Hou Hanshu* (88,12) continues that it raised doubts regarding the veracity of reports they had received about the might and grandeur of the Roman empire. Antun is a reference, McLaughlin informs us, to Antoninus Pius, which the Chinese abbreviated to Antun and signifies the Roman empire.

We know too that the *Weilüe* and *Book of Liang* record the arrival in 226 CE of a merchant named Qin Lun; Wu Miao, the Prefect of Jiaozhi, sent him to the court of Sun Quan (the ruler of Eastern Wu) who commissioned him to provide him with a report on his native country and its people.[1] The merchant was to return with ten female and ten male 'blackish coloured dwarfs' he had requested as a curiosity. According to the *Weilüe* and *Book of Liang* Roman merchants were active in Cambodia and Vietnam, a claim testified by archaeological finds in Vietnam, Thailand, Malaysia, and Indonesia.

Yule mentions that in the early-third century CE a Daqin ruler sent an envoy with gifts to the northern Chinese court of Cao Wei (220–266 CE) that included glassware of various colours. We know that top quality glass from Roman manufactories in Alexandria and Syria was exported throughout Asia, including Han China. According to An:[2]

> 'The first Roman glassware discovered in China is a blue soda-lime glass bowl dating to the early 1st century BC and excavated from a Western Han tomb in the southern port city of Guangzhou, which may have come there via the Indian Ocean and South China Sea. Other Roman glass items include a mosaic-glass bowl found in a prince's tomb near Nanjing dated to 67 AD and a glass bottle with opaque white streaks found in an Eastern Han tomb of Luoyang. Roman and Persian glassware has been found in a 5th-century AD tomb of Gyeongju [Seorabeol], Korea, capital of ancient Silla, east of China. Roman glass beads have been discovered

as far as Japan, within the 5th-century AD Kofun-era Utsukushi burial mound near Kyoto.'

There were other Roman luxury items on the shopping list: gold-embroidered rugs and gold-coloured cloth, amber, asbestos cloth, and sea silk, which was a cloth made from the silk-like hairs of a Mediterranean shellfish, the *Pinna nobilis*.

And we know all about the dissembling and duplicitous Parthians along the Silk Road who, according to McLaughlin, 'for security and profit restricted the flow of information that reached the Mediterranean concerning the distant Han Empire'. The Parthians allowed Roman traders to visit Iraq, but joining the caravans traversing Iran to Transoxiana and the silk routes leading to China was forbidden.

It was war which projected the Chinese into contact with the west, with their efforts to repel the belligerent Xiongnu nation, a confederation of nomadic tribes who populated the Mongolian Plateau from the third century BCE to the late-first century CE. In the end the Xiongnu were defeated by the Han dynasty in a conflict lasting hundreds of years, which led to the forcible resettlement of large numbers of Xiongnu within Han borders. The *Hu Hanshu* records that in *Da Quin* (Rome) the Romans 'cropped their hair and wore embroidered clothes. The people of this country are tall and honest ... are honest in business; they don't have two prices ... and the resources of the state are abundant'. A charitable if naïve assessment of the Roman trader. The Chinese also assumed that the Romans had their own silk manufactories, rearing their own silkworms and growing mulberry trees. *The Hu Hanshu* expatiates on the goods that might be bought from Roman merchants: these include gold, silver, precious stones, luminous jade, bright-moon pearls, fighting cocks, rhino horn, coral, yellow amber, opaque glass, cinnabar, gold threaded and multi-coloured embroideries and asbestos cloth. No doubt much of this would have been bought in the markets of India and transhipped to the Chinese borders. Nevertheless, excavations have uncovered Roman coins minted from the first century CE and after, including a coin of Maximian (r. 286 to 305 CE) and medallions from the reigns of Antoninus Pius (r. 138–161 CE) and Marcus Aurelius (r. 161–180 CE) in Jiaozhi (in present-day Vietnam). Roman glassware and silverware have been unearthed at Chinese archaeological sites dated to the Han period (202 BC to 220 CE). Roman coins and glass beads have also been found in the Japanese archipelago.[3]

Da Qin was clearly considered a useful ally for the Han Empire so, as we have seen, a diplomatic mission was sent to Rome in 97 CE led by Gan Ying.

For the Romans silk was undoubtedly the main prize. However, unique quality steel played its part in trade between China and the west. We admire Rome for its well-oiled war machine and its cutting edge weaponry. However, it could not compete with Chinese steel when it came to strength and sharpness. Steel was harder than iron, more flexible with a higher tensile strength, more rust resistant than iron and it stayed sharper for longer. The implications for weapons are clear; lethal armour piercing crossbow bolts were a specialty.[4] This superior steel and how to make it was initially concealed from other Steppe nations, but money prevails and the high price it commanded soon led to embargoes being broken; this is how it reached Parthia and the Parthians who lost no time in issuing it to its army. The Battle of Carrhae in 53 BCE, calamitous for Rome, offered the ideal field trial of the superiority of steel over iron with Roman shields and body armour easily penetrated and Parthian lances passing unhindered through Roman bodies. Likewise, the Roman *gladius* and javelins made little impact on steely Parthian armour. The Romans were always behind the curve when it came to steel, even though the Indians mastered the engineering and the production process, selling it in their markets where, of course, it was available to the Romans.[5] Florus describes how at Carrhae the Parthian army was resplendent in their glimmering armour and 'with their standards fluttering with gold and silk pennants'. The Romans were no doubt in awe at the sight but their amazement was short lived when the Parthians then attacked with a vengeance.[6]

Before that the Romans' experience of silk was restricted to that produced from a short-lived grub, notably on the Greek island of Cos. This Coan silk is described by Pliny as 'a luxury fabric ideal for women's clothes'.[7] As it happened, Coan silk was rougher than the oriental type and did not radiate that translucent sheen which so enchanted Propertius and Tibullus, and no doubt other young men about town.[8] By 20 CE the market for Coan was replaced by Chinese, widely regarded as the sheer height of fashion.[9]

During the first century BCE Chinese silk had been a rare thing in Rome, but in the first century availability changed dramatically. We have seen how Pliny bemoaned the effects of the financial drain of bullion from the Roman economy, much of which was expended on Chinese silks. In 14 CE the Senate tried to prohibit the wearing of silk by men, but it continued to pour in anyway. Economic concerns aside, silk clothes were thought by some, like a prim Seneca the Elder, to be decadent.

The Parthians were not the only warriors who found a military use for silk. Silk was an essential feature of Roman triumphs in the first century BCE, with both Pompey and Julius Caesar vying to out-silk each other with extravagant displays of the fabric; the crowds were amazed by this vividly coloured material with its unique translucent sheen shading them from the sun.[10] Caligula made extensive use of it in public ceremonies and receptions for impressionable foreign dignitaries.[11] Theatres and amphitheatres were decked out in it, and silk was soon showing up in all its extravagance in private houses as awnings and upholstery, guaranteed to impress and to be topped by envious neighbours and guests. During Nero's reign from 54 CE silk was piling in from the Roman ports, later decorating the Colosseum.[12]

The discerning Roman man or woman might well have wondered where this wonderful material actually came from. McLaughlin (2016) tells us that:

> 'From the Euphrates frontier in Syria a merchant caravan would have taken at least 100 days to travel across Parthian Iran with a further 50 days to traverse Bactria in the Kushan Empire. From there it was a further 25 days to a trade outpost called Tashkurgan.'

So a minimum of 150 days to cross just the western sections of the silk routes that led to the Tarim kingdoms.[13] Chinese records relating to caravans state that 'more than 10 state sponsored caravans left every year for destinations along the Tarim silk routes'. Moreover, the records suggest that each caravan might comprise up to 600 camels loaded with 10,000 silk rolls – equal to four tons of fabric'.[14] Ten caravans could effectively transport 100,000 rolls – 40 tons of silk.

But, as McLaughlin points out, only a fraction came to Rome, but it was still a prodigious amount of trade when 10 tons converted into 16 million sesterces in Roman markets, sufficient for 8,000 tunics or 16,000 dresses.

Chapter 16

The Assimilation and Adoption of Foreign Ideas and Culture through Trade

The contact between cultures engendered through trade inevitably facilitated and promoted the interchange of ideas and cultural practices, particularly in the areas of language, religion, philosophy, architecture and art.

We all know how travel broadens the mind – a bit of a cliché but true all the same. As in most of the things we do in life, it is impossible to travel without learning something – indeed, often a single journey will teach us lots of things, covering a broad range of experiences. For example, the Romans thought that silk was obtained from trees.

This chapter explores one of the important by-products of Roman travel beyond its borders: as we have seen in the preceding pages, trade was a, if not the, major compelling factor of these peregrinations, as were its corollaries: wealth – personal and state – regional hegemony, defence and political and military stability, which themselves foster and sustain trade. A sense of adventure and a desire to learn from one's experiences abroad and from other peoples and cultures may not have always been uppermost on the agendas of most journeys, but travel for the Romans beyond their *limes* often brought back a lot more than the pecuniary and fashionable benefits of silk, scent, spice and slaves.

By and large, the Romans were, as a civilization, astute enough to realize that it was good policy to learn from one's conquests and alliances and take from them what can be identified as having worked well for them and then repurpose it to benefit the motherland. Trade and religion apart, much of what Roman foreign travellers imported may have been subliminal, accidental even, but whatever, the finer points of barbarian culture, architecture, fine arts, religion, law and literature, to a greater or lesser extent, often found their way back and were assimilated into the Roman way of life, into what is termed 'Romanitas' – Roman-ness.

The Metropolitan Museum of Art in New York sums up this enduring process of culturalization and other civilising influences, following and cross fertilised with trade:

'New inventions, religious beliefs, artistic styles, languages, and social customs, as well as goods and raw materials, were transmitted by people moving from one place to another to conduct business.'[1]

It continues:

'Long-distance trade played a major role in the cultural, religious, and artistic exchanges that took place between the major centers of civilization in Europe and Asia during antiquity ... Cities along these trade routes grew rich providing services to merchants and acting as international marketplaces. Some, like Palmyra and Petra, ... also became cultural and artistic centers, where peoples of different ethnic and cultural backgrounds could meet and intermingle.'

The MMA tells us how the trade routes were the communications highways of the ancient world. These channels are reflected, for example, in the sculptural styles of Gandhara (modern-day Pakistan and northern India) and Gaul (modern-day France), both influenced by the Hellenistic styles popularized by the Romans.[2]

One very visible example of how eastern trade in particular influenced the Roman elite comes with the thousands of mosaics and wall paintings which have survived from domestic homes, temples and government buildings, and are now housed in museums throughout the world, or in situ in culture fertile places like Pompeii and Herculaneum. For example, the Villa Romana del Casale has mosaics depicting the capture of animals in India, Indonesia and Africa.[3]

'In the Ambulacro della Grande Caccia there, the hunting and capture of animals is represented in such detail that it is possible to identify the species. There is a scene that shows a technique to distract a tiger with a shimmering ball of glass or mirror in order to take her cubs. Tiger hunting with red ribbons serving as a distraction is also shown. In the mosaic there are also numerous other animals such as rhinoceros, an Indian elephant (recognized from the ears) with his Indian conductor, and the Indian peafowl, and other exotic birds. There are also numerous animals from Africa. Tigers, leopards and Asian and African lions were used in the arenas and circuses. The European lion was already extinct at that time. Probably the last lived in the Balkan Peninsula and were hunted to stock arenas. The birds and monkeys entertained the guests of many villas. Also in the Villa Romana del Tellaro there is a mosaic with a tiger in the jungle attacking a man with Roman clothes, probably a careless hunter. The animals were transported in cages by ship.'4

The Bardo Museum in Tunis is a goldmine of beautiful mosaics featuring, among other things, vivid hunting scenes.

Here is a brief summary of the salient influences which either the itinerant Roman trader took back to Rome, or else were allowed to percolate into Roman culture:

Etruscan: The Romans were greatly influenced by the Etruscans, particularly in art, architecture, religion

Greek: The Romans admired and borrowed heavily and constantly from Greek culture: notably philosophy, literature, art, and architecture. Many Greek works were translated into Latin, while Greek slaves and teachers played a crucial role in transmitting Greek culture to the Romans as teachers or scribes. Roman towns and cities are, of course, awash with Greek style buildings throughout the empire.

Hellenistic: Alexander the Great and the subsequent Hellenistic kingdoms had a profound impact on the Roman Empire. Hellenistic culture, which combined Greek elements with influences from the Middle East and Egypt, had an impact on Roman art, philosophy, and religion.

Near Eastern: As we have seen, the Roman Empire came into contact with and was influenced by various ancient Near Eastern cultures, including those of Egypt, Persia, and Mesopotamia. These cultures had an influence on Roman art, architecture, religious practices, and trade.

Celtic and Germanic: As the Roman Empire expanded into Gaul and parts of Germany and Britain, it encountered Celtic and Germanic peoples. The Romans integrated aspects of their culture, such as language, clothing, and military tactics.

Arabia: Spices revolutionised Roman cuisine, while heady incense redefined luxury in the Roman world and played a key role in Roman religion.

China: Luxury was again redefined with the import of silk into the Roman Empire on a huge scale. The Chinese also showed the Romans that they were not the only military force to be reckoned with: Chinese steel was far and away more lethal and versatile than Rome's old iron weaponry.

Such was the power of international trade: to bring with it profound changes in society, culture and established religious practices, which is evidence for the significance of material culture in the process of globalization amongst the Romans.

Cultural globalization has been defined as the process of spreading ideas, values, and meanings around the world, which can lead to increased social relations and inclusiveness and enhanced diversification.

The Silk Road and Culturalization

The Silk Road (or Silk Routes) – effectively connecting trade routes between western and eastern civilizations from the start of the second century BCE – is a late-nineteenth century term and denotes a 6,400 kilometre complex network of sea and mainly land routes linking up Central East, South, Southeast, and West Asia, along with East Africa and Southern Europe. As such, it is indicative of and exemplifies the cultural superhighways described above, bringing all manner of goods from the east to a luxury- and product-hungry Roman empire. Textiles, incense and spices were among the main cargoes, but the range and depth of the commodities was at once both profound and extensive.

For example:

- Roman glassware discovered in the archaeological sites of Gyeongju, the capital of the Silla kingdom, demonstrates that Roman artefacts were traded as far east as the Korean peninsula.[5]
- The Graeco-Roman trade with India instigated by Eudoxus of Cyzicus in 130 BCE continued apace, and according to Strabo (II.5.12), by Augustan times up to 120 ships were heading from Myos Hormos in Roman Egypt to India.
- The Roman traders connected with the Central Asian Silk Road through their ports in Barygaza (modern Bharuch) and Barbaricum (modern Karachi) and proceeded down the western coast of India.[6] All of this and much more can be found in the invaluable maritime travel resource that is the *Periplus of the Erythraean Sea* written in 60 CE.
- When Rome was not battling with Parthia it was the expedition of Maës Titianus in the early-second century CE or at the end of the first century which penetrated farthest east along the Silk Road, no doubt in a bid to eliminate the middle man forever and so reducing margins.[7]

We have noted above when mentioning how educative travel and first-hand experience was and is in the context of silk and the Roman belief that it grew on trees as affirmed by Seneca the Younger in his *Phaedra* and by Virgil in the *Georgics*. Pliny the Elder, though, put the record straight a few years later when discussing the *bombyx* or silk moth in his *Natural History*: 'They weave webs, like spiders, that become a luxurious clothing material for women, called silk'.[8] The eager Romans also bartered spices, glassware, and perfumes.[9]

But there was, obviously, an economic (and social) price to all of this. While the Chinese grew increasingly wealthy, there were those back in Rome anxiously monitoring the significant outflow of gold to pay for it all. Moreover, there were those who considered translucent and slinky silk clothing decadent and immoral in women and men. It was all not terribly Roman, and particularly embarrassing in the light of the legislation Augustus was struggling to enforce to curb the general malaise he saw in his society. The Roman Senate enacted sumptuary legislation to ban the wearing of silk, on economic and moral grounds. It is worth repeating how a strait-laced Seneca the Younger splutters:

> 'I can see clothes of silk, if materials that do not hide the body, nor even one's decency, can be called clothes. ... Wretched flocks of maids labour so that the adulteress may be visible through her thin dress, so that her husband has no more acquaintance than any outsider or foreigner with his wife's body.'[10]

We can detect the strengthening role of the powerful merchants from Bactria and Taxila in the unification of Central Asia and Northern India within the Kushan Empire between the first and third centuries.[11] They were responsible for fostering multi-cultural interaction, as evidenced by their second-century treasure hoards filled with products from Graeco-Roman, Chinese, and Indian trade, such as those excavated at Begram.

Slaves were also part of the trade and connected the Silk Road slave trade to the slave trades at Bukhara and the Black Sea, particularly for slave girls.[12]

Chapter 17

Eastern Religions in the Roman Empire

Religion was, and remains, one of the important areas in which the cross-fertilization and osmotic behaviour of cultural influences is most apparent. Matthias Helble, in the abstract to his paper, *On the Influence of World Religions on International Trade*, outlines the situation generally with the interconnection between trade and the spread and accretion of religion:[1]

'As the world economy is integrating, trade between countries is growing rapidly. The exchange of goods not only has an economic, but also a cultural dimension. This paper investigates the possible ways that religion influences international trade patterns. It studies the view of the five world religions, namely Hinduism, Judaism, Buddhism, Christianity, and Islam, on economic activity, and trade in particular. Analyzing empirically trade flows between 151 countries, the paper finds an impact of religion on trade. Furthermore, the results indicate that religious openness boosts trade performance of countries.'

In 2014, Peter Wick stated in his introductory chapter to *Religions and Trade: Religious Formation, Transformation and Cross-Cultural Exchange between East and West*:[2]

'The relationship between religion and trade is complex and multi-layered. Both impact on one another in manifold ways ... The thirteen articles of this volume engage with religions and trade from different angles and offer a kaleidoscopic view of this broad field of study. A group of international scholars investigates, from the perspective of trade, the various processes in the formation and transformation of eastern and western religions from the time of their emergence. Looking at religious dynamics from the viewpoint of trade proves to be profitable since different cultures and religions have been (and still are) brought into contact with one another in places of commerce and along transregional and transcontinental routes of trade. Trade – in the sense of a real exchange of (physical) goods between people – thus leads to contact and interaction between people of different faiths.

In this context, various ideas and religious 'commodities' are exchanged – 'offered', 'negotiated' and 'bought'. Thus, a more metaphorical notion of trade comes to the fore when religious goods are exported and imported, not exclusively but particularly on the basis of (literal) trade contacts. It is a metaphorical notion of trade not least because the exchange is not always intentional, nor does it need to be reciprocal. Both notions of trade (commercial and metaphorical) are closely intertwined and can mutually reinforce one another. Both lead to expansion and densification as well as the amalgamation of religions and religious traditions.'

The UNESCO Silk Roads Programme tells us that:

'The Silk Routes were of great importance in the passage of not only goods and crafts but also of religions and ideologies throughout Central Asia, the Near East and Europe. Buddhism spread from India into northern Asia, Mongolia, and China, whilst Christianity and Islam emerged and were disseminated by trade, pilgrims, and military conquest. The literary, architectural and artistic effects of this can be traced today in the cultures of civilizations along the Silk Routes.'
https://en.unesco.org/silkroad/themes/religion-and-spirituality?page=7

Traditional Roman religion was built around a large, gendered and incestuous polytheistic pantheon, where the gods and goddesses governed and controlled everything that happened to Romans in the real Roman world, in their current lives and in the next. Everyone had recourse and access to these divinities; everyone could see them all around – painted on walls, erected in statuary, incorporated into and onto buildings, stamped on their coins, laid out in mosaics on the floor. If they could read, they could learn about them from, for example, Homer's *Odyssey*, Lucretius' *de Rerum Natura*, Cicero's *On the Nature of the Gods*, or Ovid's *Metamorphoses*; if illiterate, then theology or mythology could be read to them verbatim or communicated in stories; they could see them on the stage, comedic or tragic; the Roman would also see his or her gods at countless festivals and in temples – in short, Roman gods were omnipresent and ubiquitous. Both Cicero and Virgil say so: 'God covers all things: the earth, the open seas and the vast skies'.[1]

The Romans enjoyed a gendered and incestuous polytheistic pantheon, where the gods and goddesses governed and controlled everything that happened to Romans in the real Roman world, in their current lives and in the next. Trade, journeys, voyages, borders, profit and communications were no exception and the god who looked after these was Mercury. Mercury, therefore, is important to us because he was important to the traders and merchants described in this book.

Over time state religion had become rather staid, spiritually bankrupt and impersonal by the end of the Republic.[2] A reverential Varro, in 47 BCE, was so concerned by this decline and indifference that he wrote a book about Roman religion, lest history allow it to be forgotten. His *Human and Divine Antiquities* contains sixteen books describing the festivals, rites, priests, temples, divinities and institutions. Ovid, too, lists the various festivals and liturgies in his *Fasti*.

Official Roman religion was essentially founded on and catered for an agricultural society. For example, Jupiter made the crops grow with his rain and sun; Saturn encouraged sowing; Ceres promoted growth. As Rome's possessions increased and more of the world was Romanized, as Rome became more urbanised and cosmopolitan, then, with the syncretization of exotic and mysterious foreign gods and goddesses, traditional Roman religion gradually lost its relevance to Roman life and culture. It became unexciting and unappealing, so men and women turned to and embraced the new, oriental, mystery religions which they came into contact with, and which percolated into Roman society. With the exception of Mithraism which was exclusively for men, these cults, particularly the cult of Isis, offered women an active role in the priesthood; the cults could be personalised and customised to meet the needs of individuals, be they man or woman, and because their eschatology often enshrined birth and rebirth they offered hope of life after death, immortality.

It was not just spices, incense, slaves and silk that poured into Rome in the wake of the fleets of merchants who sailed the seas and rivers, crossed deserts and traversed mountains as far west as Britannia, as far north as Finland, as far south as Lake Chad and as far east as India, Burma, Vietnam and China. No, something considerably less tangible was insinuating itself into Roman life, something just as exotic and foreign was percolating into Roman culture – and that something was foreign religion as practised by barbarians – eastern religions that promised a lot more for their acolytes and adherents than Jupiter and Diana; mystery religions which were all the more tantalising because of their innate mysteriousness which could only be demystified through initiation and total commitment.

Here are a few:

The *Bona Dea*

The *Bona Dea*, Good Goddess, came in from the cities of Magna Graecia, during the early or middle Republic, and was granted her own state cult on the Aventine Hill.

In vivid contrast to the more relaxed, and objective account by Plutarch,[3] Juvenal launches an excoriating attack on the patrician women performing the rites of the *Bona Dea*, describing them as drunken maenads, crazed with desire for unabated sex, which, if it cannot be satisfied by an *adulter*, can be sated by the *adulter's* son, or by slaves, or the water carrier; as a last resort an ass will take them in the arse: *inposito clunem sumittat asello*.[4] The cult first appeared in Rome around 272 BCE, during the Tarentine War; *Bona Dea* was associated with chastity and fertility and the protection of Rome. As an equivalent to Fauna she could prophesy the fates of women. She had two festivals: one at her temple on the Aventine; the other at the home of the Pontifex Maximus of the day. Her Aventine cult, in which a blood sacrifice took place on 1 May, was re-dedicated in 123 BCE by the Vestal Virgin Licinia; but this was annulled as unlawful by the Senate: Licinia was later charged with unchastity, and entombed, her life slowly ebbing away unprovisioned in isolation, darkness and unimaginable fear.[5]

Although *Bona Dea* was celebrated by men and women alike,[6] in the domestic rite which took place annually on 3 December all males were banished, even male animals and pictures or statues of males. Only *matronae* and the Vestal Virgins were present; the Vestals brought in *Bona Dea's* image from her temple and a meal of sow's entrails was eaten, sacrificed to her on behalf of the Roman people, and sacrificial wine. The 'fun' (*ludere*) lasted all night with female musicians, games and sacrificial wine, euphemistically called 'milk', from a 'honey jar'. This was not a feeble attempt to conceal clandestine drinking; rather, it came about when Faunus, married to the Good Goddess, caught her out, drinking surreptitiously and beat her to death with a myrtle branch. Myrtle was also associated with Aphrodite and with sex; as such it was alien to the rites and banned. The *matronae* refrained from sexual activity in the run up to the festival. According to Cicero, any man caught observing the rites could be punished by blinding.[7]

Bona Dea was jealously protected by its adherents, so when the high profile rites of 62 BCE hosted chez Julius Caesar as Pontifex Maximus that year were infiltrated by a high profile man, the ensuing scandal was huge, not least because Caesar's mother, Aurelia Cotta, Pompeia his wife, and his sister, Julia, and the Vestals were all there. According to Juvenal, any sexual propriety that had remained in Rome evaporated that night: Publius Clodius Pulcher (Juvenal's *lute girl with a penis – psaltria penem ... intulit*) sacrilegiously gate-crashed the rites. The scandal led to Caesar divorcing Pompeia: she was implicated – and, of course, Caesar's wife must not be under suspicion.

The Bacchanalia

The cult of Bacchus was also, at first, exclusively female, and notorious for the frenzy and shrieking of its adherents, the sonorous beat of drums and the clashing of cymbals. It had huge popular appeal even before men were admitted: Livy described its spread as an epidemic; it excited the sexual emotions in women.[8] Officially, it was regarded as an unsettling conspiracy against Rome, when an Etrurian initiate was suspected of secret and mysterious nocturnal sacrifices and soothsaying. Originally, it was relatively harmless with daytime rites three times a year and *matronae* as priestesses; we know from Cicero that nocturnal rites generally were illegal, as was initiation, except in the rites of Ceres.[9] Things changed dramatically when a priestess called Paculla Annia started initiating men, the rites were moved to night time and took place a very frequent five times every month. The intoxicating mix of wine, the dark, women and then men was explosive, with *orgia* on a grand scale involving hetero- and homosexual sex, and providing a platform for perjury, forgery, poisoning and murder. The initiation of men was seen officially as tantamount to displacing and tempting them from the sanctity of the *familia* and of the state.

It all came to a head in 186 BCE when Publius Aebutius was targeted by his greedy stepfather who, with the boy's mother, Durenia, conspired to dispose of him by enrolling him in the Bacchanalia, so sure were they that he was bound to come to harm. Aebutius' girlfriend, Hispala Faecina, a reforming prostitute who had witnessed the orgiastic rites as an initiate, was horrified when she heard this and dissuaded Aebutius from going along with it. Such was the notoriety of the cult and the hazards involved, including routine ritual male rape, any opposition to which resulted in summary sacrifice. On the advice of his aunt, Aebutia, Aebutius reported the matter to the consul, Spurius Postumius, whose wife Sulpicia then interviewed both Aebutia and Hispala to establish their integrity; Hispala, understandably reluctant at first, eventually agreed to reveal all, taking up residence in Postumius' house for safety. The outcome was that, according to Livy, 7,000 Bacchantes were prosecuted under the *Senatus Consultum de Bacchanalibus*, many of whom fled Rome or committed suicide.[10] A manhunt ensued and imprisonments and executions followed; many of the convicted women were handed over to their *paterfamilias* for the family to dispense justice; most of the Bacchic shrines in Rome and throughout Italy were then destroyed. Both whistle-blowers were handsomely rewarded, a measure of the deep concern the rite caused the authorities and of their determination to stamp it out.[11]

Cybele

An early, and officially sanctioned, import from Asia Minor was Cybele, or *Magna Mater* – a deity with obvious relevance to and association with women; she was a universal earth mother who looked out for all things maternal and represented rebirth and immortality through the resurrection of Attis. The couple are vividly celebrated in Catullus 63; Ovid describes Attis in detail in the *Fasti*.[12]

Cybele was brought to Rome in 204 BCE after consultation of the *Sibylline Books* revealed that victory over the Carthaginians could only be ensured by her presence – according to Livy the *Books* decreed that any foe will be expelled if the Idaean mother is brought from Pessinus to Rome. A delegation was promptly dispatched to Phrygia to bring back a meteoric stone symbolising the deity.[13] The stone had originally been brought from Pessinus to Pergamum by King Attalus I, and lodged in the Megalesion shrine there.[14] Publius Cornelius Scipio (the future Nasica) was the official receiver at Ostia, chosen as the noblest man (*vir optimus*) in Rome at the time; he handed the 'goddess' over to a delegation of *matronae* who took her on to Rome. One of these was Quinta Claudia, a *matrona* whose *pudicitia* (chastity) had been questioned; however, she scotched all rumours and emphatically restored her reputation that day: the boat carrying the delegation ran aground in the Tiber and soothsayers declared that it could only be refloated by a *matrona* whose reputation was above question. Claudia, seeing an opportunity, grabbed the rope and refloated the boat, and her reputation with it. The *Magna Mater* was duly installed in the Temple of Victory on the Palatine; she received her own temple there in 191 BCE and games, the *Ludi Megalenses*, were set up in her honour.

Once the cult was established, however, the Roman authorities must have wished that they had taken more care over what they had wished for. The orgiastic, frenzied rites, the eunuchs, the wild dancing, the self-castration and other acts of self-harm by adherents – the Galli – were all quite alien and objectionable to the Romans: measures were taken to control the cult and to marginalise it as far as possible. Lucretius has an excellent and vivid account of a display of Cybelean rites where he describes the Galli as 'crazy eunuch priests, and their violent frenzy'.[15]

The Cult of Isis

Herodotus (2,40) had introduced the Romans to Isis in the fifth century BCE when he told how, in her homeland, in sacrifices to Isis the stomach cavity of a sacrificial ox was richly stuffed with bread, raisins, figs, honey, frankincense and myrrh before being roasted and feasted on. The scent coming off those oxen must have been divine and intoxicating.

The distinctly oriental Cult of Isis spread rapidly and, like a rash, spread through Italy from Egypt and in Augustan Rome had instant appeal to women – not surprisingly, because Isis was associated with a number of recognisable Roman female deities such as Athena, Aphrodite, Hera, Demeter and Artemis.

Isis was universally seen as caring and compassionate to her female flock, making valued time for each of her initiates. Moreover, Isis was adaptable and versatile: she was all things to all men, or rather all women: one inscription describes her perfectly: 'goddess Isis, you who are one and all'. Moreover, as a mortal she had lived a life that was instantly recognisable to her adherents: she was a woman and a mother who had known grief and bereavement; women would have empathised with Isis' role as a mother, depicted as she often was holding an infant in her arms. This was Horus, the offspring of her incestuous relationship with Osiris, her brother. Isis had worked the streets and brothels as a prostitute in Tyre; her appeal was to the widest range of female Roman society. She was beneficent and came to be associated with fertility – every year when she saw famine afflicting Egypt, she wept in sorrow so that her copious tears replenished the Nile and irrigated the flood plains. As a kind of early feminist she instigated the Egyptian tradition of honouring queens above kings, as exemplified recently in the Roman civil war by the power and influence wielded by Cleopatra VII; in short, 'she made women just as powerful as men'. Death and resurrection was there to be seen in the rejuvenated Egyptian lands and the death and rebirth of Osiris, also her husband.

In the early-second century CE the novelist Apuleius gives us a vivid and illuminating description of the initiation of Lucius into the rites of Isis in his *Metamorphoses*: these extracts give a taste of the exotic and a glimpse of the very un-Roman nature of the cult:

> 'Then came a great throng, of men as well as women, with lamps, candles, torches, and other lights, doing honour to her that was born of the heavenly stars. After that came the musical harmony of instruments, pipes and flutes in most pleasant rhythm. Then came a fair company of young men dressed in white singing both metre and verse with a lovely grace which some studious poet had made by favour of the Muses ... then arrived the trumpeters ... Then came a great company of men and women of all ranks and every age who were initiates and had taken divine orders, whose garments, being of the whitest linen, glistened all through the streets. The women had their hair anointed, and their heads covered with light linen; but the men had their heads shaven and shining bright ... Another [initiate] carried the secrets of their glorious religion, enclosed in a coffer'.
> Apuleius, The Golden Ass or Metamorphoses 11, *7ff; translation adapted from W. Adlington (1566) and revised by S. Gaselee 1922*

Juvenal mocks and scorns women disciples to this and to other oriental cults.[16] At Isis celebrations women, dressed head-to-toe in white, sprayed their hair with perfume; they strewed the roads with flowers and perfumes and even attached mirrors on their backs to catch a reflection of Isis as she approached them from behind and with ivory combs they made as if to comb the goddesses' hair.

The accessibility and inclusiveness of the cult of Isis with its potential appeal of up to 50 per cent of the population of Rome, set it apart from traditional Roman religion: it represented an opportunity for women to attain high religious office and become priestesses. One inscription shows us six female Isis *sacerdotes* (out of twenty-six), one of which was a woman of senatorial rank, another the daughter of a freedman, Usia Prima.[17] Around one third of Isis' devotees cited in Italian inscriptions are women.

Suspicion and paranoia grew in official and state quarters in equal measure to its blossoming popularity. Augustus recognised in Isis a disturbing reincarnation of that *fatale monstrum*, Cleopatra, and a threat to his license-curbing, moral legislation: in 28 BCE he banned the building of temples of Isis within Rome and in 21 BCE extended this to an exclusion zone around the city.

The anti-Isis hysteria reached its zenith under Tiberius after a well-publicised scandal involving a well-to-do *matrona*, Paulina, and the equestrian Decius Mundus. The mischievous priests of Isis had convinced Paulina that Anubis himself would like nothing more than to have sex with her in the temple; Anubis, of course, was none other than a decked-out Decius Mundus who had bribed the conspiratorial priests to facilitate his seduction. The tactless, and foolish, equestrian boasted of his conquest and word inevitably reached Tiberius: Mundus was exiled, the priests were crucified and thousands of Isis worshippers were expelled from the Rome to exile on Sardinia.[18]

The scandal is interesting because it not only shows that it was permissible and unremarkable for a Roman *matrona* to visit a temple of Isis but it also vindicates, to some extent, Juvenal's scorn for the gullibility of women dabbling in such cults.

Caligula was the first emperor to spot the substantial political kudos to be gained from support for such a popular cult, with its huge constituency: he built a temple to Isis in the Campus Martius within the walls of Rome – and the goddess never really looked back.

Mithras

Mithraism was a mystery religion based around the god Mithras and practised in the Roman Empire from the first to the fourth century CE. The religion was inspired by Persian Zoroastrianism worship of the god Mithra. However, Roman Mithras has few similarities to his Zoroastrian precursor, although he does retain his Phrygian cap and other clothing, for example, as a visual reminder of his eastern origins. Mithras was eternally at war with the forces of evil. According to legend he captured a bull – symbolic of primeval force and vitality – and slew it in a cave (*tauroctony*), to release its concentrated power for the good of mankind. Mithraism offered an escape from darkness into light but required in return a lifelong commitment, hence its popularity with the military to whom such long-term allegiances were routine.

Mithraic temples were typically small, gloomy, semi-subterranean places, intended to evoke the legendary cave where Mithras killed the bull. Inside, secret ceremonies would be followed by ritual feasts, the devotees reclining on benches (*podia*) running along the side walls.

Michael White (1997) tells us that the cult of Mithras was especially popular in Ostia, as shown by the discovery of eighteen Mithraea. Ostia was also home to the Ostia Synagogue, the earliest synagogue yet to be discovered in Europe.[19] The building dates from the reign of Claudius (41–54 CE) and continued in use as a synagogue into the fifth century CE.

Serapis

We first meet Serapis in Memphis, a Greco-Egyptian deity of the Sun, where his cult was celebrated in conjunction with that of the bull Apis. Serapis was originally a god of the underworld but was reborn as a new Hellenised deity by Ptolemy I Soter (r. 305–284 BCE), who centred the worship at Alexandria and was looking to unify the Greek and Egyptian subjects of the Ptolemaic Kingdom.

The Serapeum at Alexandria represented Serapis as a regally robed and bearded figure, his right hand resting on the three-headed underworld guard dog, Cerberus, lying at his feet, and a sceptre in his left hand. Over time healing and fertility were added to his portfolio. He came to Rome and the wider Mediterranean on the trade routes and was especially popular in ports and commercial cities. At Rome, Serapis was worshipped in the *Iseum Campense*, the sanctuary of Isis built on the Campus Martius. The Roman cults of Isis and Serapis grew more popular in the later first century.

In York archaeologists unearthed in 1770 a dedication of a temple to Serapis by the Commander of Legio VI, Claudius Hieronymianus.

The Eleusinian Mysteries

The Eleusinian Mysteries initiations were held annually for the cult of Demeter and Persephone based at the Panhellenic Sanctuary of Eleusis. They are considered the 'most famous of the secret religious rites of ancient Greece'. Burkett tells us that 'The rites, ceremonies, and beliefs were kept secret and consistently preserved from antiquity. For the initiated, the rebirth of Persephone symbolized the eternity of life which flows from generation to generation, and they believed that they would have a reward in the afterlife'. Augustus himself was initiated into the Eleusinian Mysteries while in Athens.[20]

It seems that the different mystery religions may have attracted different, distinct socio-economic demographics: the middle classes of Roman cities inclined toward the Dionysiac societies; Isis was worshipped by lower middle class people in the seaports and trading towns, while followers of the *Magna Mater* were mainly craftsmen.

Epilogue

So, the inquisitive Roman we met in the Introduction, were he or she to have a 'book' such as this to hand, would know by now the many and various origins of all that produce and the foreign flora and fauna, laid out on display in his buzzing downtown market. Most of it, he has learnt, came not from the confines of his empire, but from mysterious far-off lands beyond the porous borders of that empire – from Britannia and the Nordic countries, from Arabia to Nubia; from India to Vietnam, from China to Burma.

Exotic birds and animals astonished and amazed him or her: flamingoes and tortoise shells, elephants, tigers and rhinos were caged and for sale: amber and diaphanous silk tempted fashion-conscious women (and some men), while beryl and amber bejewelled them; cinnamon, saffron, pepper and dill flavoured the meat, while myrrh and frankincense filled the air with their heady perfumes.

While he or she paused a while to take it all in, he or she may have been aware of the very real fiscal problems caused by traders buying up all these commodities using diminishing treasury gold and silver and almost trashing Rome's economy; but this did not stop traders scrambling for business in Africa, Arabia, Ceylon, India and Malaya.

Trade, he or she would have realized, brought with it other benefits for the Romans. Slaves and prostitutes disembarked by the boat-load and the old staid Olympian religion was revivified with exciting, vibrant, party-like and woman-friendly, decadent mystery cults celebrating eastern Isis, Mithras, Cybele and Bona Dea.

The Silk Road didn't just expedite the trade in see-through silks, nutmeg, cloves and star anise; along its various dusty tracks plodded caravans of camels burdened with tea, dyes, steel and porcelain. Our curious Roman wouldn't care, or even know that, gold apart, by comparison our mercantile offer to the Chinese and Indian was comparatively dull and unexceptional: horses, honey, wine and the like.

The Silk Road was, along with other market places, routes and roads and entrepôts like it, also an information superhighway, a precursor to our internet, disseminating culture, knowledge, language, communication skills, religion, philosophy, art, literature and architecture through convivial gatherings of salesmen, students, scholars and scribes in the many bustling bazaars along the route. Such cultural exchange, as we all know, nurtures and promotes trade and productivity. War and conflict have the opposite effect, so commerce also is an eloquent ambassador and advocate for peace – despite the ever-troublesome Parthians.

And this is exactly what our curious Roman observed and experienced when he or she cast their astonished eyes over their bustling local market.

Appendix

The Second-Hand Book Trade in Brundisium

As an example of the second-hand book trade as it operated in the port of Brundisium around 150 CE, we have the account of author Aulus Gellius when he found a second-hand bookstall, quite by chance. The books he chanced upon were what we call paradoxography – a little-known genre which contains works describing the miraculous and astonishing.[1]

As I say in the introduction to my *Miracula* (London, 2024), what survives of the literature of Greece and Rome is replete with wondrous tales, astounding facts, odd and marvellous events, that never cease to astonish and to stretch credulity to its limits. Some are well known, many others less so, recorded for us by obscure authors or left to languish in the darker corners of works by more familiar writers, such as Herodotus' *Histories*, Aristotle, Plato, Strabo (geography) and Pausanias (Greece); and then there is Pliny the Elder's encyclopaedic *Natural History*, Suetonius' *Lives of the Caesars*, the *Annals* of Tacitus (2, 24; 6, 28; 11, 21) and the work of Gaius Licinius Mucianus (*fl.* first century AD), whose natural history and geography of the East was an important source for Pliny the Elder when foraging for things miraculous for his *Natural History*.

Aulus Gellius (AD *c.* 125–180), a Roman author and grammarian, conveniently gives us a real-life instance of paradoxography, not to say serendipity, which neatly defines the genre and leaves us thirsting for more. Here is what he says:

'When I was returning from Greece to Italy and had reached Brundisium, I got off the boat and was mooching about in that famous port ... There I saw some bundles of books for sale, and I eagerly hurried over to them. Now, they were all in Greek, filled with marvellous tales, things unheard of, incredible; the writers were ancient and authoritative: Aristeas of Proconnesus, Isigonus of Nicaea, Ctesias and Onesicritus, Philostephanus and Hegesias. The volumes themselves, however, were grubby from long neglect, in bad condition and dog-eared. Nevertheless, I went up and asked their price; then, taken in by their extraordinary and unexpected cheapness, I bought lots of them for a small amount, and quickly read through all of them over the next two nights ...

'This is the sort of stuff contained in those books: the most remote of the Scythians, who live in the far north, eat human flesh and subsist on the nourishment of that food, are called "cannibals". Also there are men in the same region having one eye in the middle of the forehead and are called Arimaspi, who look like what the poets call Cyclopes. There are also in the same part of the world other men, of marvellous swiftness, whose feet are turned backwards and do not point forward, as in the rest of mankind. Further, tradition has it that in a distant land called Albania men are born whose hair turns white in childhood and who see better by night than during the day. It was absolutely certain that the Sauromatae, who dwell far away beyond the river Borysthenes, take food only every other day and fast on the intervening day.' (*Aulus Gellius*, Attic Nights 9, 4)[2]

Notes

Introduction
1. After Tacitus, in *Agricola* 10, where he was probably referring to the far-flung Orkneys.
2. Scheidel, Walter (April 2006). 'Population and demography' (PDF). *Princeton/Stanford Working Papers in Classics*. p. 9.; Hanson, J. W., Ortman, S. G. (2017). 'A systematic method for estimating the populations of Greek and Roman settlements'. *Journal of Roman Archaeology* 30: 301–324.
3. Wheeler, Sir Mortimer, (1954), *Rome Beyond the Imperial Frontiers*, p. 15
4. Horace, *Odes* 3, 29. See Rudd, N. (1991). 'Two Invitations: Tennyson 'To the Rev. F. D. Maurice' and Horace to Maecenas ('Odes' III.29)', *Hermathena*, 150, 5–19.
5. Cicero, Pro *Lege Manilia*, 7,19–66 BCE.
6. Not least Raoul McLaughlin's *The Roman Empire and the Indian Ocean* (2014) and *The Roman Empire and The Silk Routes* (2016).

Chapter 2: Roman Trade
1. Serrati, J. (2006). 'Neptune's Altars: The Treaties between Rome and Carthage (509–226 BC)', *The Classical Quarterly*, 56(1), 113–134.
2. Horace, *Epistles* 2, 1, 156–157.
3. See Temin, Peter, (2013), p. 13 and Goldsworthy, (2016), p. 392.
4. For details of other belligerent women see Chrystal, Paul, (2020), *Women at War in the Classical World* and Chrystal, Paul, (2024), *World-Changing Women: 150 Women Who Rewrote the Histories of Ancient Egypt, Israel, Greece & Rome*.
5. See Marzano, Annalisa, (2013), *Harvesting the Sea: The Exploitation of Marine Resources in the Roman Mediterranean*, Oxford University Press. pp. 270ff.
6. Livy, 21, 63.
7. Hopkins, Keith, (2017), *Sociological Studies in Roman History*, Cambridge University Press. p. 169. See also Cartwright, (2018), 'The Romans are Celebrated for their Roads but in fact, it remained much cheaper to transport goods by sea rather than by river or land as the cost ratio was approximately' 1:5:28.
8. Young, Gary K., (2003), *Rome's Eastern Trade: International Commerce and Imperial Policy 31 BC–AD 305* Routledge, p. 35–48.
9. *II Verr.* V18.
10. Cato, *De.Agr.* 1.3.
11. Livy, 21.63.3–4.
12. John H. D'Arms, (1981), *Commerce and Social Standing in Ancient Rome*, chapter 3, Harvard University Press.
13. *De.Agr. Praefatio*.
14. 6.56.1–3.
15. Tacitus, *Annals*, 4.13.2.
16. Plutarch, *Cato the Elder*, 21.5ff. Kessler, David, and Temin, Peter, (2007), 'The Organization of the Grain Trade in the Early Roman Empire', *The Economic History Review* 60, no. 2 (2007): 313–315.

17. Potter, David Stone, *A Companion to the Roman Empire*, p. 293, Blackwell.
18. (1994), *Law and Life of Rome*, p. 229, Cornell University Press, 1994.
19. Ward-Perkins, Bryan, (2005), *The Fall of Rome: and the End of Civilization*, pp. 91–92, Oxford University Press.
20. Lancaster, (2005), in her *Concrete Vaulted Construction in Imperial Rome: Innovations in Context*, p. 81, Cambridge University Press.
21. Julian Bennett (1997), *Trajan: Optimus Princeps: A Life and Times*, p. 2, Routledge.
22. J. Theodore Peña, *Roman Pottery in the Archaeological Record*, p. 174–178, Cambridge University Press.
23. https://www.archaeology.org/exclusives/articles/2892-rome-monte-testaccio-amphoras
24. https://www.worldhistory.org/article/638/trade-in-the-roman-world/
25. See Chrystal, (2021).
26. Safrai, (1994), p. 78.
27. Charles, (2009), pp. 9–12.
28. Claudius had personal experience of mob reactions to grain shortages, having been subjected to personal abuse during a bread riot.
29. Haywood, John, (2000), *Historical Atlas of the Classical World, 500 BC–AD 600*.
30. Rickman, (1980), p. 262.
31. Rickman, (2002), 114–1, 353–362.
32. Rickman, G.E. (1980), p.263. See Augustus, *Res Gestae* 15, Josephus, *Jewish War* 2,16,4 for the figures, and Hopkins (1983), *Model Ships and Staples*, p. 86.
33. *Historia Augusta: The Life of Septimius Severus*, 1.8.5; Taylor, Rabun, (2010), 'Bread and Water; Septimus Severus and the Rise of the Curator Aquarum et Miniciae', *Memoirs of the American Academy in Rome*, Vol 55, pp. 199–200.
34. Rickman (1980), pp. 262–264.
35. https://www.worldhistory.org/article/638/trade-in-the-roman-world/
36. For details of Roman York, see Chrystal, Paul, (2022), *A Historical Guide to Roman York*.
37. Harper, Kyle, (2017), *The Fate of Rome: Climate, Disease, and the End of an Empire*. See Chrystal, Paul, (2021), *A History of the World in 100 Pandemics, Plagues and Epidemics* for full details.
38. de Crespigny, Rafe, (2007), *A Biographical Dictionary of Later Han to the Three Kingdoms (23–220 AD)*, Leiden. Rafe de Crespigny mused in the 1930s that the small pox plagues afflicting the Eastern Han Empire during the reigns of Emperor Huan of Han (r. 146–168) and Emperor Ling of Han (r. 168–189) – with outbreaks in 151, 161, 171, 173, 179, 182, and 185 – were possibly connected to the Antonine plague on the western fringes of Eurasia. De Crespigny suggests that 'it may be only chance' that the outbreak of the Antonine plague in 166 coincides with the Roman embassy of 'Daqin' (the Roman Empire) landing in Jiaozhi (northern Vietnam) and visiting the Han court of Emperor Huan, claiming to represent 'Andun' (安敦; a transliteration of Marcus Aurelius Antoninus or his predecessor Antoninus Pius).
39. McLaughlin, R., (2010), *Rome and the Distant East: Trade Routes to the Ancient Lands of Arabia, India, and China*, London.

Chapter 3: The Borders of Empire (*Limes*)
1. Breeze, David J., (2011), *The Frontiers of Imperial Rome*, pp 5–6; see Lewis & Short, *ad loc*.
2. See Chrystal, Paul, (2019), *The Romans in the North of England*, Darlington
3. https://www.militaer-wissen.de/the-roman-limes-border-wall/?lang=en

Chapter 4: Communications: Getting Goods to and from Market

1. Logistics is a part of supply chain management that deals with the efficient forward and reverse flow of goods, services, and related information from the point of origin to the point of consumption according to the needs of customers. Logistics management is a component that binds the supply chain together.
2. *The Tabula Peutingeriana* (Peutinger Table) is an *itinerarium* showing the *cursus publicus*, the road network in the Roman Empire. The original map dates from the fourth century. It covers Europe, parts of Asia (India) and North-Africa. The map is named after Konrad Peutinger, a German fifteenth-sixteenth century humanist and antiquarian. The map was discovered in a library in Worms by Conrad Celtes, who was unable to publish his find before his death, and bequeathed the map in 1508 to Peutinger. It is at the Österreichische Nationalbibliothek, Hofburg, Vienna.
3. See Faigenbaum-Golovin S, et al., (2017), 'Multispectral Imaging Reveals Biblical-Period Inscription Unnoticed for Half a Century', *PLoS ONE* 12(6): e0178400.
4. This is how *ORBIS: The Stanford Geospatial Network Model of the Roman World* introduces its useful groundbreaking model of communication costs:

    'Spanning one-ninth of the earth's circumference across three continents, the Roman Empire ruled a quarter of humanity through complex networks of political power, military domination and economic exchange. These extensive connections were sustained by premodern transportation and communication technologies that relied on energy generated by human and animal bodies, winds, and currents ... For the first time, ORBIS allows us to express Roman communication costs in terms of both time and expense. By simulating movement along the principal routes of the Roman road network, the main navigable rivers, and hundreds of sea routes in the Mediterranean, Black Sea and coastal Atlantic, this interactive model reconstructs the duration and financial cost of travel in antiquity. The website allows the creation of routes along a few selected major roads across the empire, according to the setting of various variables such as fastest/cheapest/shortest, month of travel distance, time etc.'

    https://orbis.stanford.edu/orbis2012/#
5. *Libra*, the basic Roman unit of weight; after 268 BCE it was equal to 0.722 pounds avoirdupois (0.329 kg). This pound was brought to Britain and other provinces where it became the standard for weighing gold and silver and for use in all commercial transactions.
6. See the correspondence between Pliny and Trajan on the licenses; Pliny, 10, 46.
7. Pliny, 10, 120.
8. *Scriptores Historiae Augustae*, 'Hadrian', 7, 5 5.
9. Procopius, *Secret History* 30.

Chapter 5: Roman-ness and *Romanitas*, Xenophobia and Barbarians

1. See Chrystal, 2020, pp. 110–111; Dench, 2010; Gruen, 2013.
2. Dench, 2010, p.8.
3. Thompson, 1993.
4. Dench, *ibid*.
5. Tertullian (c. 155 – c. 240 AD), an early North African Christian, who coined it in his *De Pallio*, 'On the Cloak, (4, 1).
6. Plutarch, *Cato*, 23, 1–3; Polybius, 31, 24. See also Isaac, B., (2013), *The Invention of Racism in Classical Antiquity*, degruyter.com.
7. Livy, 24, 2–4; Aulus Gellius, 7, 6–8.

8. Various suggestions for the start and or cause of the decline have been made: Polybius, 31, 25, ascribes it to the victory over Macedonia; L. Calpurnius Piso (Pliny, *NH* 17, 38, 244) goes with 154 BCE; Appian, *Bellum Civili*, 1, 7, for the end of the war in Italy; Livy, 39, 6, 7, prefers 186 BCE; Valleius Paterculus, *Historiae Romanae*, and Sallust, *Catilina*, 10, opt for the end of the Third Punic War.
9. Plutarch, *Cato*, 12, 4–5.
10. Cicero (106 BCE-43 BCE), philosopher, politician, lawyer, orator, and consul.
11. Tiberius was emperor from 14 CE to 37 CE. Suetonius, *Tiberius*, 71.
12. Valerius Maximus (c. 20 BC c. 50 CE), 2, 2, 2.
13. Rubel, (2020), p. 9.

Chapter 6: The Celts and the Germani
1. Caesar, *Gallic Wars*, 4, 2.
2. Wells, (1987), p. 409.
3. VandenBoom, *Pre-Conquest Celtic and Germanic Trade with the Wider Mediterranean*.
4. Cunliffe, (1988), p.87.
5. *ibid*.
6. *ibid*.
7. Cunliffe, (1988), p. 147.
8. Strabo 4, 5,2. For a survey on the Romanization of Gaulish culture, see Woolf, Greg (1998), *Becoming Roman: The Origins of Provincial Civilization in Gaul*, Cambridge.
9. *The Oxford Classical Dictionary* defines *Interpretatio Romana*, lit. 'Latin translation' (Tac. *Germ*, 43. 3) as a phrase used to describe the Roman habit of replacing the name of a foreign deity with that of a Roman deity considered somehow comparable. At times this process involved extensive identification of the actual deities, while in other cases, the deities, though sharing a name, continued to be sharply distinguished. Different Latin names could sometimes be substituted for the same foreign name, depending on which characteristic of the god was chosen as the basis for comparison. The earliest of these 'translations' were from Greek: thus 'Zeus' was translated by 'Iuppiter' (see Zeus; Jupiter). The process continued as the Romans came into contact with other cultures, so that the German 'Wodan' was called 'Mercurius' by Roman writers. Only in a few cases were foreign divine names adopted directly into Latin, e.g. 'Apollo' and 'Isis'.
10. *Pollini, (2002)*.
11. Inse Jones, (1995).
12. Todd, (2004), p. 2.
13. See Chrystal, *Roman Military Disasters*, Chapter 9.
14. Caesar, *Gallic Wars* 2, 15; Tacitus, *Germania* 23.
15. Op cit p. 21.
16. Dio, 53, 26.
17. Pliny the Elder, *Nat. Hist*, 37, 45.
18. Tacitus, *Germania*, 41.
19. Dio, 72, 15.
20. Beresford Ellis, (1998), p. 132.
21. Levick (2009), p. 64–65.
22. Strabo, *Geography* 4,4,1; Ptolemy, 2, 8, 6.
23. Wells, Kelheim, p. 401.
24. Op cit p. 406.
25. Op cit p. 404.

Chapter 7: Rome and the Nordic Countries
1. Waldman & Mason, (2006), p. 786. Much of this chapter is inspired by Anderrson's web article cited below.
2. Ränk, (1976), pp. 7–9.
3. https://cohorsllcimbria.com/the-roman-empire-and-scandinavia
4. Dobson, (1936), p. 73.
5. An ornament or plate of thinly beaten precious metal, typically a thin gold disc.
6. Green, Thomas R. G., (May 2007), 'Trade, Gift-Giving and *Romanitas*: A Comparison of the Use of Roman Imports in Western Britain and Southern Scandinavia', *The Heroic Age*, 10.
7. See Parker, (2021), pp. 16–17.
8. https://undark.org/wp-content/uploads/2023/01/ChatGPT.pdf.
9. The following archaeology owes much to Paul Mercer's article, '*Romans in Norway? Surely Not*' at https://www.epiacumheritage.org/blog/post/romans-in-norway-surely-not%EF%BF%BC/.
10. Marit Synnøve Vea, https://avaldsnes.info/en/informasjon/storhaug-kongen/.
11. *Lorange's Excavation in 1869–70 and the Message in a Bottle*, Raknehaugen, Akershus Kulturnett.
12. The Roman *spathe* was a long combat sword, it had a straight, double-edged blade, a descendant of the more famous *gladius*. Originally the spatha was used by the Roman cavalry and as horsemen were regularly recruited from Gallic tribes the sword owes its origin to the Celts who when recruited were issued chainmail shirts, oval shields, helmets and swords of their own native style. Early spathae are depicted on tombstones with hilts and scabbards very close to legionary types. It is likely that the auxiliary cavalry units copied legionary fashions, making these swords essentially a hybrid between Celtic and Roman weapon design.

    The spatha began to replace the shorter gladius as the primary Roman sword from about AD 100 onwards. The Romans continued to use their spathae right up until the fall of the Roman Empire.
13. Haakon Shetelig (1877–1955) was a Norwegian archaeologist, historian and museum director. He was a pioneer in archaeology known for his study of art from the Viking era in Norway. He is most frequently associated with his work on the Oseberg ship near Tønsberg, Norway.
14. Tacitus, *Germania*, 46.
15. Ptolemy, 2,11; 3, 5. See Whitaker (1980). 'Tacitus' "Fenni" and Ptolemy's "Phinnoi", *The Classical Journal*, 75(3), 215–224.
16. Eduard Norden, (1920), *Die germanische Urgeschichte in Tacitus Germania*, p. 442, Leipzig. The Romans were in possession of Baltic amber and doubtless were in commercial contact with this area.
17. 'Reinhard Hiussler, Tacitus und das historische Bewusstsein (Bibliothek Altertumswirtschaften New Series), Heidelberg 1965, 191, cf 207.
18. Jordanes, *Getae*, 3.
19. Olaus Magnus *(1658) [1555]*, *'The Description of Scricfinnia'*, *Historia de Gentibus Septentrionalibus*, Rome.

Chapter 8: Eastern Europe
1. Herodotus, 4, 44.
2. See Chrystal, Paul, (2019), *Rome: Republic into Empire*, chap. 4.
3. See Chrystal, Paul, (2023), *Bioterrorism and Biological Warfare*, page 53ff.

4. See Chrystal, Paul, (2017), *Women in Ancient Greece.*
5. See Chrystal, Paul, (2020), *Women at War in the Classical World*, chap 4.
6. See Chrystal, Paul, (2015), *Wars and Battles of the Roman Republic.*
7. Symonenko, (2003).
8. Appian, *Mithr.* 57.
9. Symonenko, (2002).
10. For details see Chrystal, (2019), 70, 73.
11. In his *Germania.* See Olcott, M.D., (1985), 'Tacitus on the Ancient Amber-Gatherers: A Re-evaluation of Germania', *Journal of Baltic Studies, 16*(3), 302–315.
12. Bunkse, (1994).
13. Singer, (2008).
14. Reeves, C.N., (1990), *The Complete Tutankhamun: The King, the Tomb, the Royal Treasure:* Serpico, M.; White, R., (2000), 'Resins, Amber, and Bitumen', in Nicholson, P.T., Shaw, I. (eds.). *Ancient Egyptian Materials and Technology*, Cambridge Part II, chapter 18, pp. 430–475, esp. 451–454, as cited by Gestoso Singer: Hood, S. (1990), 'Amber in Egypt', written at Liblice, PL., in Beck, C.W., Bouzek, J., (eds.), *Amber in Archaeology: Second International Conference on Amber in Archaeology*, Institute of Archaeology, Prague.
15. Beck, Curt W., (1972), 'Analysis and Provenance of Mioan and Mycenaean Amber', [part] IV Mycenae', *Greek, Roman, and Byzantine Studies,* 13 (4): 359–385: Anna J. et al., (2008), 'The Qatna Lion: Scientific Confirmation of Baltic Amber in Late Bronze Age Syria' (PDF), *Antiquity,* 82: 49–59.
16. Jovaiša, E., (2001), 'The Balts and Amber' (PDF), *Acta Academiae Artium Vilnensis*, 22: 149–156.
17. *The Ancient Transport of Amber*, https://www.getty.edu/publications/ambers/intro/11/
18. J. Kolendo, (1981), *A la recherche de l'ambre baltique: L'expédition d'un chevalier romain sous Néron*, Warsaw.
19. Hammarlund, Anders, (2001), 'The Amber Road, Center and Periphery', published in the print edition of *Baltic Worlds* pages 4–10, Vol III:1, 2010. Published on Balticworlds. com 24 March, 2010.
20. Kristiansen, Kristian, Suchowska-Ducke, Paulina, (2015), 'Connected Histories: The Dynamics of Bronze Age Interaction and Trade 1500–1100 BCE', *Proceedings of the Prehistoric Society*, 81: 361–392: Jones, Gwyn, (2001), *A History of the Vikings*, Oxford.
21. Tac. *Germ.* 4.4.
22. Dio Chrys. *Or.* 79.4.
23. Tac. *Ger.* 45.5.
24. Bliujienė, (2006), 85. Amber finds are surprisingly sparse also in earlier prominent Germanic cultures, such as the Hallstatt culture, according to Marková & Stegmann-Rajtár (2006).
25. Timberlake, Luke, https://www.saltshack.co.uk/amazing-amber/
26. Kurlansky, Mark (2003), *Salt: A World History*, London. For two interesting articles on amber, see *Ancient Literary Sources on the Origins of Amber*: https://www.getty.edu/publications/ambers/intro/9/ and https://amberinternational.net/amber-history/
27. Strong, D.E., (1966), *Catalogue of the Carved Amber in the Department of Greek and Roman Antiquities,* pp. 91–96, London.
28. Hammarlund, *op. cit.*
29. Swift, (2002), 49–52; Lundgren, (2018), p. 20.
30. Pliny, *HN* 37. 50.

Chapter 9: Britannia

1. Plutarch, *Life of Caesar*, 23, 2.
2. Strabo, *Geography*, 2,4,1.
3. Herodotus, 3, 115.
4. Pliny, *NH*,7,1, 97.
5. Diodorus, 5, 38, 4.
6. Pliny, *NH,* 2,169a.
7. Lucretius, *DRN*, 6, 1105.
8. Cicero *DND,* 2, 34, 88.
9. Balsdon, J.P.V.D, *Julius Caesar,* p. 82.
10. Grant, Michael, *Julius Caesar,* p. 65.
11. Strabo, *Geography,* 4, 4.
12. A *supplicatio* is a day of public prayer when the men, women, and children of Rome processed to religious sites around the city praying for divine aid in times of crisis. It also served as a thanksgiving, when a great Roman victory had been won, usually decreed as soon as official intelligence of the victory had been received by a report from the general in command.
13. Cicero, *Ad Familiares*, 7, 6.
14. Suetonius, *Caesar,* 47.
15. *Natural History*, 9, 116, 9.169; Juvenal, *Satire,* 4, 141
16. Dio, 49, 38.
17. Strabo, *Geography,* 2, 5, 8.
18. Virgil, *Georgics*, 1,30 and 3.25.
19. Horace, *Odes*, 1, 35, 29–31.
20. See Chrystal, Paul, (2015) *Roman Military Disasters.*
21. Tacitus, *Agricola*, 13.
22. Suetonius, *Caligula,* 44–46; Cassius Dio, *Roman History,* 59, 25.
23. Cassius Dio, 60, 19.
24. Suetonius, *Claudius,* 17.
25. *Ibid.*
26. Josephus, *Bellum Judaicum,* 3, 1, 2.
27. Tacitus, *Annals,* 12, 31–40.
28. Scriptores Historia Augustae, *Hadrian,* 9,2.

Chapter 10: Africa – Sub-Sahara and West Africa, Egypt, Nubia, Lake Chad

1. Pliny the Elder, *NH,* 2.75.1; Diodorus Siculus, 3.41.1.
2. *NH,* 2.183, 6.168.
3. https://www.khanacademy.org/humanities/art-africa/east-africa2/ethiopia/a/the-kingdom-of-aksum
4. Munro-Hay, Stuart (1991), *Aksum: An African Civilisation of Late Antiquity,* Edinburgh, p. 17.
5. 216 CE–274 CE.
6. https://www.libertarianism.org/columns/commerce-trade-ancient-africa-aksum. Boardman, Sheila, *The Agricultural Foundation of the Aksumite Empire,* pp. 137–147.
7. Mango, Marlia Mundell, *Byzantine Trade, 4th-12th centuries: the Archaeology of Local, Regional and International Exchange*, p. 278.
8. *Geography,* 16.4.
9. A *periplus* (or *periplous,* is a manuscript document that lists the ports and coastal landmarks, in voyage order and with approximate intervening distances, to enable the

captain of a vessel to know what he or she could expect to find along a shore. So, the *periplus* was a type of log and served the same purpose as the later Roman *itinerarium* of road stops. However, the Greek navigators added various notes, which, if they were professional geographers, as many were, became part of their own contributions to Greek geography. See Chrystal, *Roman Record Keeping and Communications*, 2018:

'The form of the *periplus* is at least as old as the earliest Greek historian, the Ionian Hecataeus of Miletus. Herodotus and Thucydides contain passages that appear to have been based on *peripli*.'

10. Mortimer Wheeler, (1954), p. 138.
11. See *Eggermont, Pierre (1968), 'The Date of the Periplus Maris Erythraei', 1960, Oriental Monograph Series, Vol. IV, pp. 94–96*: and Casson *(1989); Chami, (2002)*.
12. Hancock, J., 2021.
13. Huntingford, (1980).
14. For details, see Chrystal, Paul, (2018), *Roman Record Keeping and Communications*, Stroud.
15. *The Periplus of Hanno: a Voyage of Discovery Down the West African Coast*, Translated by Schoff, H., 1912.
16. Apuleius, *Metamorphoses*, 2.10.
17. Pliny the Elder, *Natural History*, 14, 7.
18. Berenice Troglodytica, also called Berenike (Βερενίκη) or Baranis, is an ancient seaport of Egypt on the western shore of the Red Sea.
19. Seneca, *On Benefits*, 7.
20. Dalrymple, William (2024), *The Golden Road: How Ancient India Transformed the World*, London.
21. See Rathbone, Dominic W., 'Muziris Papyrus', *OCD* https://doi.org/10.1093/acrefore/9780199381135.013.8258.
22. Petrie, William Matthew Flinders, *A History of Egypt. Volume 3: From the XIXth to the XXXth Dynasties*, Adamant Media Corporation, p. 366.
23. Redmount, Carol A., 'The Wadi Tumilat and the Canal of the Pharaohs', *Journal of Near Eastern Studies*, Vol. 54, No. 2 (Apr. 1995), pp. 127–135.
24. The *Description de l'Égypte* was a series of publications, appearing first in 1809 and continuing until 1829, which aimed to comprehensively catalogue all known aspects of ancient and modern Egypt as well as its natural history. It is the collaborative work of about 160 civilian scholars and scientists, known as the savants, who accompanied Bonaparte's expedition to Egypt in 1798 to 1801 as part of the French Revolutionary Wars, as well as about 2000 artists and technicians, including 400 engravers, who would later compile it into a full work. At the time of its publication, it was the largest known published work in the world.
25. Hall, Linda., *The Search for the Ancient Suez Canal*, Kansas City, MO.
26. *Carte hydrographique de l'Basse Egypte et d'une partie de l'Isthme de Suez*, (1855, 1882), Volume 87, page 803. Paris.
27. By The Abbasid Caliph al-Mansur; see Redmount, *op cit*.
28. McLaughlin, (2010), *Rome and the Distant East*, 160–168; ibid (2014), p. 14.
29. Strabo, 17, 1, 13. 1m sesterces = roughly £995,896; 1 bn sesterces = roughly £995,896,000. Strabo, 17, 1, 13; De Romanis, 2020, pp. 132133, 180181, 277297, 312. See McLaughlin, (2014), p. 19; he suggests that the first tax was a Mediterranean *portaria* tax exacting 1/40th.
30. Suetonius, *Augustus*, 49,2; *Res Gestae*, 17; Dio, 54.2.
31. For more on this see Cobb, Matthew Adam, 'The Roman State and Red Sea Trade Revenue', in Durand, Caroline et al (ed), (2002), *Networked Spaces: The Spatiality of Networks in the Red Sea and Western Indian Ocean*, Lyon.

32. Dio, 51, 17.
33. Dio. 51, 21.
34. Suetonius, *Augustus*, 41; Dio, 51, 21.
35. Strabo, 2, 5, 12/
36. https://www.webpages.uidaho.edu/~rfrey/PDF/166/Judaism%20Christianity/166%20Book%20of%20Revelation.pdf.
37. McLaughlin, (2014), p. 27.
38. Welsby, Derek A. (1996), *The Kingdom of Kush*, London, pp. 64–65.
39. Jackson, Robert B., (2002), *At Empire's Edge: Exploring Rome's Egyptian Frontier*, Yale University Press.
40. Pliny, *NH*, 5, 5, 36.

Chapter 11: Arabia
1. Pliny, *Natural History*, 12.84.
2. Livy, 34.7. See Chrystal, *Women in Ancient Rome* (2014) p. 9: 'The proposal in 195 BCE to repeal the *lex Oppia* of 215 BCE evoked distaste and condemnation when women came out from their homes and demonstrated in the Forum to support the repeal. The law had restricted the use of luxuries by women in the wake of the Battle of Cannae some twenty years before. It limited the amount of gold women could own and required that all the assets of wards, single women, and widows be handed over to the State; the wearing of dresses with purple trim and riding in carriages within Rome or nearby towns was also prohibited, except during religious festivals. The feeling amongst women was that the law had served its purpose and had run its course'.
3. Women were also constricted by the 169 BCE *lex Voconia* in terms of the value of wealth they could inherit. Only sisters of a deceased woman could inherit in cases of intestacy and women were prohibited from inheriting large legacies. Property was allowed so long as the value did not exceed the heir's legacy. This effectively overturned the *XII Tables* law permitting women to inherit and to be named in wills: the presumption now was that the family's money would evaporate if left to a woman and that women frittered away their wealth on frivolous things. Chrystal, (2014), pp. 74–75.
4. *Rome's Eastern Trade:* https://depts.washington.edu/silkroad/exhibit/rome/essay.html
5. McLaughlin, Raoul, (2016), *The Roman Empire and the Silk Routes.*
6. Strabo, 11,11, 1.
7. Dean, Riaz, (2022), *The Stone Tower: Ptolemy, the Silk Road, and a 2,000-Year-Old Riddle*, Delhi, pp. 130, 154–55.
8. J. Oliver Thomson, (1948), located the Stone Tower in his *History of Ancient Geography*, Cambridge, pp. 179–180. See also Galli, (2017), pp. 3–9.
9. McLaughlin, *op. cit.*
10. Pliny, *NH,* 12, 32; *Matthew,* 22.
11. Persius, *Satires,* 3, 103, 5. Pliny was not happy though, questioning how much.
12. Arrian, *Periplus of the Black Sea,* 1–2.
13. *Feriale Duranum* – a calendar of religious observances for a Roman military garrison at Dura-Europos in Roman Syria, in the reign of Severus Alexander (224–235 CE).
14. See Chrystal, Paul, (2018), *Roman Record Keeping and Communications,* chapter 9.
15. Department of Ancient Near Eastern Art, (2000), 'Nabataean Kingdom and Petra', in *Heilbrunn Timeline of Art History*, New York: The Metropolitan Museum of Art.
16. Strabo, 16, 780–783; Cassius Dio, 53, 29; Pliny, *Natural History,* 6. 32.
17. Bowerstock, (1983), pp. 47f.
18. Pliny, *NH,* 6, 162.

Chapter 12: Parthia and the Sasanian Empire
1. https://depts.washington.edu/silkroad/exhibit/parthians/essay.html
2. Plutarch, *Crassus*, 31, 7. For details see Chrystal, Paul, (2015), *Roman Military Disasters*.
3. McLaughlin, R., (2016), *The Roman Empire and the Silk Routes*, Barnsley.
4. Brosius, (2006), pp. 90–91; Watson, (1983), pp. 540–542; Garthwaite, (2005), pp. 77–78.
5. Garthwaite, (2005), p. 78; Brosius, (2006), pp. 122–123.
6. Brosius, (2006), pp. 123–125.
7. Wang, (2007), pp. 100–101.
8. Kurz, (1983), p. 560.
9. Ebrey, (1999), p. 70; for an archaeological survey of Roman glasswares in ancient Chinese burials, see An, (2002), pp. 79–84.
10. Howard, (2012), p. 133.
11. Watson, (1983), 543–544.
12. Gregoratti, (2017), pp. 131.
13. Watson, (1983), 543–544.
14. Yu, (1986), 460–461.
15. For details, see Chrystal, Paul, (2022), *A History of the World in 100 Pandemics, Plagues and Epidemics*.
16. Department of Ancient Near Eastern Art, 'Trade between the Romans and the Empires of Asia', in *Heilbrunn Timeline of Art History*, New York: The Metropolitan Museum of Art, 2000. http://www.metmuseum.org/toah/hd/silk/hd_silk.htm. The Sogdians were an Iranian people whose homeland, Sogdiana, was located at the junction of several trade routes, in present-day Uzbekistan and Tajikistan.
17. Hourani, p. 87.
18. Sitwell, p. 111.
19. Nicolle, p. 6.
20. *'Sassanids Used Commercial Labels: Iranian Archeologists'*, *Payvand*, 21, August 2009.
21. https://web.archive.org/web/20070929120428/http://www.payvand.com/news/04/aug/1199.html
22. Frye, (2005), p. 325.
23. Sarfaraz, p. 353.
24. Nicolle, p.6.
25. McLaughlin, (2016), p. 84.
26. Aurelius Victor (*Epitome*, XV, 4), and Appian (*Praef.* 7).
27. Hill, (2009), p. 31.
28. McLaughlin, (2016), p. 86.
29. Strabo, 2, 5, 12.

Chapter 13: India
1. See Rao, S.R., 'Shipping and Maritime Trade of the Indus People', *Expedition Magazine* 7, no. 3 (May, 1965): https://www.penn.museum/sites/expedition/shipping-and-maritime-trade-of-the-indus-people/. See also Caspers, E. C. L. D., (1973), 'Harappan Trade in the Arabian Gulf in the Third Millenium BC', *Proceedings of the Seminar for Arabian Studies*, 3, 3–20.
Dhavalikar, M. K., (1985), 'Review of Harappan Trade with West Asia, by S. Ratnagar', *Bulletin of the Deccan College Research Institute*, 44, 189–193.
https://thefridaytimes.com/27-Sep-2019/trade-networks-of-the-indus-civilization
2. (2014), pp. 152–153.

3. Pliny, *NH*, 34, 55.
4. *Arathashastra*, 2, 22. *Arathashastra* is an Ancient Indian Sanskrit treatise on statecraft, political science, economic policy and military strategy.
5. Suetonius, *Augustus*, 21.
6. Strabo, 15, 1, 71.
7. Strabo, *idem*.
8. *NH*, 37,76; Chapter 37.
9. Sinopoli, (2001), p. 178.
10. Higham, p. 299.
11. The Konkan is a stretch of land on the western coast of India, bound by the River Daman Ganga at Damaon in the north, to Anjediva Island. It includes Goa.
12. Tomber, (2008), pp. 230–232.
13. *Periplus*, 50.
14. Caldwell, Robert, (1881), *A Political and General History of the District of Tinnevelly*, Asian Educational Services, p. 20.
15. Subrahmanian, N., (1972), *History of Tamilnad: 1565–1956*, Koodal Publishers.
16. Krishnamurthy. R., *Sangam Age Tamil Coins*, Madras, p. 6.
17. Husaini: *The History of the Pandya Country*, p. 18.
18. Pliny, *NH*, 35, 32.
19. Gurukkal, Rajan, (2015), 'Classical Indo-Roman Trade: A Misnomer in Political Economy', *Economic and Political Weekly*, 48, 26–27. McLaughlin, (2010).
20. Pliny, *NH*, 6, 26; 12, 41. See McLaughlin, (2014), p. 191 for verification of this.
21. Akananura, 149, 7–11.
22. McLaughlin, (2014), p. 172.
23. Sasisekharan, B., (1999), 'Technology of Iron and Steel in Kodumanal', *Indian Journal of History of Science*, 34 (4).
24. Florus, 2, 34–62.
25. Suetonius, *Augustus*, 30.
26. Strabo, 15, 1, 73.
27. *Periplus*, 61.
28. Ptolemy, *Geographia*, 7,2.
29. Pliny, *NH*, 6, 21; Servius, *Commentary on Virgil*, 1, 9, 30.

Chapter 14: Sri Lanka and Myanmar (Burma)
1. *Periplus*, 60.
2. *Periplus*, 64; Strabo, 2, 1, 14; Pliny, *NH*, 9, 5, 4.
3. Pliny, *NH*, 6, 23, 84.
4. Cosmas Indicopleustes, Christian Topography, 11.17–19.
5. Strabo, 2, 1, 14.
6. Bopearachchi, p. xviii, in Weerakody.
7. McLaughlin, (2014), p. 196.
8. McLaughlin, (2014), p. 197.
9. *Periplus*, 64: Ptolemy, 72.
10. Martial, *Spectacles*, 86.
11. Near modern Ho Chi Min City; see Young, *Rome's Eastern Trade*, p. 29.
12. Ptolemy, 7, 3
13. McLaughlin, (2014), p. 206.

Chapter 15: China and the Silk Road
1. Hirth, Friedrich, (2000), [1885], (ed.), *East Asian History Sourcebook: Chinese Accounts of Rome, Byzantium and the Middle East, c. 91 B.C.E. – 1643 C.E.*, Fordham University.
2. An, Jiayao, 82–83.
3. *Hou Hanshu*, 88, 12: McLaughlin, (2016), xix.
4. British Library, 'Detailed Record for Harley 7182'. www.bl.uk
5. See McLaughlin, (2016), pp, 2–5 for details.
6. *Hou Hanshu*, 18, 12; *Periplus*, 49, 56; 64.
7. Florus, 46, 3, 11.
8. Pliny, *NH*, 11, 26, 7.
9. Propertius, 1,2; Tibullus, 2,3.
10. See Rashke, *New Studies in Roman Commerce with the East*, (1978), 625.
11. Pliny, *NH*, 19,6; Dio, 43, 24.
12. Dio, 5, 9, 12.
13. *Periplus*, 49, 56; 64; Pliny *NH*, 19,6; Tacitus, *Annals*, 13, 31; Dio, 63, 6, 2.
14. McLaughlin, (2016), pp 27–28.
15. *Zhou shu*, 50, 2340c.
16. McLaughlin, (2016), *op.cit.*

Chapter 16: The Assimilation and Adoption of Foreign Ideas and Culture Through Trade
1. Department of Ancient Near Eastern Art, 'Trade Routes between Europe and Asia during Antiquity', in *Heilbrunn Timeline of Art History*, New York, The Metropolitan Museum of Art, 2000–. http://www.metmuseum.org/toah/hd/trade/hd_trade.htm (October 2000).
2. Gandhāra was an ancient Indo-Aryan civilization centred in present-day north-west Pakistan and north-east Afghanistan. The core of the region of Gandhara was the Peshawar and Swat valleys, though the cultural influence of 'Greater Gandhara' extended across the Indus River to the Taxila region in Potohar Plateau and westwards into the Kabul valley in Afghanistan, and northwards up to the Karakoram range.
3. The Villa Romana del Casale is a fine Roman villa located about two miles from Piazza Armerina, Sicily.
4. 'Il Blog sulla Villa Romana del Casale Piazza Armerina', *villadelcasale.it*.
5. Liu, Xinru (2010), *The Silk Road in World History*, Oxford University Press.
6. Liu, (2010), p. 40.
7. Cary, Max (1956), 'Maes, Qui et Titianus', *The Classical Quarterly*, 6.3/4 (1956), pp. 130–134.
8. *NH* 11, 26, 76.
9. Liu, (2010), p. 21.
10. Seneca the Younger (c. 3 BCE–65 CE), *Declamations*, Vol. I.
11. Modern-day Tajikistan, Uzbekistan, Afghanistan, Pakistan, Eastern Iran and Northern India.
12. See Mayers, K. (2016), *The First English Explorer: The Life of Anthony Jenkinson (1529–1611) and His Adventures on the Route to the Orient*. Storbritannien: Matador, pp. 122–123.

Chapter 17: Eastern Religions in the Roman Empire
1. Helble, Matthias, (2006), *On the Influence of World Religions on International Trade:* https://jpia.princeton.edu/sites/g/files/toruqf1661/files/2006-11.pdf.

See also Lewer, J. J., & Van den Berg, H., (2007), 'Religion and International Trade: Does the Sharing of a Religious Culture Facilitate the Formation of Trade Networks?', *The American Journal of Economics and Sociology*, 66(4), 765–794.
2. Wick, P., & Rabens, V., (Eds.), (2014), in *Religions and Trade: Religious Formation, Transformation and Cross-Cultural Exchange between East and West*, (pp. i–vi), Brill. See also https://festival.si.edu/2002/the-silk-road/the-silk-road-crossroads-and-encounters-of-faith/smithsonian.
3. Cicero, *de Deorum Natura*, 2, 70–72; Virgil, *Georgics*, 4, 221ff.
4. Cf, however, Beard, *Rome*, pp. 25ff who argues against this view.
5. *Caesar*, 9.
6. Juvenal, 6, 314–334.
7. Cicero, *De Domo Sua*, 53,136.
8. See Brouwer, *Bona Dea*.
9. *De Haruspicum Responsis*, 17, 37–18, 38.
10. Livy, 39, 15, 6; 39, 8.
11. *De Legibus*, 2, 9, 21.
12. Livy, 39, 17.
13. Livy, 39, 19–22.
14. 4, 223ff.
15. Livy, 29, 10; 29, 14, 10–14.
16. Juvenal, 6, 511–541.
17. 11, 9–10.
18. Tacitus, Annals, 2, 85; Suetonius, Tiberius, 36.
19. *CIL*, 6, 224.
20. Tacitus, *Annals*, 2, 85; Suetonius, *Tiberius*, 36.

Appendix: The Second-Hand Book Trade in Brundidium
1. Chrystal, Paul, *Miracula: Weird and Wonderful Stories of Ancient Greece and Rome*, London, 2025.
2. For a detailed treatment of the book trade in ancient Greece and Rome, see my: *The Book in the Ancient World: How the Wisdom of the Ages Was Preserved*, Barnsley, 2025.

Further Reading by Chapter

Introduction
Cartwright, M., (2018, April 12), 'Trade in the Roman World', *World History Encyclopedia*, Retrieved from https://www.worldhistory.org/article/638/trade-in-the-roman-world/
Evers, Kasper Grønlund, (2017), *Worlds Apart Trading Together: The Organisation of Long-Distance Trade between Rome and India in Antiquity*, 32, Archaeopress
Heilbrunn Timeline of Art History, Trade between the Romans and the Empires of Asia Essay, The Metropolitan Museum of Art
McLaughlin, Raoul, (2014), *The Roman Empire and the Indian Ocean*, Barnsley
McLaughlin, Raoul, (2016), *The Roman Empire and The Silk Routes*, Barnsley
Terpstra, Tac T., (2013), *Trading Communities in the Roman World: A Micro-Economic and Institutional,* Leiden
Tomber, Roberta, (2008), *Indo-Roman Trade: From Pots To Pepper*, Bristol

Chapter 2: Roman Trade
Archibald, Zosia, *Moving Upcountry: Travel from Ancient Ports to Inland Harbours*
Arnaud, P., (2012), 'La mer, vecteur des mobilités grecques', in 'Mobilités grecques', Capdetrey & Zurbach (eds.), *Scripta Antiqua* 46, Ausonius, Bordeaux, (p 89–135)
Bocquelet, David, (2022), 'Roman Ships – From SPQR to the Imperium', *Naval Encyclopedia*
Bond, Sarah, (2016), *Trade and Taboo: Disreputable Professions in the Roman Mediterranean*, University of Michigan Press
Bowman, Alan K., (2009), *Quantifying the Roman Economy: Methods and Problems*, Oxford
Callataÿ, François de., (2014), *Quantifying the Greco-Roman Economy and Beyond*, Bari: Edipuglia
Cartwright, M., (2018), *Trade in the Roman World*, https://www.worldhistory.org/article/638/trade-in-the-roman-world/
Casson, Lionel., 1990, 'New Light on Maritime Loans: P. Vindob. G 40822', in *Zeitschrift für Papyrologie und Epigraphik* 84, (pp 195–206), – a complete translation into English. The papyrus is presently housed in the Austrian National Library in Vienna. It is one of the very few surviving maritime contracts presently available to us (see also: http://papyri.info/ddbdp/sb;3;7169)
Casson, Lionel, (1991), *The Ancient Mariners: Seafarers and Sea Fighters of the Mediterranean in Ancient Times* (2nd ed.), Princeton University Press
Casson, Lionel, (1995), *Ships and Seamanship in the Ancient World*, Johns Hopkins University Press
Charles, Michael, (2005), 'Transporting the Troops in Late Antiquity: Naves Onerariae, Claudian and the Gildonic War'. *Classical Journal*, (3): 275–299
Chrystal, Paul, (2022), *A Historical Guide to Roman York,* Barnsley
Cioffi, Robert L., (2016), *Travel in the Roman World*, https://www.academia.edu/23290586/Travel_in_the_Roman_World_Oxford_Handbooks_Online_?hb-g-sw=10259552

Crawford, M.H., (1977), 'Rome and the Greek World: Economic Relationships', *The Economic History Review*, 30(1), 42–52
Denny, Mark, (2009), *Float Your Boat!: The Evolution and Science of Sailing*, Baltimore
De Romanis, F., (2012), 'Playing Sudoku on the Verso of the 'Muziris Papyrus': Pepper, Malabathron and Tortoise Shell in the Cargo of the Hermapollon', *Journal of Ancient Indian History*, 27, 75–101, gives a brilliant reconstruction of the cargo on board the Hermapollon
De Souza, P., (2002), *Piracy in the Graeco-Roman World*, Cambridge University Press
Duncan-Jones, Richard, (1990), *Structure and Scale in the Roman Economy*, Cambridge
Friedman, Zazara, (2004), 'The Ships Depicted in the Lod Mosaic Reconsidered', *International Journal of Nautical Archaeology, Portsmouth* (1): 164–168
Gambash G., (2017), 'Between Mobility and Connectivity in the Ancient Mediterranean: Coast-Skirting Travellers in the Southern Levant', *Impact of Empire*, 12, 155–172
Garnsey, P., (1989), *Famine and Food Supply in the Graeco-Roman World: Responses to Risk and Crisis*, Cambridge
Garnsey, Peter, (2015), *The Roman Empire: Economy, Society and Culture*, 2nd edition, Oakland, CA
Gates, Charles, (2011), *Ancient Cities: The Archaeology of Urban Life in the Ancient Near East and Egypt, Greece and Rome*, (2nd ed.), London
Goldsworthy, Adrian Keith, (2016), *Pax Romana: War, Peace, and Conquest in the Roman World*, New Haven
Greene, Kevin, (1986), *The Archaeology of the Roman Economy*, Berkeley
Haddad, Elie & Avissar, Miriam, (2003), 'A Suggested Reconstruction of One of the Merchant Ships on the Mosaic Floor in Lod (Lydda) Israel', *International Journal of Nautical Archaeology, Portsmouth* 32(1): 73–77
Henrichs, A., (1995), '*Graecia Capta*: Roman Views of Greek Culture', *Harvard Studies in Classical Philology*, 97, 243–261
Hermansen, Gustav, (1982), *Ostia: Aspects of Roman City Life*, Edmonton
Hopkins, Keith, (1983), *Models, Ships and Staples*
Jones, A.H.M., 'The Greeks Under the Roman Empire, *Dumbarton Oaks Papers*, 17 (1963): 1–19
Jones, A.H.M., (1974), *The Roman Economy: Studies in Ancient Economic and Administrative History*, Oxford
Keay, S.J., (2006), *Portus: An Archaeological Survey of the Port of Imperial Rome*, British School at Rome
Levick, B., (2004), 'The Roman Economy: Trade in Asia Minor and the Niche Market', *Greece & Rome*, 51(2), 180–198
Lewit, Tamara, (1991), *Agricultural Production in the Roman Economy, A.D. 200–400*, Oxford: Tempus Reparatum
Linn, Jason, (2012), 'The Roman Grain Supply, 442–455', *Journal of Late Antiquity*, Vol. 5, No. 2, pp. 320–321
Marsh, Frank Burr, (1926), 'In Defense of the Corn-Dole'. *The Classical Journal*, 22(1): 10–25
Meiggs, R., (1960) [1973], *Roman Ostia*, 2nd ed., Oxford University Press
Meijer, Fik, (1986), *A History of Seafaring in the Classical World*, Routledge
Morris, I., (2004), 'Economic Growth in Ancient Greece', *Journal of Institutional and Theoretical Economics (JITE)/Zeitschrift Für Die Gesamte Staatswissenschaft*, 160(4), 709–742
Peacock, D.P.S., (1986), *Amphorae and the Roman Economy: An Introductory Guide*, London
Rankov, Boris, (1995), 'Fleets of the Early Roman Empire, 31 BC–AD 324', in Morrison, John S. & Gardiner, Robert, (eds.), *The Age of the Galley: Mediterranean Oared Vessels Since Pre-Classical Times*, Conway Maritime Press

Rickman, G.E., (1980), 'The Grain Trade Under the Roman Empire', *Memoirs of the American Academy in Rome*, 36: 263
Rickman, Geoffrey, (2002), 'Rome, Ostia and Portus: The Problem of Storage', *Mélanges de l'école française de Rome*, Année
Russell, Ben, (2013), *The Economics of the Roman Stone Trade*, New York
Safrai, Ze'ev, (1994), *The Economy of Roman Palestine*, London
Scheidel, Walter, (2007), *The Cambridge Economic History of the Greco-Roman World*, Cambridge
Scheidel, Walter, (2012), *The Cambridge Companion to the Roman Economy*, Cambridge
Serrati, J., (2006), 'Neptune's Altars: The Treaties between Rome and Carthage (509–226 B.C.)', *The Classical Quarterly*, 56(1), 113–134
Skinner, Frederick George, (1967), *Weights and Measures: Their Ancient Origins and their Development in Great Britain up to A.D. 1855*, H.M.S.O
Stephenson, Stephen K., (July 7, 2010), *Ancient Computers*, IEEE Global History Network
Sugden, Keith F., (1981A), 'History of the Abacus', *Accounting Historians Journal*, Fall 1981, Vol. 8, No. 2, pp. 1–22
Syme, R., (1957), 'The Greeks under Roman Rule', *Proceedings of the Massachusetts Historical Society*, 72, 3–20
Temin, P., (2001), 'A Market Economy in the Early Roman Empire', *The Journal of Roman Studies*, 91, 169–181
Temin, Peter, (2013), *The Roman Market Economy*, Princeton
Tomber, R., (2008), *Indo-Roman Trade: From Pots to Pepper*, London
Van Nijf, (2014), *Trade, Transport and Society in the Ancient World*, London
Vrba, Eric Michael, (2008) *Ancient German Identity in the Shadow of the Roman Empire: The Impact of Roman Trade and Contact Along the Middle Danube Frontier, 10 BC–AD 166*, Oxford
Wells, B.W., (1923), 'Trade and Travel in the Roman Empire', *The Classical Journal*, 19(1), 7–16
White, L. Michael, (1997), 'Synagogue and Society in Imperial Ostia: Archaeological and Epigraphic Evidence', *The Harvard Theological Review*, 90.1
Whitewright, Julian, 'How Fast is Fast? Technology, Trade and Speed Under Sail on the Roman Red Sea, https://www.academia.edu/1112629/How_fast_is_fast_Technology_trade_and_speed_under_sail_on_the_Roman_Red_Sea?hb-g-sw=10259552
Wilson, A.I. and Bowman, A.K., (2018), 'Introduction: Trade, Commerce, and the State', in
Wilson, A.I. and Bowman, A.K. (eds), *Trade, Commerce, and the State in the Roman World*, 1–24, Oxford
Woolf, G., (1994), 'Becoming Roman, Staying Greek: Culture, Identity and the Civilising Process in the Roman East', *Proceedings of the Cambridge Philological Society*, 40, 116–143

Chapter 3: The Borders of Empire (*Limes*)
Breeze, D.J., (1982), *The Northern Frontiers of Roman Britain*
Breeze, David J., (2011), *The Frontiers of Imperial Rome*, Barnsley
Chrystal, Paul, (2019), *The Romans in the North of England*, Darlington
Collins, R., & McIntosh, F., (Eds.), (2014), *Life in the Limes: Studies of the People and Objects of the Roman Frontiers*, Oxbow Books
Dyson, Stephen, (1985), *The Creation of the Roman Frontier*, Princeton
Heckster, Olivier, and Kaizer, Ted, (eds) (2011), *Frontiers in the Roman World: Proceedings of the Ninth Workshop of the International Network Impact of Empire*, Leiden
Isaac, Benjamin, (1988), 'The Meaning of 'Limes' and 'Limitanei' in Ancient Sources', *Journal of Roman Studies*, 78 (1988), pp. 125–147
Isaac, Benjamin, (1992), *The Limits of Empire: The Roman Army in the East*, Oxford

Kennedy, David, L., (2012), *Rome's Desert Frontiers*, London
Poidebard, A., (1934), *La Trace de Rome dans le désert de Syrie*
Spring, Peter, (2015), *Great Walls and Linear Barriers*, Barnsley
Timmerman, Erik, (2024), 'The Roman Impact on the Economy of the Lower Germanic Limes Region', *Impact of Empire*, Volume 48, Leiden
Wacher, J., (ed.), (1987), *The Roman World*, pt. 4: 'The Frontiers'
Whittaker, C., (1994), *The Frontiers of the Roman Empire*
Zietsman, J.C., (2009), 'Crossing the Roman Frontier: Egypt in Rome (and Beyond)', *Acta Classica* 52: 1–21

Chapter 4: Communications: Getting Goods to and from Market
Boetto, Giulia, *Merchant Vessels and Maritime Commerce in Roman Times*
Chrystal, Paul, (2018), *Roman Record Keeping and Communications*, Stroud
Erdkamp, Paul, (2002), 'No Respect: Urban Markets and Food Riots in the Roman World, 100 BC–400 AD', in *The Transformation of Economic Life under the Roman Empire*, edited by John Rich and Lukas de Blois, 93–115, Amsterdam: 2002
Erdkamp, Paul, (2005), *The Grain Market in the Roman Empire: A Social, Political, and Economic Study*, Cambridge, 2005
Finley, M.I., (1985), *The Ancient Economy*, Berkeley
Garnsey, Peter, (1988), *Famine and Food Supply in the Graeco-Roman World*, Cambridge
Harris, William V., (2000), 'Trade', in *Cambridge Ancient History, Vol. XI*, edited by Bowman, Alan K., Garnsey, Peter, & Rathbone, Dominic, 710–740, Cambridge, 2000
Jones, A.H.M., (1974), *The Roman Economy: Studies in Ancient Economic and Administrative History*, Totowa
Lo Cascio, Elio, (2000), 'The Roman Principate: The Impact of the Organization of the Empire on Production', in *Production and Public Powers in Classical Antiquity*, edited by Lo Cascio, Elio & Rathbone, Dominic, 77–85, Cambridge
Rickman, Geoffrey, (1980), *The Corn Supply of Ancient Rome*, Oxford
Rickman, Geoffrey, (2008), 'Ports, Ships, and Power in the Roman World', *Memoirs of the American Academy in Rome, Supplementary Volumes, Vol. 6, The Maritime World of Ancient Rome*, pp. 8–9
Sirks, Boudewijn, (1991), *Food for Rome: The Legal Structure of the Transportation and Processing of Supplies for the Imperial Distribution in Rome and Constantinople*, Amsterdam: Gieben
Stone, David L., (2014), 'Africa in the Roman Empire: Connectivity, the Economy, and Artificial Port Structures', *American Journal of Archaeology*, Vol. 118, No. 4, pp. 565–593
Suharoschi, Dan-Alexandru, (2020), 'The Limes Germanicus: Trade and the Roman Army in Rubel', in Alexander, (ed), *Experiencing the Frontier and the Frontier of Experience: Barbarian Perspectives and Roman Strategies to Deal with New Threats*
Tengström, Emin, (1974), *Bread for the People: Studies of the Corn-Supply of Rome during the Late Empire*, Stockholm

Chapter 5: Roman-ness and *Romanitas*, Xenophobia and Barbarians
Chrystal, Paul, (2023), 'Two Case Studies on Receptions of Sex & Power: Lucretia and Verginia' – Chapter 16', in *The Routledge Companion to the Reception of Ancient Greek and Roman Gender and Sexuality*
Chrystal, Paul, (2020), *Woman at War in the Classical World*, Barnsley
Dench, Emma, (2010), 'Roman Identity', in Barchiesi, Alessandro & Scheidel, Walter (eds.), *The Oxford Handbook of Roman Studies*, Oxford

Gruen, Erich S., (2014), 'Romans and Jews', in McInerney, Jeremy, (ed.), *A Companion to Ethnicity in the Ancient Mediterranean*, John Wiley & Sons
MacMullen, Ramsay, (2000), *Romanization in the Time of Augustus*, Yale
Pohl, Walter, (2018), 'Introduction: Early medieval Romanness – a multiple identity', in Pohl, Walter et al, (eds.), *Transformations of Romanness: Early Medieval Regions and Identities*, De Gruyter
Rubel, Alexander, (2020), 'What the Romans Really Meant When using the Term 'Barbarian': Some Thoughts on 'Romans and Barbarians'', in Curcă, Roxana-Gabriela et al, (eds.), *Rome and Barbaricum: Contributions to the Archaeology and History of Interaction in European Protohistory*, Archaeopress Publishing Ltd
Thompson, Lloyd, (1993), 'Roman Perceptions of Blacks', *Electronic Antiquity: Communicating the Classics*, 1(4)

Chapter 6: The Celts and the Germani
Beresford Ellis, Peter, (1998), *A Concise History of the Celts*, London
Brogan, O., (1936), "Trade between the Roman Empire and the Free Germans', *The Journal of Roman Studies*, 26:2: pp.195–222
Cary, M., (1929), *The Ancient Explorers*, London
Chrystal, Paul, (2015), *Roman Military Disasters*, Barnsley
Chrystal, Paul, (2015), *Wars and Battles of the Roman Republic*, Stroud
Chrystal, Paul, (2019), *From Republic to Empire*, Barnsley
Chrystal, Paul, (2021), *A Historical Guide to Roman York*, Barnsley
Collis, S. (2003), *The Celts: Origins, Myths and Inventions*, Tempus Publishing
Cunliffe, B., Greeks, (1988), *Romans and Barbarians: Spheres of Interaction*, London
Cunliffe, B., (1997), *The Ancient Celts*, Oxford
Dyck, L.H., (2016), *The Roman Barbarian Wars*, Barnsley
Erickson, Brice, (2002), 'Falling Masts, Rising Masters: The Ethnography of Virtue in Caesar's Account of the Veneti', *American Journal of Philology*, 123(4): 601–622
Inse Jones, Prudence, (1995), *History of Pagan Europe*, London
James, S. (2005), *The World of the Celts*, London
King, A., (1990), *Roman Gaul and Germany*, Berkeley
Levick, Barbara, (2009), 'The Veneti Revisited: C.E. Stevens and the Tradition on Caesar the Propagandist', in Welch, Kathryn & Powell, Anton, (eds.), *Julius Caesar as Artful Reporter: The War Commentaries as Political Instruments*, Classical Press of Wales
Maier, B., & Windle, K., (2003), *The Celts: A History from Earliest Times to the Present*, Edinburgh
Millet, M., & McGrail, S., (1987), 'The Archaeology of the Hasholme Logboat', *The Archaeological Journal*, 144: 69–155
Omrani, Bijan, (2017), *Caesar's Footprints: Journeys to Roman Gaul*, Head of Zeus
Pollini, John, ed., (2002), 'Gallo-Roman Bronzes and the Process of Romanization: The Cobannus Hoard', *Monumenta Graeca et Romana, Vol. 9*, Leiden
Rankin, H.D., (2002), *The Celts and the Classical World*, 2nd ed., London
Riggsby, A.M., (2010), *Caesar in Gaul and Rome: War in Words*, Austin TX
Tchernia, A., (2011), *Les Romains et le commerce*, Napels: Centre Jean Bernard
Todd, M., (2004), *The Early Germans*, Oxford
VandenBoom, Becki, *Pre-Conquest Celtic and Germanic Trade with the Wider Mediterranean*, https://www.academia.edu/5081476/Pre-%20conquest_Celtic_and_Germanic_trade_with_the_wider_Mediterranean
Wells, P.S., (1987), 'Industry, Commerce and Temperate Europe's First Cities: Preliminary Report on 1987 Excavations at Kelheim, Bavaria', *Journal of Field Archaeology*, 14:4

West, L.C., (1937), 'Roman Gaul: The Objects of Trade', *Classical Philology*, Vol. 32, No. 3
Wilcox, P., (2000), *Barbarians against Rome: Rome's Celtic, Germanic, Spanish and Gallic Enemies*, Osprey
Woolf, Greg, (1998), *Becoming Roman: The Origins of Provincial Civilization in Gaul*, Cambridge
http://www.academia.edu/5081476/Pre- conquest_Celtic_and_Germanic_trade_with_ the_wider_Mediterranean
http://upload.wikimedia.org/wikipedia/commons/thumb/b/ba/Map_Gallia_Tribes_ Towns.png/640px-Map_Gallia_Tribes_Towns.png
http://bluenetworks2014.weebly.com/trade-between-gauls-and-romans-in-gaul.html

Chapter 7: Rome and the Nordic Countries
Alonso-Núñez, J.M., (1988), 'Roman Knowledge of Scandinavia in the Imperial Period', *Oxford Journal of Archaeology*, 7, 47–64
Andersson, Kent, 'The Roman Empire and Scandinavia, Nordic Tales Byzantine Paths – https://nordictalesbyzantinepaths.ku.edu.tr/en/article/the-roman-empire-and-scandinavia-t3
Axboc, M., (1981), 'The Scandinavian Gold Bracteates: Studies on their Manufacture and Regional Variations', *Acta Archaeologica*, 52: 1–100, 52–55
Bakka, E., (1971), 'Scandinavian Trade Relations with the Continent and the British Isles in Pre-Viking Times', in *Anrikvariskl arkiv 40 Early Medieval Studies 3*, (1971): 37–51 (39)
Behr, C., (2006), 'Using bracteates as evidence for long-distance contacts', *Reading Medieval Studies*, XXXII. pp. 15–25. https://centaur.reading.ac.uk/84536/
Brogan, O., (1936), 'Trade between the Roman Empire and the Free Germans', *The Journal of Roman Studies*, 26(2), 195–222
Campbell, E., (1996a), 'Trade in the Dark-Age West: A Peripheral Activity?', in *Scotland in Dark Age Britain*, edited by B. E. Crawford, Edinburgh
Campbell, E., (1996c), 'The Archaeological Evidence for External Contacts: Imports, Trade and Economy in Celtic Britain AD 400–800', in *External Contacts and the Economy of Late Roman and Post-Roman Britain*, edited by K. R. Dark, Woodbridge
Dobson, Dina, P., (1936), 'Roman Influence in the North', *Greece & Rome* 5.14, pp 73–89
Fulford, M., (1985), 'Roman Material in Barbarian Society, c. 200 BC–c. AD 400', in *Settlement and Society: Aspects of West European Prehistory in the First Millennium B.C.*, edited by T. Champion and J. Megaw, Leicester
Grane, Thomas, (2007), *The Roman Empire and Scandinavia – a Northern Connection*, submitted as PhD dissertation at the SAXO-Institute, University of Copenhagen by Thomas Grane
Hansen, U., (1989), 'Beyond the Roman Frontier, in *The Birth of Europe: Archaeology and Social Development in the First Millennium A.D.*, edited by K. Randsborg, Rome: L'Erma di Bretschneider
Hedeager, L., (1978a), 'A Quantitative Analysis of Roman Imports in Europe North of the Limes (0–400 A.D.), and the Question of Romano-Germanic Exchange', in *New Directions in Scandinavian Archaeology*, edited by K. Kristiansen and C. Paludan-Müller, National Museum of Denmark
Hedeager, L., (1987), 'Empire, Frontier and the Barbarian Hinterland: Rome and Northern Europe from AD 1–400', in *Centre and Periphery in the Ancient World*, edited by M. Rowlands et al., Cambridge
Imer, Lisbeth M., (2010), 'Runes and Romans in the North', *Futhark International Journal of Runic Studies* 1

Jankuhn, H., (1982), 'Trade and Settlement in Central and Northern Europe up to and During the Viking Period', *The Journal of the Royal Society of Antiquaries of Ireland*, 112, 18–50

Lyttkens, Carl Hampus, (2012), 'The Roman Bazaar. A Comparative Study of Trade and Markets in a Tributary Empire, *Scandinavian Economic History Review*, 60:1, 108–111

Museer, Malmö, (1996), *Roman Reflections in Scandinavia*, Rome: L'Erma di Bretschneider

Mercer, Paul, *Romans in Norway? Surely Not*B at https://www.epiacumheritage.org/blog/post/romans-in-norway-surely-not%EF%BF%BC/

Parker, David Stuart, (2021), 'Vestiges of Roman Cult Religion and Household Deities' in the *Northern Barbaricum: A Study of Statuettes and other Anthropomorphic Figures from Barbaricum, Britannia Superior and the Roman Heartlands*, Lunds Universitet Bachelor's Degree in Archaeology

Ränk, Gustav, (1976), *Old Estonia, The People and Culture*, Indiana University

Roberts, S.H., (1994), 'Bronze Statuettes Found in Denmark', *Akten der 10. Internationalen Tagung über antike Bronzen – Freiburg*, 18–22. Juli 1988, Stuttgart, Landesdenkmalamt Baden-Württemberg

Waldman, Carl; Mason, Catherine, (2006), *Encyclopedia of European Peoples*, Infobase Publishing

Wells, S.P., (1999), *The Barbarians Speak: How the Conquered Peoples Shaped Roman Europe*, Princeton

Whitaker, I., (1980), 'Tacitus' 'Fenni' and Ptolemy's 'Phinnoi'', *The Classical Journal*, 75(3), 215–224

Wicker, N.L., (2005), 'Display of Scandinavian Migration Period Bracteates and Other Pendant Jewelry as a Reflection of Prestige and Identity', in *De Re Metallica. The Uses of Metal in the Middle Ages*, eds. R. Bork, et aL, AVIST A Studies in the History of Medieval Technology, Science, and Art 4, Aldershot, 2005, 49–61 (54f.)

Wooding, J.M., (1996), 'Cargoes in Trade along the Western Seaboard', in *External Contacts and the Economy of Late Roman and Post-Roman Britain*, edited by K. R. Dark, Woodbridge

Chapter 8: Eastern Europe

Bliujienė, A., (2006), 'Amber in the Eastern Baltic Region during the Roman Iron Age. Some aspects of Barbarian Fashions', in *Amber in Archaeology: Proceedings of the Fifth International Conference on Amber in Archaeology*, eds. A. Palavestra, C. Beck & J. Todd, Belgrade, 80–95

Bojtár, Endre, (1999), *Foreword to the Past: A Cultural History of the Baltic People*, Budapest

Bunkśe, E.V., & Tietze, W., (1994), 'Baltic Peoples, Baltic Culture, and Europe: Introduction', *GeoJournal*, 33(1), 5–8

Chrystal, Paul, (2015), *Wars and Battles of the Roman Republic*, Stroud

Chrystal, Paul, (2017), *Women in Ancient Greece*, Stroud

Chrystal, Paul, (2019), *Rome: Republic into Empire*, Barnsley

Chrystal, Paul, (2020), *Women at War in the Classical World*, Barnsley

Chrystal, Paul, (2023), *Bioterrorism and Biological Warfare*, Barnsley

Causey, F., (2012), *Amber and the Ancient World*, Los Angeles

Cunliffe, B., (1988), *Greeks, Romans & Barbarians, Spheres of Interaction*, London

de Navarro, J.M., (December 1925), 'Prehistoric Routes between Northern Europe and Italy Defined by the Amber Trade', *The Geographical Journal*, 66(6): 481–503

Gimbutas, Marija, (1963), *The Balts*, London

Grimaldi, D.A., (1996), *Amber: Window to the Past*, New York

Istvánovits, E., & Kulcsár, V., (2020), 'Sarmatians on the Borders of the Roman Empire: Steppe Traditions and Imported Cultural Phenomena', *Ancient Civilizations from Scythia to Siberia*, 26(2), 391–402

Kiaupa, Zigmanta, (2008), *The History of the Baltic Countries*, Estonia
Kulakov, V., (2005), *The Amber Lands in the Time of the Roman Empire*, Oxford
Lundgren, O., (2018), *The Gold of the North: Amber in the Roman Empire in the First Two Centuries AD*, Bachelor Thesis in Classical Archaeology and Ancient History, Department of Archaeology and Ancient History, Uppsala Universitet
Madsen, Jesper Majbom, (2010), 'Mithradates VI: Rome's Perfect Enemy', in *Proceedings of the Danish Institute in Athens*, Vol. 6, 2010, pp. 223–237
Marková, K. & Stegmann-Rajtár, S., (2006), 'Amber in the Context of Cultural Interactions in the Carpathian Basin in the Early Iron Age', in *Amber in Archaeology. Proceedings of the Fifth International Conference on Amber in Archaeology*, eds. A. Palavestra., C. Beck., & J. Todd, Belgrade, 110–123
Mayor, Adrienne, (2009), *The Poison King: The Life and Legend of Mithradates, Rome's Deadliest Enemy*, Princeton
McGing, B.C., (1986), *The Foreign Policy of Mithradates VI Eupator, King of Pontus*, Mnemosyne, Supplements: 89, Leiden
Miller, F., (1981), *The Roman Empire and Its Neighbours*, London
Mordvintseva, V., (2017), 'The Sarmatians in the Northern Black Sea Region: (On the Basis of Archaeological Material)', in V. Kozlovskaya (Ed.), *The Northern Black Sea in Antiquity: Networks, Connectivity, and Cultural Interactions*, pp. 233–283, Cambridge
Navarro, J.M. de., (1925), 'Prehistoric Routes Between Northern Europe and Italy Defined by the Amber Trade', *The Geographical Journal*, 66, 481–503
Pitts, L.F., (1989), 'Relations between Rome and the German 'Kings' on the Middle Danube in the First to Fourth Centuries A.D.', *The Journal of Roman Studies*, 79, 45–58
Ross, A., (1998), *Amber: The Natural Time Capsule*, London
Singer, Graciela Gestoso, (2008), "Amber in the Ancient Near East', *i-Medjat* No. 2 (December 2008), Papyrus Electronique des Ankou
Spekke, A., (1957), *The Ancient Amber Routes and the Geographical Discovery of the Eastern Baltic*, Stockholm
Strong, D.E., (1966), *Catalogue of the Carved Amber in the Department of Greek and Roman Antiquities*, London
Sulimerski, T., (1970), *The Sarmatians*, London
Swift, E., (2003), 'Transformation in Meaning: Amber and Glass Beads Across the Roman Frontier', *Theoretical Roman Archaeology Journal*, 2002, 48–57
Symonenko, Oleksandr V., (2013), 'Trade and Trophy: Near East Imports in the Sarmatian Culture', *Mousaios*, 18
Trusted, M., (1985), *Catalogue of European Ambers in the Victoria and Albert Museum*, Wisbech
Wallace-Hadrill, A., (1990), 'Pliny the Elder and Man's Unnatural History', *Greece & Rome*, 37(1), 80–96.

Chapter 9: Britannia
Allason-Jones, Lyndsay, (2002), *The Jet Industry and Allied Trades in Roman Britain*, in, Wilson & Price
Blagg, T.F.C., & King, A., (eds.), (1984), *Military and Civilian in Roman Britain: Cultural Relationships in a Frontier Province*, Oxford: British Archaeological Reports
Chrystal, Paul, (2020), *The Romans in the North of England*, Darlington
Chrystal, Paul, (2022), *The Making of Roman York*, Lancaster
Chrystal, Paul, (2022), *A Historical Guide to Roman York*, Barnsley
du Plat Taylor, Joan, & Cleere, Henry, (eds.), (1978), *Roman Shipping and Trade: Britain and the Rhine Provinces*, London: Council for British Archaeology

Fulford, Michael, (1977), *Pottery and Britain's Foreign Trade in the Later Roman Period*, pp. 35–84. In Peacock (1977)
Fulford, Michael, (1984), *Demonstrating Britannia's Economic Dependence in the First and Second Centuries*, in Blagg & King (1984)
Fulford, Michael, (1989), *The Economy of Roman Britain*, in Todd (1989)
Fulford, Michael, (1991), *Britain and the Roman Empire: The Evidence for Regional and Long Distance Trade*, in Jones (1991)
Fulford, Michael, (2007), *Coasting Britannia: Roman Trade and Traffic Around the Shores of Britain*, in Gosden et al.
Peacock, D.P.S., and Williams, D.F., (1986), *Amphorae in the Roman Economy*, London
Ireland, Stanley, (2008) [1986], *Roman Britain: A Sourcebook*, London
Margary, Ivan D., (1973) [1967], *Roman Roads in Britain*, 3rd ed., London: J. Baker
Mattingly, David, (2006), *An Imperial Possession: Britain in the Roman Empire*, London: Penguin
Millet, Martin, (1992) [1990], *The Romanization of Britain: An Essay in Archaeological Interpretation*, Cambridge University Press
Moorhead, Sam, & Stuttard, David, (2012), *The Romans Who Shaped Britain*, London
Tyers, Paul, (1996a), *Roman Pottery in Britain*, London
Tyers, Paul, (1996b), 'Roman Amphoras in Britain', *Internet Archaeology:* Council for British Archaeology
Wilson, Peter R., & Price, Jennifer, (eds.), (2002), *Aspects of Industry in Roman Yorkshire and the North*, Oxford

Chapter 10: Africa – Sub-Sahara and West Africa, Egypt, Nubia, Lake Chad

Carpenter, Rhys, (1966); Nef, Evelyn Stefansson, (ed.), *Beyond the Pillars of Heracles: The Classical World Seen through the Eyes of its Discoverers*, The Great Explorers: New York
Celentano, C., (2016), 'Palmyrenes Abroad: Traders and Patrons in Arsacid Mesopotamia', *Greek and Roman Studies*, 19, 2016, pp. 30–57
Cary, Max, & Warmington, Eric Herbert, (1929), *The Ancient Explorers*, London
Cobb, M.A., (2015), 'Balancing the Trade: Roman Cargo Shipments to India', *OJA* 34/2, 2015
Cobb, M.A., (2018), *Rome and the Indian Ocean Trade from Augustus to the Early Third Century CE*, Leiden
Coleman De Graft-Johnson, John, (1986), *African Glory: The Story of Vanished Negro Civilizations*, New York
Dalby, Andrew, (2002), *Dangerous Tastes*, University of California Press
De Romanis F., (2014), 'Ivory from Muziris', *ISAW Papers* 8, 2014, pp. 134, http://dlib.nyu.edu/awdl/isaw/isaw-papers/8
De Romanis, F., (2015), 'Comparative Perspectives on the Pepper Trade', in F. De Romanis, & M. Maiuro (eds.), *Across the Ocean. Nine Essays on Indo-Mediterranean Trade*, Leiden 2015
De Romanis, F., (2020), *The Indo-Roman Pepper Trade and the Muziris Papyrus*, Oxford
Eichel, Marijean H., (1976), 'A Note on Polybius' Voyage to Africa in 146 BC', *Classical Philology* 71
Habinger, Sophie, B., (2020), 'Mobility and Origin of Camels in the Roman Empire through Serial Stable Carbon and Oxygen Isotope Variations in Tooth Enamel', *Quaternary International* 557, 80–91
Hourani, George F., (1995), *Arab Seafaring in the Indian Ocean in Ancient and Early Medieval Times*, Princeton University Press
Hyde, Walter Woodburn, (1947), *Ancient Greek Mariners*, New York
Kaeppel, Carl, (1936), *Off the Beaten Track in the Classics*, New York

Kirpan, L.P., (1957), 'Rome beyond the Southern Egyptian Frontier', *Geographical Journal*
Kroupa, Sebestian, (2019), 'Humanists and Travellers, Gorgons and Gorillas: Hanno the Navigator's 'Periplus' and Early Modern Geography (1530–1630) (PDF), *International History Review*, 41(4): 793–820
Law, R.C.C., (1978), 'North Africa in the Period of Phoenician and Greek Colonization, c. 800 to 325 BC', in Fage, John Donnelly, & Oliver, Roland Anthony (eds.), *The Cambridge History of Africa*, Vol. 2, Cambridge
Lendering, Jona, (2020) [1998], 'Hanno the Navigator', *Livius*
Mauny, Raymond, (1955), 'La navigation sur les côtes du sahara pendant l'antiquité', *Revue des Études Anciennes* (in French), Bordeaux Montaigne University, 57(1): 92–101
McLaughlin, R., (2010), *Rome and the Distant East*, Continuum
McLaughlin, R., (2014), *The Roman Empire and the Indian Ocean*, Barnsley
McLaughlin, R., (2016), *The Roman Empire and the Silk Routes: The Ancient World Economy and the Empires of Parthia, Central Asia and Han China*, Barnsley
McLaughlin, R., (2019), 'Indian Ocean Commerce in Context: The Economic and Revenue Significance of Eastern Trade in the Ancient World', in M.A. Cobb (ed.), *The Indian Ocean in Antiquity: Political, Cultural, and Economic Impacts*, London, 2019, pp. 117134
Moore, Frank Gardner, (1950), "Three Canal Projects, Roman and Byzantine', *American Journal of Archaeology*, Vol. 54, No. 2, pp. 97–111
Munro-Hay, Stuart, (1991), *Aksum: An African Civilization of Late Antiquity*, Edinburgh
Oikonomides, Al. N., (1977) [1974], Oikonomides, Al. N. (ed.), *Periplus, or Circumnavigation (of Africa)*, 2nd ed., Chicago
Phillipson, David, (1998), *Ancient Ethiopia, Aksum: Its Antecedents and Successors*, London
Phillipson, David, (2009), 'The First Millennium BC in the Highlands of Northern Ethiopia and South–Central Eritrea: A Reassessment of Cultural and Political Development', *African Archaeological Review*, 26: 257–274
Phillipson, David, (2012), *Foundations of an African Civilization: Aksum and the Northern Horn, 1000 BC–AD 1300*, Addis Ababa
Rappoport, S., (1904), *'History of Egypt'*, Volume 3, Chapter V: 'The Waterways of Egypt', pp. 250–253, London
Rathbone, Dominic W., (2003), 'The Financing of Maritime Commerce in the Roman Empire, I–II AD.', in *Credito e moneta nel mondo romano*, edited by Elio Lo Cascio, 197–229, Bari, Italy: Edipuglia
Raven, Susan, (2012), *Rome in Africa*, London
Roth, Jonathan, *The Roman Army in Tripolitana and Gold Trade with Sub-Saharan Africa*
Seland, E.H., 'The Persian Gulf or the Red Sea? Two Axes in the Ancient Indian Ocean Trade, Where to Go and Why' *World Archaeology*, 43, 2011, pp. 398–409
Sidebotham, Steven E., (2019), *Berenike and the Ancient Maritime Spice Route*, University of California Press
Singer, C., (2021), 'The Incense Kingdom of Yemen: An Outline History of the South Arabian Incense', in *Food for the Gods*, edited by Peacock, D. P. S. and Williams, D. F. (eds.), Oxbow Books, 2021
Stone, David L., (2014), 'Africa in the Roman Empire: Connectivity, the Economy, and Artificial Port Structures', *American Journal of Archaeology*, Vol. 118, No. 4, pp. 565–593
Swanson, J.T., (1975), 'The Myth of Trans-Saharan Trade during the Roman Era', *The International Journal of African Historical Studies*, 8(4), p. 582–600
Thorley, J., (1969), 'The Development of Trade between the Roman Empire and the East under Augustus'. *Greece & Rome*, 16(2), 209–223

Tomber, Roberta, (2008), *Indo-Roman Trade: From Pots to Pepper*, London
Turner, Jack, (2005), *Spice*, Vintage
Watt, Martin, (2013), *Frankincense & Myrrh*, C W Daniel

Chapter 11: Arabia
Bloggs, G.W., (1986), 'Tyre and Tylos: Bahrain in the Graeco-Roman World', in Rice, Michael (ed.), *Bahrain through the Ages: The Archaeology*, Routledge.
Boulnois, Luce, (2004), *Silk Road: Monks, Warriors & Merchants on the Silk Road*, Hong Kong
Bowerstock, G.W., (1983), *Roman Arabia*, Cambridge
Cary, Max, (1956), 'Maes, Qui et Titianus', *The Classical Quarterly*, 6, pp. 130–134
Charlesworth, M.P., (1974) [reprint of 1926 ed.], *Trade-Routes and Commerce of the Roman Empire*, 2nd ed., Chicago
Corn, Charles, & Glasserman, Debbie, (1999), *The Scents of Eden: A History of the Spice Trade*, Kodansha America
Fisher, Greg, (2019), *Rome, Persia, and Arabia: Shaping the Middle East from Pompey to Muhammad*, London
Galli, Marco, (2017), 'Beyond Frontiers: Ancient Rome and the Eurasian Trade Networks', *Journal of Eurasian Studies*
Hill, John E., (2009), *Through the Jade Gate to Rome: A Study of the Silk Routes during the Later Han Dynasty, First to Second Centuries CE*, BookSurge
Hirth, Friedrich, (2000) [1885], Jerome S. Arkenberg (ed.), *East Asian History Sourcebook: Chinese Accounts of Rome, Byzantium and the Middle East, c. 91 B.C.E.–1643 C.E.*, Fordham.edu.
Hirth, Friedrich, (1939) [1885], *China and the Roman Orient: Researches Into Their Ancient and Mediaeval Relations as Represented in Old Chinese Records*, (reprint), Leipzig
Keay, John, (2006), *The Spice Route: A History*, University of California Press
Klotz, David, (2015), 'Darius I and the Sabaeans: Ancient Partners in Red Sea Navigation', *Journal of Near Eastern Studies*, 74(2): 267–280
Korotayev, Andrey, (1995), *Ancient Yemen*, Oxford
Leslie, D.D., & Gardiner, K.H.J., (1996), 'The Roman Empire in Chinese Sources', *Studi Orientali*, Vol. 15, Rome
Markoe, Glenn, (ed.), (2003), *Petra Rediscovered: Lost City of the Nabataeans*, New York
McLaughlin, Raoul, (2016), *The Roman Empire and the Silk Routes*, Barnsley
Millar, Fergus, (ed.), (1967), *The Roman Empire and its Neighbours*, New York
Miller, J. Innes, (1969), *The Spice Trade of the Roman Empire 29 B.C. to A.D. 641*, Oxford
Nabhan, Gary Paul, (2014), *Cumin, Camels, and Caravans: A Spice Odyssey*, University of California Press
Nebes, Norbert, (2023), 'Early Saba and Its Neighbors', in Radner, Karen, Moeller, Nadine, & Potts, D. T., (eds.), *The Oxford History of the Ancient Near East: The Age of Persia*, Vol. 5, Oxford University Press, pp. 299–375
Pulleyblank, Edwin G., (1999), 'The Roman Empire as Known to Han China', *Journal of the American Oriental Society*, Vol. 119, No. 1 (1999), pp. 71–79
Rawlinson, Hugh George, (2001), *Intercourse Between India and the Western World: From the Earliest Times to the Fall of Rome*, Asian Educational Services
Sidebotham, S. E., (1986), 'Aelius Gallus and Arabia', *Latomus: Revue d'études latines*, 45.3: 590–602
Tabulae Geographicae, (2017), 'New inscriptions from Saudi Arabia and the Extent of Roman Rule Along the Red Sea', *Tabulae Geographicae*, March 31, 2017

Taylor, Jane, (2002), *Petra and the Lost Kingdom of the Nabataeans*, Cambridge, Mass
Young, Gary K., (2001), *Rome's Eastern Trade: International Commerce and Imperial Policy, 31 BC–AD 305*, London

Chapter 12: Parthia and the Sasanian Empire
Brosius, Maria, (2006), *The Persians: An Introduction*, London
Casson, L., (1954), 'The Grain Trade of the Hellenistic World', *TAPhA* 85 (1954): 168–187
Casson, L., (1980), 'The Role of the State in Rome's Grain Trade', *MAAR* 36 (1980): 21–33
Davis, Richard, (2002), 'Greece ix. Greek and Persian Romances', *Encyclopaedia Iranica*, Vol. XI, Fasc. 4. pp. 339–342
Ebrey, Patricia Buckley, (1999), *The Cambridge Illustrated History of China*, Cambridge
Frye, R.N., (2005), 'The Sassanians', in Eiddon, Iorwerth, & Edwards, Stephen (eds.), *The Cambridge Ancient History – XII – The Crisis of Empire*
Garthwaite, Gene Ralph, (2005), *The Persians*, Oxford
Grainger, J. D., (2013), *Rome, Parthia and India*, Barnsley
Gregoratti, Leonardo, (2017), 'The Arsacid Empire', in Daryaee, Touraj (ed.), *King of the Seven Climes: A History of the Ancient Iranian World (3000 BCE–651 CE)* , UCI Jordan Center for Persian Studies
Hill, John E., (2009), *Through the Jade Gate to Rome: A Study of the Silk Routes during the Later Han Dynasty, First to Second Centuries CE*, BookSurge
Hill, Steven, (2013), *Defining the alter orbis: The Roman View of Parthia in the Early Principate*, dissertation: University of Wales, Trinity Saint David
Hourani, Albert, (1991), *A History of the Arab Peoples*, London
Howard, Michael C., (2012), *Transnationalism in Ancient and Medieval Societies: The Role of Cross Border Trade and Travel*, Jefferson: McFarland & Company
Isaac, B., (2004), *The Invention of Racism in Classical Antiquity*, Princeton
Kurz, Otto, (1983), 'Cultural Relations Between Parthia and Rome', in Yarshater, Ehsan (ed.), *The Cambridge History of Iran, Volume 3(1): The Seleucid, Parthian and Sasanian Periods*, Cambridge
Lukonin, V.G., (1983), 'Political, Social and Administrative Institutions: Taxes and Trade', in Yarshater, Ehsan (ed.), *The Cambridge History of Iran, Volume 3(2): The Seleucid, Parthian and Sasanian Periods*. Cambridge
McLaughlin, R., (2016), *The Roman Empire and the Silk Routes*, Barnsley
Nicolle, David, (1996), *Sassanian Armies: The Iranian Empire Early-3rd to Mid-7th Centuries AD*, Stockport
Patterson, L.E., (2015), 'Antony and Armenia', *TAPA* 145(1), 77–105
Rickman, G., (1980), 'The Grain Trade under the Roman Empire', *MAAR* 36 (1980): 261–27
Schoff, Wilfred H., (1914), *Parthian Stations by Isidore of Charax: The Greek text, with a Translation and Commentary*, Philadelphia: Commercial Museum
Simpson, St. John, (ed.), (2002), *Queen of Sheba: Treasures from Ancient Yemen*, London: British Museum Press
Tao, W., (2007), 'Parthia in China: A Re-examination of the Historical Records', in *The Age of the Parthians*, edited by V. Curtis and S. Stewart, 87–104, London
Whitfield, Susan, (1999), *Life along the Silk Road*, Berkeley
Whitfield, Susan, with Ursula Sims-Williams, (eds.), (2004), *The Silk Route: Trade, Travel, War and Faith*, London
Wang, Tao, (2007), 'Parthia in China: A Re-examination of the Historical Records', in Curtis, Vesta Sarkhosh and Stewart, Sarah (eds.), *The Age of the Parthians: The Ideas of*

Iran, Vol. 2, London in association with the London Middle East Institute at SOAS and the British Museum

Watson, William, (1983), 'Iran and China', in Yarshater, Ehsan, (ed.), *The Cambridge History of Iran, Volume 3(1): The Seleucid, Parthian and Sasanian Periods*, Cambridge

Young, Gary K., (2001), *Rome's Eastern Trade: International Commerce and Imperial Policy, 31 BC–AD 305*, London

Yü, Ying-shih, (1986), 'Han Foreign Relations', in Twitchett, Denis and Loewe, Michael (eds.), *Cambridge History of China: the Ch'in and Han Empires, 221 B.C.–A.D. 220*, Vol. 1, Cambridge

Chapter 13: India

Higham, Charles, (2009), *Encyclopedia of Ancient Asian Civilizations*, Infobase

Husaini, S.A.Q., (1962), *The History of the Pandya Country*, Karaikud

McCrindle, J.W., (1884), 'Ptolemy's Geography of India and Southern Asia', *The Indian Antiquary*, Bombay 372 ff

McCrindle, J.W., (1927), *Ancient India as Described by Ptolemy*, Calcutta

Mukund, Kanakalatha, (1999), *The Trading World of the Tamil Merchant*, Hyderabad

Parker, Grant, & Rife, J. L., (2014), 'The Making of Roman India by Grant Parker (review)', *American Journal of Philology*, vol. 135 no. 4, 2014, pp. 672–675: Project MUSE

Rawlinson, H.G., (2001), *Intercourse Between India and the Western World: From the Earliest Times of the Fall of Rome*, Asian Educational Services

Sinopoli, Carla M., (2001), 'On the Edge of Empire: Form and Substance in the Satavahana Dynasty", in Alcock, Susan E et al. (eds.), *Empires: Perspectives from Archaeology and History*, Cambridge

Tomber, R., (2008), *Indo-Roman Trade: From Pots to Pepper*, London

Warmington, E.H., (1974), *The Commerce Between the Roman Empire and India*, 2nd edition, London

Wendrich, W.Z., 'Berenike Crossroads: The Integration of Information', *Journal of the Economic and Social History of the Orient*, 46(1): 59–60

Chapter 14: Sri Lanka and Myanmar (Burma)

McLaughlin, R., (2014a), 'Ancient Contacts: The Roman Emperor and the Sinhalese King', *Classics Ireland*, 21–22, 1–40

Munasinghe, D.S.A., (2021), 'Sri Lanka and Greco-Roman Trade Relations', *Journal of Archaeological Studies in India*, Vol. 1, No. 2, 2021, pp. 241–249

Szekelyy M., (2018), *Senedipity: The Roman Discovery of Taprobane. Borders and Crossings*: International and Multidisciplinary Conference on Travel Writing (Pula – Brijuni, 15 September 2018. https://emuni.si/wp-content/uploads/2019/11/2018-11-2_49-62.pdf

Weerakkody, D.P.M., *Sri Lanka and the Roman Empire*, Digital Library @ University of Peradeniya http://dlib.pdn.ac.lk › bitstream

Weerakkody, D.P.M., (1997, ed.), *Taprobanê: Ancient Sri Lanka as Known to Greeks and Romans. Indicopleustoi. Archaeologies of the Indian Ocean*, Turnhout: Brepols

Young, G., (2001), *Rome's Eastern Trade: International Commerce and Imperial Policy*, London

Chapter 15: China and the Silk Road

An, Jiayao, (2002), 'When Glass Was Treasured in China', in Annette L. Juliano and Judith A. Lerner (eds.), *Silk Road Studies VII: Nomads, Traders, and Holy Men Along China's Silk Road*, 79–94, Turnhout

Bang, Peter F., (2009), 'Commanding and Consuming the World: Empire, Tribute, and Trade in Roman and Chinese History', in Walter Scheidel (ed.), *Rome and China: Comparative Perspectives on Ancient World Empires*, pp. 100–120, Oxford

Bueno, André, (2016), 'Roman Views of the Chinese in Antiquity', in *Sino-Platonic Papers*, (PDF), Sino-platonic.org

Christopoulos, Lucas, (2012), 'Hellenes and Romans in Ancient China (240 BC–1398 AD)', in Victor H. Mair (ed.), *Sino-Platonic Papers*, No. 230, Chinese Academy of Social Sciences, University of Pennsylvania Department of East Asian Languages and Civilizations

Leslie, D.D., & Gardiner, K.H.J., (1996), 'The Roman Empire in Chinese Sources', *Studi Orientali*, Vol. 15, Rome: Department of Oriental Studies, University of Rome

Pulleyblank, Edwin G., (1999), 'Review: The Roman Empire as Known to Han China: The Roman Empire in Chinese Sources by D. D. Leslie; K. H. J. Gardiner', *Journal of the American Oriental Society*, Vol. 119, No. 1 (1999), pp. 71–79

Schoff, W.H., (1915), *The Eastern Iron Trade of the Roman Empire*, New Haven

Schoff, W.H., (1917), 'Navigation to the Far East under the Roman Empire', *Journal of the American Oriental Society*, Vol. 37 (1917), pp. 240–249

Thorley, John, (1971), 'The Silk Trade between China and the Roman Empire at Its Height, 'Circa' A. D. 90–130', *Greece and Rome*, Vol. 18, No. 1 (1971), pp. 71–80

Thorley, John, (1979), 'The Roman Empire and the Kushans', in *Greece and Rome*, Vol. 26, No. 2 (1979), pp. 181–190 (187f.)

Wen, Xin, On the Road, *History Today* 73, 2023

Young, Gary K., (2001), *Rome's Eastern Trade: International Commerce and Imperial Policy, 31 BC–AD 305*, London

Chapter 16: The Assimilation and Adoption of Foreign Ideas and Culture through Trade

Bentley, Jerry, (1993), *Old World Encounters: Cross-Cultural Contacts and Exchanges in Pre-Modern Times*, Oxford

Boateng, Daniel, *The Silk Road: A Timeless Lesson in Cultural Competency and Innovation*, The Future List, 2023

Frank, Tenney, (1916), 'Race Mixture in the Roman Empire', *The American Historical Review*, 21, no. 4 (1916): 689–708

Henrichs, Albert, (1995), 'Greece in Rome: Influence, Integration, Resistance', *Harvard Studies in Classical Philology*, Vol. 97, pp. 243–261

Hingley, Richard, (2005), 'Globalizing Roman Culture: Unity, Diversity and Empire', *Psychology Press*

Hingley, Richard, (2009), 'Cultural Diversity and Unity: Empire and Rome', in *Material Culture and Social Identities in the Ancient World*, Cambridge: Cambridge University Press, pp. 54–75

Hope, Valerie, (2013), 'Status and Identity in the Roman World', in *Experiencing Rome: Culture, Identity and Power in the Roman Empire*, edited by Janet Huskinson, Routledge, pp. 125–152

Jones, A.H.M., (1963), 'The Greeks under the Roman Empire', *Dumbarton Oaks Papers*, Vol. 17 (1963), pp. 13–19

Mathers, C.J., (1991), 'Review of 'The Rise of Merchant Empires: Long-Distance Trade in the Early Modern World', by J. D. Tracy', *The Business History Review*, 65(1), 201–203

MacMullen, Ramsey, (2000), *Romanization in the Time of Augustus*, Yale University Press

Milleker, Elizabeth J., (ed.), (2000), *The Year One: Art of the Ancient World East and West*, Exhibition catalogue, New York

Simpson, St. John, (ed.), (2002), *Queen of Sheba: Treasures from Ancient Yemen*, London
Moore, Clifford Herschel, (1909), 'Individualism and Religion in the Early Roman Empire', *The Harvard Theological Review* 2, no. 2, 221–34
Pollitt, Jerome, J., (1978), 'The Impact of Greek Art on Rome', *Transactions of the American Philological Association*, Vol. 108, pp. 155–174
Tracy, J.D., (ed.), (1990), *The Rise of Merchant Empires: Long-Distance Trade in the Early Modern World*, Cambridge
Wedeck, Harry E., (1929), 'The Roman Attitude toward Foreign Influence, Particularly Toward the Greek Influence during the Republic', *The Classical Weekly*, Vol. 22, No. 25 pp. 195–198
Whitfield, Susan, (1999), *Life Along the Silk Road*, Berkeley
Wen, Xin, On the Road, *History Today* 73, 2023
Whitfield, Susan, and Sims-Williams, Ursula, (eds.), (2004), *The Silk Route: Trade, Travel, War and Faith*, London: 2004
Woolf, G., (1994), 'Becoming Roman, Staying Greek: Culture, Identity and the Civilising Process in the Roman East', *Proceedings of the Cambridge Philological Society*, 40, 116–143

Chapter 17: Eastern religions in the Roman Empire
Alvar, Jaime, (2008), *Romanising Oriental Gods: Myth, Salvation, and Ethics in the Cults of Cybele, Isis, and Mithras*, Brill
Ball, Warwick, (2016), *Rome in the East: The Transformation of an Empire*, London
Beard, M., Price, S., & North, J., (1998), *Religions of Rome: Volume 1, A History*, Cambridge
Beck, Roger, (2006), *The Religion of the Mithras Cult in the Roman Empire: Mysteries of the Unconquered Sun*, Oxford
Boulnois, Luce, (2004), *Silk Road: Monks, Warriors & Merchants on the Silk Road*
Bowden, Hugh, (2010), *Mystery Cults of the Ancient World*, Princeton University
Bulliet, Richard W. (1975), *The Camel and the Wheel*, Harvard University Press
Burkert, Walter, (1987), *Ancient Mystery Cults*, Harvard University Press
Christian, David, (2000), 'Silk Roads or Steppe Roads? The Silk Roads in World History', in the *Journal of World History*, 2.1 1.
de la Vaissière, E. (2005), *Sogdian Traders: A History*, Leiden
Foltz, Richard, (1999), *Religions of the Silk Road: Overland Trade and Cultural Exchange from Antiquity to the Fifteenth Century*, New York
Hill, John E. (2009), *Through the Jade Gate to Rome: A Study of the Silk Routes during the Later Han Dynasty, 1st to 2nd centuries CE*, BookSurge, Charleston
Meyer, Marvin W., (1999), *The Ancient Mysteries, a Sourcebook: Sacred Texts of the Mystery Religions of the Ancient Mediterranean World*, University of Pennsylvania Press
Pitts, M. and Versluys, M.J., (2014), (eds.), *Globalisation and the Roman World: World History, Connectivity and Material Culture*, Cambridge University Press
Staples, Ariadne, (1998), *From Good Goddess to Vestal Virgins: Sex and Category in Roman Religion*, Routledge.
Takács, Sarolta A., (1995), *Isis and Sarapis in the Roman World*, E.J. Brill
Versnel, H.S., (1992), 'The Festival for Bona Dea and the Thesmophoria', *Greece & Rome*, 39(1): 31–55
Wen, Xin, On the Road, *History Today* 73, 2023
Wicher, Robert, (2017), 'The Globalized Roman World', in Hodos, Tamar (ed. 2017), *The Routledge Handbook of Archaeology and Globalization*, London

Index

Abacus, 2, 29–30
Africa, xvi–xvii, xx, 2, 7–8, 21, 25, 33–4, 43–4, 47, 55, 110, 112–13, 116–27, 129, 132, 135, 143–6, 152, 161, 164, 167, 177, 183, 185, 197
Aksum, 121–4
   trade with Rome, 124
Alexandria, xviii, 4–5, 17, 115, 129, 133, 135–6, 138, 140–1, 153–4, 163, 171, 178, 195
Alexandria the Great and geography, 7
Althiburos mosaic, Bardo, Tunis, 33
Amber, 3, 10, 58, 64, 68, 70, 75, 77, 79ff, 83–90, 92, 152, 179
   and Tacitus, 88–90
   and women, 89–90
Anaximander of Miletus, atlas, 6
Animals/birds, exotic trade in, 169, 173, 183–4
Antonine Itinerary, 8, 132
Antonine Plague, impact on trade, 41–2, 160
Antonine Wall, 43–4, 61, 109
Apicius, and pepper, 134
Apuleius, and Isis, 193
   Metamorphoses, 133–4
Arabia, xvii–xviii, 7, 10, 113, 115–17, 122, 126–31, 134–5, 143, 146–7, 149–55, 172, 174, 177, 184
   and civil engineering projects, 153
Aristagoras, 6
Atlases, 8
Augustus and Britannia, 101–102
   and geography, 7
   and India, 164–5
   and the Pandyans, 173
   and Red Sea ports, 126
   and Saka, 168
   and Tamil kingdoms, 170
   and trade, 1, 141–2

Bacchanalia, 190–1
Bahrain, 153–4
Balts and their trade, 68, 83ff
Barbaricum (Barbarikon), 63, 72, 128, 167, 185

Barbaroi, the Romans' attitude to foreign traders, 49, 53, 121
   and the converse, 172
Berenike, 23, 116–17, 129, 135–6
Bona Dea, 189–90, 197
Book of Revelation, The, and Roman opulence, 142
Books, as merchants' research tools; as goods, 4–5
Book trade, Appendix
Borders (*limes*), xix, 43–4, 69, 86, 182
Bottomry (insurance), 29
Boudica's revolt, 55, 62–3, 106–107
Bread, 23
Britannia, 61f
   Caligula's farcical invasion plan, 103
   and Herodotus, 94
   and its mystery, 93, 97–9, 102, 105
   and tin, 94, 99
   trade, 58–9, 91ff, 105
      with Nordic countries, 71
British Library Harley MS 7182, 9
Buddhism, 168, 187–8

Cambodia, 178
Camels, 46, 116–18, 128–30, 135, 151–2, 160, 170, 181
Canabae, 40, 87, 110–11
Canal of the Pharaohs, xv, 138–40
Capital, 30
Cargo stamps (weight, content, authenticity, etc.), 40
Cargoes, 22, 25–6, 33, 35–6, 38, 128, 136, 169
Cargo ships, *see* merchant ships
Carnuntum, 85–7
Carthage-Roman trade, 11–14
Cassiterides (Britannia, tin islands), 94–5
Cato the Elder, 23–4, 51
Catullus, xviii, 65, 96–7, 102
Celtic Britannia, 61ff
Celtic coinage, 59–61
Celtic language, 65
Celtic trade goods, 58
Celtic transportation, 65
Celts and Germani, Chapter 6

Chera, 23, 116, 128, 169–70, 172
China, Roman glass imports, 178
China, silks, 129, 133, 137, 147
China, spices, 23
China, steel, 179–80
China, trade with, 147–8, 175, Chapter 15, 176ff
Cicero, 51–2, 97, 99–100
Coan silk, 180
Coinage, 30, 77–78
Colaeus of Samos, 55
Coptos and its markets, 135
Crates of Mallus, 7
Crews, ships, 35
Cultural exchange with Rome, 182–4
and the Silk Road, 185–6
Culture, Gallo-Roman, 60
Cura Annona, corn dole, 30, 36, 38–40
Cursus publicus, the state-run courier and logistics service, 8, 45
Cybele (Magna Mater), 191–2, 196

Dacians, 80–1
Dio Cassius, 16
Diodorus Siculus and Britannia, 93, 95

Eastern Europe, Chapter 8, 79ff
Economic impact on Rome through the importations of luxuries, 186
Economy, Roman and impact of trade with India, 136
with Red Sea Route, 136
in perfumes, 140–1, 146
Egypt, 140
Elephants, 122, 124, 166
Eleusinian Mysteries, 195
Eleventh Map of Asia, 9
Eratosthenes, 7–8
Eudoxus of Cyzicus, 114–15
Extortion and deception in trade, 23, 153

Farasan Command, The, 151
Feeding Rome, *see* Cura Annona
Flag Mound at Avaldsnes, Kermøy, 73–6
Food flavourings, 152
Forum Cuppedenis market, 19
Fora venalia, 19–20
Frankincense Kingdom, 130
Free-trade economy, 30

Gallo-Roman culture, 60
Gallus, Gaus Aelius, and his expedition, 154–5
Gan Ying, 177
Geography, Roman, 6

Gemstones, from Saka, 168
Germani and Celts, Chapter 6, 54ff, 63–4
Ginger, 134
Global trade, Rome and, xvi
Gold, Roman and India, 136
Graeco-Roman trade, 14–15
Grain, 29
Grave goods, 125
Nordic, 73, 74, 89–90

Hadrian's Wall, and trade, 107–108
Hallstatt, Austria, 55
Han Dynasty, 16, 157
Hanno the Navigator, 6, 112–13
Hecataeus of Miletus, 6
Herodotus, *Histories* and geography 6, 79
and Arabia
Himilco, 95–6
Hippalus, 115–16
Homer, and Mediterranean geography, 6
Horn of Africa ('Spice Promontory'), 126

Incense, 149–50, 152–3
depressing effect on Roman economy, 149–50
market amongst elite women, 150
and Poppaea's funeral, 134
public health benefit, 134
in Roman religion, 150
sexual and sensory impact in Rome, 133
Incense Route, the, 149, 152
India and Indian Ocean, 23, 79, 114, 126–7, 129, 136, 138, 140–1, 148, 160–2, 167, Chapter 13, 164ff
and impact on Roman economy, 136
Indian steel, 172
Indus River Valley Civilization (Harappan), 165–6
Industrialization, lack of, 31
Interpretatio Romana, 60
Isis, 189, 192–6
Ivory, 124–5

Jacobus Angelus map, 8–9
Julius Caesar and Bona Dea, 190
Britannia, 61–4, 97
and Celtic trade, 65
and geography, 7
and Germania, 61–3
and Gallic ships (the Veneti), 66
Juvenal, and Bona Dea, 189–90
and misogyny, 146

Kelheim, 67
King of the Great Mound (Storhaug), 72–3

Kush, *see* Nubia
Kushan Empire, 163

Lake Chad, xix, 143–4, 189
lex Claudia (218 BCE), 23
Livy, and sexism, 147
Lod mosaic, Israel, 35
Lucian, *Navigium*, 25
Lucretius, 96

Maës Titianus, 147–8
Magi (Three Wise Men), and incense, 152
Magna Mater, *see* Cybele
Malaya, 175
Maps, 8–9
Marcian of Heraclea, 92
Marcus Aurelius and the Antun delegates, 177
Marine insurance, 28–9
Marinus of Tyre, 7–8, 92
Markets, 19–20
Market size, 31
Medicinal herbs, 151–2
Merchant/cargo ships, 31–2, 34–5
Mercuralia, 23
Mercury, god of commerce, xvi
Misogyny, 146
Mithraism, 189, 194–5
Mithridates, 80, 157
Monopoly, state, 30
Monte Testaccio tip, 22, 26–8, 40
Muziris, Kerala, 128, 135
Muziris Papyrus, 35–6, 136
Myanmar (Burma), 175

Naval superiority, Rome's, 32–3
Necho II, 6, 113
Nordic countries trade, Chapter 7, 68ff
Nubia, 143, 197

Oikumene (the entire inhabited world), 6
Ostia, 37–8
Ovid, *Fasti*, 188–9

Paint pigments, 171
Palmyra, 137
Pandyas, 23, 116, 128, 169, 172
Parthia and the Sasanian Empire, Chapter 12, 156ff
  China, 159
Parthian Stations, 160
Paulus Orosius, 142
Pausanias, *Description of Greece*, 7–8
Pax Romana and trade, 1, 15
Pax Sinica, 16

Pepper, 134
Perfumes, 140–1, 146
Peripli, 132
Periplus of the Erythraean Sea, 9, 127ff, 172, 173, 175
Periplus Maris Exteri, 92
Persian Gulf Corridor, 133, 136–8
Petronius, *Satyricon* and Trimalchio as trader, 25
Peutinger Table, 8, 46, 132
Pirates, 17–19, 22, 125
Plautus, *Mercartor*, 25
Pliny the Elder and geography, 7
  and Britannia, 92
  and negative impact on Roman economy, 146, 171
  and Rome's global trade, xvi, 10
Plutarch, 24
Polybius, 24, 114
Portus, 36–7
Port Vendres II wreck, 22
Procopius, 47
Production, 31
Provisioning trading ships, 5–6
Ptolemy, 167
  and Britannia, 92, 94
  Geographia, 6–7, 79
  and Nordic trade, 76–7
  and xenophobia, 175
Ptolemy's map, 8
Pyrrhus at war with Rome, 13–14
Pytheas of Massalia, 6, 92

Ravenna Cosmography, 8
Red Sea ports, 126
Red Sea Route, 133
  impact of trade on Roman economy, 136
Religion, Roman, and incense, 150
  and trade, 187–8
  exotic, eastern religions, 188
Roads and bridges, 20–1, 47–8, 110
'Romanization' and Romanitas, 49–50, 60, 92, 182–3
  in Britannia, 108–109
  in Nordic countries, 69, 71
Rome, impact of spices, silks and other fine imports on, 133, 136–7

Sabaea, 155
Saka (Indo-Scythian) Kingdom, 168–9
Salt, 89
Sarmatia, 79–83
  and Mithridates, 80–3
Sasanian Empire, 168
Sataspes, 113–14

Satavahana Dynasty, 169
Scythia, 79–80
Sea trade, 21
Seneca the Younger and Rome's global trade, xvi
   on the decadence of silk, 134–5, 180, 186
   sexual frenzy caused in women by eastern/mystery religions, 190–1
Serapis, 195
Shipwrecks, 34, 37, 58
Silk trade, 147–8, 161 (Sasanian), 188
Silk, and opulence, 134–5
Silk Road, the, 116–17, 137, 146ff, 157
Slave trade, 11, 24–5, 50, 186
Somalia, 130
Sostratos of Aegina, 55
Sri Lanka (Ceylon), 174–5
Statius and Rome's global trade, xvi
Steel, 172, 179
Stone Tower, 147–8
Strabo, *Geographia*, 6–7
   and Britannia, 92, 97–8, 102
   and frankincense, 112
Syria, *limes*, 44

Tabula Peutingerana, see *Peutinger Table*
Tacfarinas, 120
Tacitus and Britannia, 103
   and the Fenni, 76–7
   and geography, 7
   and Germania, 64
   and Germanic trade, 24, 64
   and Nordic trade, 69, 76
   and Tacfarinas, 120
   and xenophobia, 121
Tamil kingdoms, 168
Tetarte tax, 141
   and impact on Roman economy/international trade, 141
      military spending, 141
      disposable income for Romans, 141
Teuta, pirate queen, 17–19
Thailand, 175, 177
Tiber river as a trade artery, 32

Tooth whitener, 151
Trade, Roman, before China, 176
Trade (im)balance, 152, 177
Trade protection as a *casus belli*, 18
Trade, Roman, expansion, 10–11
Traders, 31
Trade, stigma surrounding, 24
Transportation, 46, 65, 66, 116–17, 166
'Travel guides', 8

Uluburun shipwreck, 2–4

Varazze shipwreck, 33–4
Varro, and religion, 189
Vietnam, 175, 177
Virgil and Britannia, 102

Weights and measures, 29–30, 165
West Africa, 118–19, 143–4
White marble, 151
Women and amber, 84, 89
Women, in Balts, 83
Women, and eastern religions, 189
   and Cybele, 191–2
   economic impact of finery, 171, 177, 186
   in the Fenni tribe, 76–7
   impact of war on, 63
   and incense, 150
   and Isis, 192–4
   and misogyny, 146–7
   rulers of Pandyas, 172
   Sarmatian, 80
   sexual frenzy caused by eastern/mystery religions, 190–1
   and silk, 134–5

Xenophobia, 51–3, 85, 108, 156–7, 175

York, 40, 63, 109–10

Zannone shipwrecks, 34
Zhang Qian, 157, 177

Dear Reader,

We hope you have enjoyed this book, but why not share your views on social media? You can also follow our pages to see more about our other products: facebook.com/penandswordbooks or follow us on X @penswordbooks

You can also view our products at www.pen-and-sword.co.uk (UK and ROW) or www.penandswordbooks.com (North America).

To keep up to date with our latest releases and online catalogues, please sign up to our newsletter at: www.pen-and-sword.co.uk/newsletter

If you would like a printed catalogue with our latest books, then please email: enquiries@pen-and-sword.co.uk or telephone: 01226 734555 (UK and ROW) or email: uspen-and-sword@casematepublishers.com or telephone: (610) 853-9131 (North America).

We respect your privacy and we will only use personal information to send you information about our products.

Thank you!